WITHDRAWN

Race and Racism in Britain

Also by John Solomos

Racism and Equal Opportunity Policies in the 1980s (editor, with
  Richard Jenkins)
The Roots of Urban Unrest (editor, with John Benyon)
Black Youth, Racism and the State
Race and Local Politics (editor, with Wendy Ball)
Racism and Migration in Western Europe (editor, with John Wrench)

Race and Racism in Britain

Second Edition

John Solomos
Reader in Public Policy
Birkbeck College
University of London

St. Martin's Press   New York

First published in Great Britain in 1989 as
Race and Racism in Contemporary Britain
First published in the United States of America in 1993

Printed in Hong Kong

ISBN 0-312-09980-0 (pbk.)

Library of Congress Cataloging-in-Publication Data
Solomos, John.
Race and racism in Britain / John Solomos. — 2nd ed.
p. cm.
Rev. ed. of: Race and racism in contemporary Britain. 1989.
Includes bibliographical references and index.
ISBN 0-312-09980-0 (pbk.)
1. Great Britain—Race relations. 2. Racism—Great Britain–
–History—20th century. 3. Blacks—Great Britain—Politics and
government. 4. Blacks—Great Britain—Social conditions.
I. Solomos, John. Race and racism in contemporary Britain.
II. Title.
DA125.A1S62   1993
305.8'00941—dc20   93–15200
                                                         CIP

To the memory of Cleopatra, Solomos, Styliani and Yiannis, who missed out on the opportunities I have enjoyed, but whose experiences remain with me

Contents

Preface to the First Edition   xi

Preface to the Second Edition   xiii

Introduction   1
   Recent trends and developments   2
   Key questions   3
   Racism in contemporary Europe   5
   Focus of study   6
   Plan of the book   9

1 Theories of Race and Racism   13
   Introduction   13
   Approaches to the study of race relations   14
   The sociology of race in Britain   17
   Politics, power and racism   21
   Critiques of the race relations problematic   25
   Culture, community and identity   31
   What kind of alternative?   33
   Summary and conclusion   35

2 Historical Background and Context   38
   Introduction   38
   The historical context of racism in Britain   39
   Anglo-Saxons and Celts   40
   Political and ideological responses to Jewish immigration   43
   Race and labour in the early twentieth century   47
   Summary and conclusion   51

3 The Politics of Race and Immigration since 1945   52
   Introduction   52
   The post-1945 conjuncture and European migration   53
   Migration, colonial labour and the state: 1945-62   56
   Immigration and racialised politics   59
   Immigration controls and state racism   61

The 1962 Commonwealth Immigrants Act 63
The changing terms of political debate 64
Institutionalising immigration controls 68
Immigration and race since 1979 70
Prospects for reform 74
Summary and conclusion 77

4 Race Relations Policies and the Political Process **78**
Introduction 78
Racism and racial discrimination 79
Race relations legislation in context 80
The origins of anti-discrimination legislation 82
The genesis of race relations policies 83
The 1976 Race Relations Act 85
From policy to practice 89
Proposals for reform 91
Summary and conclusion 93

5 Urban Politics and Racial Inequality **95**
Introduction 95
Concepts and models of local politics 95
Race and local politics in historical perspective 96
Processes of racialisation 98
Models of policy change 101
Policy change and conflict 102
Pressures for change and their impact 105
Resistance to change 106
Positive action and new initiatives 108
Training and racial equality 113
Changing forms of local governance 116
Summary and conclusion 118

6 Race, Policing and Disorder **120**
Introduction 120
Race, crime and disorder 120
Alienated youth and ghetto life 124
Policing minority communities 127
Mugging and street violence 130
Racialisation and popular images 136
Policing and violent disorder 139

Race, crime and statistics   143
Summary and conclusion   146

7 Protest, Racism and Urban Unrest in the 1980s   147
Introduction   147
Disorder and urban unrest   147
Explanations of urban unrest   149
Law and disorder   152
Racial disadvantage and urban unrest   156
Alienation and powerlessness   158
Power, legitimacy and political disorder   160
Policing after the riots   165
Scarman and beyond   169
The changing politics of policing   174
Summary and conclusion   178

8 Racism, Nationalism and Political Action   180
Introduction   180
Changing forms of racial ideology   181
Conceptions of race and nation   184
New-right ideologies and national identity   186
Neo-fascist politics   188
The politics of racial attacks   191
Racialised politics and the enemy within   192
Naturalisation of racism   193
Anti anti-racism   194
Nationalism and the interests of the majority   196
Summary and conclusion   197

9 Race, Politics and Mobilisation   198
Introduction   198
Political participation and exclusion   199
The context of black political participation   200
Origins of black political mobilisation   202
Forms of black political organisation   203
Anti-racist politics and political alliances   211
The politics of race and class   212
Politics, social movements and reform   214
Summary and conclusion   216

10 Race, Culture and Social Change   **218**
    Introduction   218
    Imagined communities   219
    Multiculturalism, identity and the nation   221
    Rushdie and Islam   222
    Nationality and immigration   227
    Social and economic change   229
    Summary and conclusion   231

11 Changing Dynamics of Race and Racism   **233**
    Introduction   233
    Racism, politics and ideology   234
    Equality or symbolic reforms?   235
    Protest and social change   239
    Rethinking the politics of racism   241
    Racism and nationalism in Europe   244
    What kind of future?   246

Guide to Further Reading   249

Bibliography   252

Index   273

Preface to the First Edition

I would like to thank all the colleagues, students and friends who have helped me to articulate the arguments which are developed in this book. Since 1982 I have taught a number of courses on the politics of racism and related issues, and this has allowed me to test out some of the early versions of chapters included in this volume. I also owe a special debt to my former colleagues at the Centre for Research in Ethnic Relations, University of Warwick, who provided support and a challenging intellectual environment in the initial stages of writing. My present colleagues in the Department of Politics and Sociology at Birkbeck College have given me the space and encouragement to complete this study, and without their support it would have been much delayed. A number of other academic colleagues have given me help and support, in particular Bob Benewick, John Benyon, Mike Cowen, Andrew Gamble, Clive Harris, Bob Jessop, Michael Keith, Bob Miles and Solomos Solomou. Equally I have benefited from the superb collection of materials on race relations brought together by Heather Lynn at Warwick, which has no doubt saved me many hours of searching. At Warwick I received valuable administrative and secretarial support from Rose Goodwin, Gurbakhsh Hundal and Charlotte Wellington. At Birkbeck I have benefited from the invaluable secretarial support of Audrey Coppard and Harriet Lodge. My students at Birkbeck during 1987–88 were the unknowing recipients of some parts of this book in the form of lectures, and their comments helped me to sharpen my ideas and to organise this volume somewhat differently.

I owe a deep debt to my publisher, Steven Kennedy, for his support of the project despite unforeseen delays. At a personal level my family has provided me with necessary emotional support. Friends in Birmingham and London have seen the project develop and helped me to relax when I needed to. George and Ian were good company on our various trips to watch West Bromwich Albion, and they and the 'Baggies' deserve a special thanks. Christine Dunn helped to keep me going even when the labour got too much. This book is dedicated with much love to my grandparents.

Birkbeck College, London   JOHN SOLOMOS

Preface to the Second Edition

For the second edition of this book I have chosen to rewrite all the chapters and to add additional material. This is partly the result of the pace of change even in the relatively short period since the first book was produced. Already in the past few years political debates about racial and ethnic issues have taken on new forms in both Britain and other European societies. Racist and nationalist movements have helped to further politicise debates about the role of immigration and the position of ethnic minorities. We have also seen the emergence of new forms of political and social mobilisation by minorities themselves. The changes I have introduced also reflect my own continuing attempts to come to terms with some of the key issues which this book covers. This can be seen in the new material included in Chapters 1, 5, 6 and 10, as well as in the changes I have introduced in other chapters. In including this material I have listened to the suggestions both of my students and my colleagues, and I hope this makes this edition more useful to both the specialist and the general reader.

In producing the second edition of this book I am grateful for the help and advice I have received from a number of colleagues and friends, who have helped me to revise and elaborate my argument. My greatest debt is to Les Back with whom I have worked closely over the past three years and who has influenced the content of a number of chapters in ways too numerable to mention. My students at Birkbeck College have proved a critical and supportive audience and they have helped me to clarify my ideas. The participants in the Workshop on the Politics of Racism, which has met at Birkbeck since 1988, have helped me to develop my ideas in a number of productive directions. In particular I am grateful to Clive Harris, Michael Keith and Syd Jeffers who have all helped to keep the Workshop a friendly place to try out tentative ideas. Terry Mayer and Joanne Winning have provided a supportive environment at Birkbeck while I was producing this second edition and made sure I was not overwhelmed by administration and that I kept to my deadline. Steven Kennedy once again encouraged and supported the production of this edition. Since the production of the first edition the 'Baggies' have introduced me to the delights of third division football, an experience that has proved too much at times but which has at least allowed me to visit many new grounds and produced many enjoyable Saturday afternoons looking on the bright side of life.

Birkbeck College, London   JOHN SOLOMOS

Introduction

The past decade has seen a flowering of theorising and research on changing understandings of race and racism. This has helped to stimulate the development of a number of research paradigms and has been reflected in work emanating from a variety of national contexts and disciplinary backgrounds. Such a development is to be welcomed, given the importance of racial ideologies in shaping social relations in a number of societies. It is also clear that we are still a long way from a clear understanding of the variety of processes which shape contemporary racial and ethnic relations in Britain and elsewhere.

It is against this background that this book has been written, and it has two main objectives. First, to provide an analysis of race and racism in contemporary Britain. This involves a detailed overview of the historical context of race and immigration in British society and the political responses to black immigration and the growth of multiculturalism in British society. It also includes an analysis of the pressures for legislative controls and restrictions on immigration, national and local policy developments, the role of policing and urban unrest and the shifts in racial ideologies that have taken place from the 1940s onwards.

The second aim is to analyse key aspects of the racialisation of political life and social relations in British society. This is done through an analysis of the growth of ideologies which have focused on race as an important political symbol, the role of anti-racist and black political mobilisation, and of the impact of social and economic restructuring on racial and national identities in British society. This part of the book also includes a detailed account of the possibilities for social reform and change within the current context of socio-economic restructuring and political crisis management, and reviews current debates about the role of public policy in this field.

In trying to fulfil these objectives this study draws on a range of research findings and on theoretical approaches emanating from a number of paradigms and disciplines. What has been particularly interesting in recent years has been the growing interest in issues of race and racism by researchers from a variety of disciplines, including

1

sociology, political science, anthropology, history, geography, literary theory, socio-legal studies and cultural studies (Rex and Mason, 1986; Goldberg, 1990). There has also been a notable growth of interest in these issues by feminists working in a variety of fields and this is evident in many recent studies (Ramazanoglu, 1989; Collins, 1990; hooks, 1992; Ware, 1992; Brah, 1992). This has extended the range of concerns that we are now looking at beyond the narrow confines that dominated the study of race relations up to the early 1980s and has led to a valuable dialogue across disciplinary boundaries.

My main concern has been to give a clear, explicit and, as far as possible, straightforward introduction to a complex set of historical and contemporary issues. This is not to say that the account given here is fully comprehensive or neutral. But in reviewing the role of race and racism in contemporary British society I hope that this volume will help to shed light on both the reasons we have arrived at our current state of affairs and the prospects for the future. Before moving on to this account it may be useful to comment on some of the recent trends that have influenced the course of debate about this issue in Britain as well as elsewhere in Europe.

Recent trends and developments

The early 1990s have been a period of rapid change in relation to the politics of race and immigration in Britain, the United States and many European societies. We have seen a resurgence of racist social and political movements in both West and East Europe, the development of new patterns of migration and heated political debate about the best ways to respond to the challenge posed by these developments. Widespread reportage in the media has highlighted the emergence of new forms of racism and their impact in a wide variety of specific national contexts. Indeed in many societies questions about immigration and the position of minorities have become a key issue on the political agenda.

At the same time it has also become clear that debates about immigration are inextricably tied up with wider considerations about the social and political position of established ethnic and racial minorities. The future of minority communities that have become established since the Second World War has been placed as much on the political agenda by recent developments as the question of how to respond to new waves of migrants and refugees (Castles and Miller, 1993). As second and third generation migrants establish themselves their future social and political status is still the subject of intense, and in many cases hostile, public debate.

Developments in Britain, France, Holland, Germany and elsewhere in Europe over the past decade have highlighted the volatility of this issue and the ease with which it can lead to conflict and disorder. There has been mounting evidence of growing racism and hostility to migrants, with neo-fascist and right-wing political parties using immigration as an issue with which to attract support (Husbands, 1991; Balibar, 1991). At the same time there have also been numerous forms of policy and political intervention to deal with the social and economic position of minority communities. All these events can be seen as important watersheds in terms of the racialisation of politics and the resurgence of avowedly racist political movements.

Such trends have led to widespread concern in Britain and the rest of Europe about the prospects for the 1990s. A number of key questions have been hotly debated. Are we witnessing the emergence of a new racism? What are the prospects for developing an adequate response to this phenomenon? Is there evidence that minority communities themselves are developing their own political responses and strategies for the future? What can best be done to develop policies to tackle the root causes of racism and racial inequality in contemporary Europe?

These are some of the questions that will be addressed in this volume, with a focus on the particular experience of Britain during the period since 1945. But it should be clear from what has been said already that the present situation is best characterised as inherently unstable and contradictory. It is important to go beyond the obvious and carry out substantive research on key aspects of the current situation before we can make a reasoned assessment of likely trends and possibilities for action. This volume can best be read therefore as a provisional map of developments in Britain over the past four decades.

Key questions

There are two key questions which arise when one looks at the changing face of the politics of immigration and race in contemporary

Britain. First, can we say that there is something unique about the debates about race and immigration in British society? Is there something about Britain's colonial past that holds the key to everyday notions about race and colour in contemporary British culture? Second, why have we not seen the emergence in Britain of mass racist movements and parties which are able to mobilise popular support? A point of comparison in this regard is the role of the *Front Nationale* in France over the past decade, and similar organisations in other societies.

Both of these questions have been widely debated in recent years. As regards the specificity of the British situation, for example, there have been a number of interesting attempts in recent years to compare the situation in Britain with trends in other European societies. And, although it is quite clear that there are substantial differences between the situation of immigrants in Germany and Holland and the position of minority communities in Britain, there are also areas of comparison. Similar points have been made about the comparability between the British situation and trends in the US. Part of the concern of this book is to show that although we need to be aware of the role of national differences there are dangers of reducing complex contemporary processes to essentialist notions about the role of colonialism in shaping the present.

The absence of a mass racist political movement is at one level a clear feature of the current situation in Britain. During the 1992 general election, for example, although questions about race and immigration were on the political agenda they were by no means key issues. Despite warnings that the race card was likely to be played during the election campaign there was little public debate about this issue. Certainly the question of race was an important issue in some localities, such as Cheltenham and East London, but there was a plethora of other issues which attracted more public attention. Yet it is also clear that other trends have shown that issues about race and immigration are by no means static items on the political agenda. Debates about such issues as the Rushdie affair, the role of religious differences, immigration from Hong Kong, refugee and asylum policy, and the role of immigration in a broader European context have highlighted the changing dynamics of the politics of race and ethnicity. Moreover there have been persistent concerns that tension in many inner city areas between the police and young blacks may lead to further urban unrest along the lines of the 1980s.

Taken together such debates indicate that the political value of race and immigration has by no means disappeared, though it may be taking on new forms. It is precisely the changing nature of contemporary processes of racialisation and racism that forms the central theme of this study.

Racism in contemporary Europe

What recent events in the broader European context have highlighted is the way in which debates about these issues do not make sense outside particular social, political and economic contexts. It is not possible to draw a direct comparison, for example, between the situation in France and Britain. The discussion in Britain about race and race relations is not to be found in other European societies (Bovenkerk *et al.*, 1990; Lloyd, 1991). There is a need therefore to be aware of the complex processes of migration and settlement that have shaped the situation in various national political contexts.

What is also clear, however, is that during the early 1990s political debates about race and immigration have been fundamentally transformed by trends that have had an impact on European societies as a whole. Two immediate factors are often singled out as having helped to shape recent developments. First, it is argued that developments in Eastern Europe and the former Soviet Union have helped to create fears about the likelihood of mass emmigration from the former Communist states to countries as diverse as Germany, Italy and Austria. Indeed this issue has been widely debated since 1989, though it is not easy to draw any clear conclusions about future patterns of migration or to predict the nature of the political responses that are likely to arise (Cohen, 1991). Second, it is argued that the question of immigration from North Africa has become a key political issue in France and other societies. It is argued that political instability and demographic changes are likely to lead to pressures to migrate in the North African region as a whole and that this is likely to have a major impact on countries such as France and Italy.

These transformations have taken place at a time of uncertainty and confusion over the economic and political orientation of the 'new Europe'. Questions are being asked about what it is that we mean when we talk about the construction of a new 'European identity', and the interplay with established national and ethnic boundaries. It is perhaps not surprising, therefore, that in this environment the position of ethnic and racial minorities who are already within Europe is intimately bound up with the overarching issue of the politics of immigration.

What is even more disturbing, however, is that the rapid transformation experienced by a number of societies over the past two decades, particularly in relation to the economic and social infrastructure, has provided fertile ground for extreme right wing parties and movements to target ethnic and racial minorities as 'enemies within' who are ultimately 'outsiders' or 'foreigners'. In Britain this has led, for example, to the racialisation of issues such as employment, housing, education and law and order. Although it has not led to the emergence of a mass racist social movement it has led to a resurgence of racial attacks and violence in some areas of the country.

This process has moved public and political debate beyond the question of immigration per se, with the focus moving towards the identification and resolution of specific social problems perceived as linked to ethnicity and race. But the link with the immigration question is maintained at another level, because it is the size of the minority populations, whether in the schools or the unemployment queue which is identified as the source of the problem. Such developments have fuelled the growth of political movements that uphold racist and anti-immigrant political views. In this environment it seems quite clear that the issue of immigration policy cannot be seen separately from a broader set of policy agendas about the social, economic and political position of migrant communities. This is evident from recent debates about immigration in a number of West European societies, and as will be argued in this book it has long been evident in the development of public policies about the position of ethnic minority communities in British society.

Focus of study

The study of racial relations in British society has, until recently, concentrated on a narrow range of issues. Sociological studies have focused on particular communities or on discrimination in specific employment, housing and service delivery situations. Yet we have no substantive body of research on the interrelationship between racial categorisation and social and political relations in contemporary Britain. This neglect is hard to understand, given the relatively high profile occupied by racial questions on political and public policy agendas since the 1950s.

It has become clear since the early 1980s, however, that any rounded analysis of contemporary British politics and society has to include the study of racial relations and racism as key issues. The outbreaks of urban violence which occurred in many inner city areas during the 1980s and subsequently have provided one stimulus for the increased political and academic interest in this field. In addition, recent developments in the Labour Party have led to important changes in the role of race issues and black politicians at both local and national levels. Similar trends seem to be at work in the other major political parties. It has also become clear over the years that questions about employment policy, welfare provision, local government, policing, housing and youth provision have a strong racial element which needs to be taken more fully into account.

All these issues help to explain why, particularly from the late 1960s onwards, race came to play an increasingly important role in public political debates and official policy analysis. For many on the right wing, immigration and race are important issues because of their supposed impact on the cultural and political values of British society. Statements made by politicians, press commentators, the police and government agencies have helped to build up the view that without drastic steps to control immigration and to help deal with the internal impact of race at local and national levels, the whole fabric of British society could come under threat. For the left wing too the emergence of race as a theme in political debate represents a challenge to many received wisdoms about working class politics and processes of class formation. While rejecting many of the most extreme images of the impact of immigration and race on British society, for example, the Labour Party found itself during the 1960s and 1970s taking up positions which were influenced by a wish to protect itself from accusations that it was soft on immigration.

In the present context it is clear that the changing forms of racial discourse form an important component of social and political relations in British society. The events surrounding the Rushdie affair illustrated the political confusion about both immigration and race that still exists in British society, and highlighted the need to situate an analysis of the position of ethnic and racial minorities against the background of wider changes in the political economy of postwar Britain and the social and cultural transformations which are being faced at the present time. This book seeks to outline such a framework of analysis for the study of race and racism in contemporary Britain, and suggests some avenues for more research and analysis. The prime focus will be on developing a critical analysis of the major processes which can help us to understand the use of race as a political symbol and the growing importance of debates about racism and anti-racism in contemporary Britain.

In the course of this account it will be necessary to address some of the recent conceptual and theoretical debates which have surrounded the study of race and racism. This is partly because although the concerns of this study are not with theoretical debates as such it is necessary to address some of the conceptual problems raised by key notions such as 'race' and 'racism'. It is also because contemporary social theorists are not in agreement about the meaning of the concepts of race and racism, and often use them in a haphazard fashion (Miles, 1989; Goldberg, 1990; Solomos and Back, 1993). Indeed in recent years a lively debate has developed around the terminology used by social scientists to discuss these issues. It is first necessary therefore to clarify how these concepts will be used in the course of this book.

Taking the concept of race first, it has long been recognised that, notwithstanding the long history of debates about this category, races do not exist in any scientifically meaningful sense. Yet it is also clear that in many societies people have often acted and continue to act as if race exists as a fixed objective category, and these beliefs are reflected in political discourses and at the level of popular ideas. Common sense conceptions of race have relied on a panoply of classificatory variables such as skin colour, country of origin, religion, nationality and language to define different groups of people. What are the consequences of racial categorisation for politics, ideology and social action? How does the meaning attached to race as a social category generate political debate and discourses? These are some of the questions that this book addresses in the context of contemporary British society, and its central focus is the construction of and changing meanings attached to the category of race and how in specific contexts race becomes a signifier for a range of social problems and conflicts.

Moving on to the concept of racism, in this study racism is broadly defined in the sense that it is used to cover those ideologies and social processes which discriminate against others on the basis of their putatively different racial membership. There is little to be gained from seeing racism merely as a signifier for ideas of biological or cultural superiority, since it has become clear in recent years that the focus on attributed biological inferiority is being replaced in contemporary forms of racist discourse by a concern with culture and ethnicity as historically fixed categories. This is why a central theme in this book is the argument that racism is not a static phenomenon. In societies such as Britain racism is produced and reproduced through political discourse, the media, the educational system and other institutions. Within this wider social context racism becomes an integral element of diverse social issues, such as law and order, crime, the inner cities and urban unrest.

These are complex issues and we shall address them in more detail in the course of the review of theoretical perspectives that forms the core of Chapter 1. But within the context of the substantive concerns of this book they are also questions that we shall inevitably come across when we explore the changing usage of ideas about race and racism in political discourse and public policy.

Plan of the book

The general rationale for this book has already been outlined, as well as some of the key questions that it addresses. However, there is a need to make explicit the structure of the volume, the concerns which guide the choice of particular issues to analyse and the themes covered in specific chapters.

Chapter 1 outlines some of the basic theoretical concerns that have guided the writing of this book. The guidelines proposed are basically research criteria that will be developed and expanded upon in the rest of this book, particularly in relation to the history and contemporary forms of racialised politics in Britain. The main emphasis will be on the identification and analysis of the historical context of the politics of race and racism in British society, the role of the state and political institutions in the formation of a racialised politics, and the interplay between racist political action, anti-racism and social movements.

From this starting point, the book aims to develop a critical assessment of existing theoretical approaches to the study of racism. This will be done specifically through an analysis of some of the most important facets of political debates about race and immigration since 1945, and a critical assessment of the role of political ideologies and practices in framing the racialisation of British politics and society.

A volume of this size cannot hope to take up all the themes of this chapter in any great detail. But the following chapters, taken together, are intended as a critical and historically grounded introduction to the politics of racism in contemporary Britain. Each chapter will explore the question from a specific angle, but they will all be linked up by the theme which resonates throughout the volume as a whole: namely that the analysis of racism in its various forms requires us to move beyond both abstract generalisations and reductionist assertions, recognising first and foremost the historical specificity and autonomy of racialisation as a political process.

The next two chapters reconstruct the history of debates about immigration and race in British society over the past century. Chapter 2 examines the historical background and context of more recent developments by exploring some aspects of debates about race and immigration during the late nineteenth and early twentieth centuries. Part of the concern of this chapter is to explore the linkages between developments since 1945 and processes which have a longer history. This account is continued in Chapter 3 through an analysis of the main trends since 1945, including pressures to introduce controls on immigration through legislative measures and the genesis of state agencies which regulated the entry of black labour into Britain. This chapter pays particular attention to the debates among political parties about immigration and the reasons why a political consensus in favour of regulation was established.

The overview of post-1945 developments is followed by four chapters which look at specific areas of political debate and conflict about race relations. Taken together Chapters 4, 5, 6 and 7 explore the history, mechanisms and outcomes of state intervention aimed at regulating and managing key areas of racial relations in Britain from the 1960s onwards. Chapter 4 takes up the issue of the role of race relations legislation in dealing with discrimination in such key areas as employment and housing. Legislation against discrimination has been a major plank of government policy since the mid 1960s and it has played an important role in recent political debates. Yet it remains unclear as to how far legislation can deal with the root causes of racial inequality. A key concern of this chapter therefore is the question of how effective race relations policies have been in tackling racial inequality. This is followed in Chapter 5 by a review of policies which have as their focus the urban politics of race. The local dimension of racial politics has been a key factor in political debates since the 1980s and this chapter explores the changing dynamics of the local politics of race.

Chapters 6 and 7 look at the politics of race, policing and urban unrest. The issue of the relationship between the police and minority communities has long been a question of concern in many urban localities. Aspects of this relationship are explored in Chapter 6, which focuses particularly on the wider social and political context within which the role of the police in multiracial localities has come to be viewed. Since the 1980s the outbreak of urban unrest and violent confrontations between the police and black communities has led to widespread debate about the role of racial inequality and racism in producing the conditions for public disorder. Much of the recent political debate on race-related issues has been dominated by the experience of violent street disorders in the 1980s, and Chapter 7 provides a critical analysis of both the background and the wider social and political impact of the unrest.

The focus of the book moves on in Chapter 8 to the analysis of the impact of ideologies of race and nation on political mobilisation. By analysing the continuities and discontinuities between various forms of racist ideologies and mobilisation it illustrates the material basis for the reproduction of racism in contemporary Britain and the implications this has for struggles against racism. Chapter 9 takes up the question of the role of political mobilisation by black and ethnic minority communities, and the impact of anti-racist politics and oppositional social movements on the political agenda. As well as dealing with the current forms of this mobilisation this chapter also explores the historical antecedents and the reasons for the limited success of anti-racist strategies in challenging entrenched racist practices.

This is followed in Chapter 10 by a more detailed discussion of the interplay between race, culture and social change in British society, and the role of wider social and economic relations in shaping the course of such change. Questions about culture, religion and ethnic identity have become increasingly important in recent debates and this chapter seeks to draw out some of the broader implications for the future of race relations in British society.

The final chapter reviews the main changes currently affecting race relations in contemporary Britain. It provides an overview of the main themes examined in the book and outlines some of the processes that are likely to transform future race relations. In this context developments in Britain are presented in a broader comparative context, particularly in relation to developments in other European societies and the United States.

Together the eleven chapters provide an introduction to the key issues that make up the study of race and racism in contemporary Britain. A number of the questions raised cannot be fully answered in a single volume, but this book will have achieved its task if it convinces the reader of the need for a critical approach to the analysis of race and racism in British society, and the urgency for more theorisation and research.

1 Theories of Race and Racism

Introduction

Over the past few decades there has been a flowering of studies of racial and ethnic differences and their social meaning in various historical, social, political and economic contexts. Theoretical and political debates have raged during this time, and have sometimes led to bitter conceptual and political arguments. At the same time the analysis of race and racism has become an established field of study in a number of social science disciplines, most notably in sociology, political science, economics, anthropology, cultural studies and geography (Rex and Mason, 1986; Goldberg [ed.], 1990). The literature emanating from all these disciplines has multiplied over the years, particularly in the US, Britain and other European societies and South Africa.

Such developments are certainly a step forward, particularly in a context where the role of state agencies and government policies is increasingly important to any full understanding of the dynamics of race and racist ideologies in contemporary British society. Certainly this volume would not have been possible without the growing interest in the politics of race and racism over the last few years, and the growth of theoretical and empirical investigations around this issue. The distinctive contribution of this book, however, lies in its attempt to construct a political analysis of contemporary racism which goes beyond the narrow boundaries of existing political science literature on the subject and uses insights from a critical theoretical framework which draws on the approaches of a number of disciplines and scholarly traditions in order to fathom the complex meanings attached to race and politics within contemporary Britain.

There seem to be two major reasons for this growing interest in the study of race and racism. First, and most importantly, as mentioned, there has been an evident preoccupation with racial issues in a variety of societies. Studies have shown that racial inequalities and injustices continue to be reproduced at a number of levels, ranging from the economic, social, political to the cultural. Second, associated with this awareness of the persistence of racial inequalities there has been a realisation that racism continues to be a vital, and some would say growing, force in contemporary societies.

Whatever the explanation for the recent flowering of interest it is clear that current debates have led to the emergence of a variety of schools of thought. What is also interesting, however, is that there has been little debate between researchers and scholars, apart from personalised exchanges and critiques. There is even little agreement about what it is that researchers in this field are actually investigating. The definition of key concepts such as race, race relations and racism remains an area of disagreement.

A good example of this type of disagreement is the debate on the limits of the 'race relations problematic', and the utility of race as a social scientific concept (Miles, 1982, 1989 and 1993; CCCS, 1982; Banton, 1987; Gilroy, 1987 and 1990a). Some scholars argue that the concept of race has no relevance for social analysis, while others have questioned whether racism exists as a unified category or whether it is a general term that is used to describe a variety of political and social discourses.

Rather than attempt to cover all aspects of theoretical debates on racism this chapter will focus on some of the strands that are of particular interest to this study. Each strand will be analysed both in its own right and with particular emphasis on the fundamental theoretical questions which are associated with it. This will then allow us to explore some of the main criticisms of each strand, particularly as exemplified in some of the recent standard works that have been produced within each framework. From this critical review will follow a discussion of the alternative analytic framework developed in the rest of this book.

Approaches to the study of race relations

The study of race as a field of social scientific inquiry and research can be seen as originating in the earlier part of this century with the work of a number of American sociologists and anthropologists, most notably during the 1920s and 1930s. They were influenced by the work of Robert Park, one of the key early sociological writers in this field. During the period from the 1920s to the 1950s the works of these scholars helped to establish what came to be defined as the study of race relations, particularly through their studies of segregation, immigration and race consciousness in the US. During the interwar period these works helped to develop a body of sociological concepts which were later to be refined into a sociology of race relations. Their studies of the specific contexts within which ideas about race became socially meaningful remain some of the classics in this field of study.

Many of the American studies of race up to the 1960s were influenced by the ideas of this group of writers and concentrated on the analysis of the social and economic inequalities suffered by blacks, their cultural and psychological make-up, family relations and political isolation. Following Park, the dominant assumption seemed to be that race relations were types of social relations between people of different racial characteristics, particularly morphological features. In his classical definition of the notion of race relations Park argued that the main feature of such relations was consciousness of racial differences:

> Race relations, as that term is defined in use and wont in the United States, are the relations existing between peoples distinguished by marks of racial descent, particularly when these racial differences enter into the consciousness of the individuals and groups so distinguished, and by so doing determine in each case the individual's conception of himself as well as his status in the community (Park, 1950: 81).

Although in some of his, and his students', work there is acknowledgement of the economic and social conditions which can help produce race consciousness the focus is on the nature of relationships between races. Thus Park and his followers tended to see the development and perpetuation of racial conflicts in terms of the ways in which phenotypical differences came to be understood in terms of racial definitions and identities. The emphasis was on a 'cycle of race relations', leading to the assimilation of different racial groupings into a common culture. The cycle was seen as consisting of four stages of contact, conflict, accommodation and assimilation (Park, 1950: 82–4).

While Park's work was by and large descriptive and untheorised it was instrumental in leading to the development of a distinct sub-field of sociological studies of race relations in the US. This trend was helped by the publication of Gunnar Myrdal's *An American Dilemma* in 1944, which documented the history of black inequality and racial prejudice in the US. Arguing forcefully for the integration of blacks into mainstream American life, Myrdal predicted that the process of integration and assimilation would eventually replace the processes of conflict and segregation (Myrdal, 1969a, 1969b).

From the late 1940s to the 1960s this model of assimilation became a dominant influence on research in this field in the US. Pierre L. van den Berghe, for example, characterised the American studies of race in the following way:

> The field has been dominated by a functionalist view of society and a definition of the race problem as one of integration and assimilation of minorities into the mainstream of a consensus based society (1967: 7).

Sociological theorising on race and racism in the US thus developed around notions of race relations and the race problem as an outcome of processes of group contact and social interaction. Race was considered a relevant empirical referent only with regard to the extent to which cultural and social meanings were attached to the physical traits of a particular social group. This in turn helped to popularise notions about the origins of racial conflicts and prejudice which concentrated on situations of cultural contract. The emphasis in sociological studies of the race problem during these decades was on the origins of racial prejudice, the interplay between prejudice and conflict, the impact of assimilation on the life of black Americans and the processes through which racial conflicts could be mediated or overcome.

Sociological studies of other race relations situations in a number of societies were influenced from the beginning by various aspects of the American literature, as well as by the experience of racial differentiation in South Africa. This was certainly the case in the British context, where the study of race began to establish itself during the 1940s and 1950s. At this time the emergent field of race studies in Britain was dominated by two main themes. First, the issue of 'coloured immigrants' and the reaction to them by white Britons. Second, the role of colonial history in determining popular conceptions of colour and race within British society. Most studies of this period concentrated on the interaction between specific groups of 'coloured immigrants' and whites in local situations. Little theorising was attempted, and writers such as Sheila Patterson and Ruth Glass were in fact critical of attempts to subsume the situation of the black immigrants under generalised categories of race relations (Glass, 1960; Patterson, 1963).

These early studies of race did not actually talk about racism as such. This is a more recent concept and its usage was linked to the rise of Nazism in Germany. As the Nazis came to power and articulated and put into practice their ideas about racial superiority the term racism came to be used to refer to ideas which defined some racial or ethnic groups as superior and others as inferior. This usage of the term was first suggested by Ruth Benedict in her book *Race and Racism* which defined racism as 'the dogma that one ethnic group is condemned by nature to congenital inferiority and another group is destined to congenital superiority' (Benedict, 1943: 97). In this context racism was seen as referring to those sets of ideas that defined ethnic and racial groups on the basis of claims about biological nature and inherent superiority or ability.

Since the 1960s heated political and theoretical debates have led to what Miles refers to as a process of 'conceptual inflation' (Miles, 1989: 41), resulting in the usage of racism to cover disparate sets of ideas and socio-political relations. Additionally, radical and neo-Marxist researchers have argued that the focus of research needs to be on the analysis of the dynamics of racism and not on what is called race relations.

The sociology of race in Britain

Since 1945 a number of developments outside the US have encouraged interest in the study of race and racism in other societies. An important development in this context was the emergence of migrant labour as an important social group in many West European societies. Migration from the ex-colonies and Southern Europe led to the creation of racial and ethnic minorities in countries such as Britain, France, Germany and Holland. Another important development was the entrenchment of the apartheid system in South Africa, a process which aroused the interest of both social scientists and political activists, particularly in relation to the role of the political and legal system in enforcing racial segregation and the 'separate development' of different racial groups.

In Britain, and other European societies, the growth in the theorisation of race and racism ran parallel to these developments, providing a number of important and sophisticated analyses of the politics and ideology of racism. There were two central concerns in these early European attempts to theorise racial and ethnic relations. First, the patterns of immigration and incorporation into the labour market of black and other ethnic communities. Second, the role of colonial history in determining popular conceptions of colour, race and ethnicity in European societies.

A number of early studies of what in Britain came to be called 'race relations' were carried out in the 1950s and 1960s by scholars such as Michael Banton, Ruth Glass, John Rex and Sheila Patterson. Most studies of this period concentrated on the interaction between minority and majority communities in employment, housing and other social contexts. What is interesting in hindsight, given the virulence of some of the theoretical debates since the early 1980s, is the relative absence of a clear theoretical perspective about (a) what constituted the object of analysis of these specific studies and (b) the absence of a wider socio-political perspective about the interplay between 'race relations' and other kinds of social relations.

By the 1960s, however, there was a noticeable growth of interest in the theoretical study of the new forms of migration and settlement being experienced in Britain and elsewhere and in other types of 'race relations'. Michael Banton's book *Race Relations* represents a good example of the texts of this period. It looks at race relations from a global and historical perspective, concentrating particularly on situations of cultural contact, beliefs about the nature of race, and the social relations constructed on the basis of racial categories. By looking at the historical experience of changing patterns of interaction Banton argued that six basic orders of race relations could be identified: institutionalised contact, acculturation, domination, paternalism, integration and pluralism (Banton, 1967).

It was during the 1960s that what Banton and others have called the 'race relations problematic' became the dominant approach in this field (Banton, 1991). Banton quite rightly points out that the preoccupation with race relations was reflected in both the research agenda and in public policy. In other words both social scientists and policy makers were talking increasingly about the need to understand

and deal with the nature of race relations and forms of racial discrimination in British society. It was perhaps not surprising, in this context, that the 1969 conference of the British Sociological Association took as its theme 'The Sociology of Race and Racialism', with the explicit concern to encourage the sociological study of race relations (Zubaida, 1970).

It was at this time that John Rex's influential text *Race Relations in Sociological Theory* first appeared. This text has exercised a major influence over this field since its publication and it remains one of the most ambitious attempts to provide a theoretical grounding for research in this field. According to Rex's analytic model the definition of social relations between persons as race relations is encouraged by the existence of certain structural conditions: frontier situations of conflict over scarce resources, the existence of unfree, indentured, or slave labour, unusually harsh class exploitation, strict legal intergroup distinctions and occupational segregation, differential access to power and prestige, cultural diversity and limited group interaction, and migrant labour as an underclass fulfilling stigmatised roles in a metropolitan setting (Rex, 1983). He defines the field of race relations in the following terms:

> Race relations situations and problems have the following characteristics: they refer to situations in which two or more groups with distinct identities and recognisable characteristics are forced by economic and political circumstances to live together in a society. Within this they refer to situations in which there is a high degree of conflict between the groups and in which ascriptive criteria are used to mark out the members of each group in order that one group may pursue one of a number of hostile policies against the other. Finally, within this group of situations true race relations may be said to exist when the practices of ascriptive allocation of roles and rights referred to are justified in terms of some kind of deterministic theory, whether that theory be of a scientific, religious, cultural, historical, ideological or sociological kind (ibid.: 159–60).

From this perspective the study of race relations is concerned with situations in which such structured conditions interacted with actors' definitions in such a way as to produce a racially structured social reality.

In developing his own empirical work on Britain Rex was particularly interested in two fundamental questions. First, the question of to what extent black immigrants were incorporated into welfare state institutions and enjoyed equal access to housing, education and employment. Second, he explored the consequences of the development of racial inequality for the development of a 'racialised' consciousness among both the white and black and white working class. In one way or another those questions provided the focus of his studies of Sparkbrook and Handsworth, and his work on general aspects of race relations policies (Rex and Moore, 1967; Rex and Tomlinson, 1979).

Other attempts were made during the late 1960s and 1970s to develop a generalised sociological framework for the analysis of race and racism. Spurred on by the increasing politicisation of racial issues in the US, Britain and elsewhere, a mass of sociological theorising, monographs and case studies was produced during this period and British sociologists began to show serious interest in the subject, both as it concerned Britain and as a global phenomenon.

These concerns were articulated clearly by Rex in two studies of race relations in Birmingham during the 1960s and the 1970s. In the study conducted by Rex and his associates in Handsworth during the mid 1970s (Rex and Tomlinson, 1979) the basic research problem was to explore the degree to which immigrant populations shared the class position of their white neighbours and white workers in general. The substance of the analysis goes on to outline a class structure in which white workers have been granted certain rights which have been won through the working class movement via trade unions and the Labour Party. The result was the development, in the 1970s, of a state of class truce between white workers and subordinate classes. The position of immigrant workers and their children was located outside the negotiation that had taken place between the white workers and capital. They experienced discrimination in all the areas where the white workers had made significant gains, that is employment, education and housing. It follows from this that immigrant workers were placed outside the working class as an 'underclass':

> The concept of underclass was intended to suggest . . . that the minorities were systematically at a disadvantage compared with their white peers and that, instead of identifying with working class culture, community and politics, they formed their own organisa-

tions and became effectively a separate underprivileged class (Rex and Tomlinson, 1979: 275).

From this point Rex and Tomlinson develop a model of political action and even a political agenda for black populations as they become a 'class for themselves'. Immigrant minorities are forced into a series of reactive/defensive political strategies. This process takes on different forms within Asian and West Indian communities. Within Asian communities this results in a concentration on capital accumulation and social mobility. In the West Indian community it takes the form of withdrawal from competition altogether with an emphasis on the construction of a black identity. This all leads to what Rex refers to elsewhere as the 'politics of defensive confrontation' (Rex, 1979).

The work of both Banton and Rex helped therefore, though from rather different starting points, to establish the study of race relations as an emerging field in the social sciences during the 1960s and 1970s. They also helped to institutionalise research on race relations by their work in running, at different stages, the major research centre in this field.

Politics, power and racism

With a few notable exceptions most studies of race relations in Britain during the 1950s and 1960s did not analyse questions of power and politics in any detail. Zubaida wrote in 1972, of the atheoretical and ahistorical nature of many sociological studies of race relations which led them to ignore the political context of political parties, trade unions, local and central government in their analysis of the British situation:

> In spite of the great importance of this issue, this political area of race relations appears to be little researched at any significant level. There is a plethora of studies . . . which are concerned with 'attitudes', 'prejudice' and 'discrimination'. They are remarkably uninformative; for the most part, they tell us about the relative readiness of sections of the population to subscribe to one set of verbal formula rather than another. What we need are studies of the way the race relations issues enter into the structures, strategies

and ideologies of political parties and trade unions and governmental bodies (Zubaida, 1972: 141).

The work of authors such as Rex did raise the issue of politics and
power, but it remained a secondary influence on the mainstream
sociological studies of race relations. Moreover few of the influential
studies of this period analysed the political context which structured
the meanings attached to race and racism in Britain. At a descriptive
level some of the issues which Zubaida mentions were analysed, but
they were not integrated into the wider conceptual debates about the
theory of racism or into the analysis of processes of racialisation in
contemporary Britain.

This relative neglect of the political dimension of racial issues
continued well into the 1970s, and was heightened by the absence of
racial questions from the agenda of both radical and mainstream
political science during this period. Dominant approaches within
political science have concentrated almost entirely on the class and
status determinants of political ideology and behaviour in the belief
that the logic of politics in advanced capitalist societies springs from
the nature of the social structure. Questions about issues such as
gender, race, environmental policy and novel forms of political
organisation received relatively little attention, and even then they
had generally been added on to existing analytic models. This neglect
is even more noticeable when compared to the voluminous literature
on the sociology of race relations and the social anthropology of
immigrant and black communities, fields of study which have
expanded greatly since the early 1970s.

Nevertheless what is also clear is that the dominant focus of the
texts that have looked at the politics of race has been a limited set of
issues relating only to some aspects of the integration of black
minorities into established political institutions. Since the 1970s
these issues have received some attention, although not always from
a political science perspective, and have led to a small but growing
body of literature on each subject. Many of the questions asked in
these studies have related narrowly to the role of political parties,
Parliament and interest groups. The preoccupation of much of the
literature on British politics with what John Dearlove and Peter
Saunders call a 'narrow view of politics and power' (1984: 3–4) has
thus been reproduced in the literature concerned with the politics of
racism.

In the body of work produced since the early 1960s surprisingly little attention has been paid to the question of the substance of the state interventions in this area and who benefited from them; the causes of changes in ideology and policy; the interrelationship between policy changes in the race sphere and other areas of economic, social and welfare policy; and, perhaps more importantly, the mediations between state and society which bring about changes in political and ideological relations.

The relative absence of race from the agenda of mainstream political analysis needs to be contextualised against the background of a number of factors. First, as a number of writers have pointed out (Leys, 1983: chapter 1; Coates, 1984; Moran, 1985) political science in Britain has developed along conventional lines and often has not linked up directly with the changing realities of political life. Dearlove has pointed out that, unlike most other social science disciplines, British political science was left largely untouched by the intellectual unrest of the 1960s. It was only in the acute economic, social and ideological crisis of the 1970s, which resulted in a period of soul searching and critical self-evaluation among political scientists, that the discipline experienced the intellectual turmoil and strife which other disciplines had experienced during the 1960s. It was this turmoil that led to a strong feeling among many political scientists that 'the established discourse is no longer an adequate basis for understanding contemporary British politics' (Dearlove, 1982: 437) and a lively debate about the theoretical and empirical basis for the study of the political context of economic, social and political inequalities.

Within this broader context of the development of postwar political science it is possible to begin to make sense of how the encounter with race was dealt with, an encounter which broadly covers the two terms of Dearlove's periodisation. During the 1960s and early 1970s the political study of racism remained noticeably underdeveloped, particularly when compared with the massive growth of the sociology of race relations over the same period. Having produced little in the way of textbooks and monographic studies during the previous two decades, the political science approach to race issues was boosted by the growth of the National Front's political impact during the late 1970s and the series of violent disorderly protests which took place during 1980–1 and 1985. With the breakup of what Dearlove has called the established understandings of British political life, issues such as gender and race began to receive more serious attention from mainstream political science, even if only at the margins of established political issues such as inner city policy and unemployment.

A number of sociological and neo-Marxist writings on racism provide a useful starting point for rethinking the interrelationship of race to power relations and political structures, although there are few analytically clear studies of this aspect of racism. During the 1960s and 1970s some studies of voting behaviour, immigration and race relations legislation were carried out within the framework of political science. But what is interesting is that few of these studies became part of the teaching syllabus in politics departments or attracted the attention of non-race specialists, whether in the mainstream or in the radical sections of the discipline. This gap has been bridged in recent years by the attention given to race issues in some of the new politics textbooks, though this is by no means the case in all of them.

Studies such as these have made some important contributions to the political analysis of racism in contemporary Britain, but there remain many gaps which can only be filled if the contribution of the studies referred to above can be integrated within a theoretically rigorous and empirically grounded political analysis of racism. Such theoretical and empirical clarification of the roots of racism has not been forthcoming however. Indeed racism remains a sadly neglected issue in most discussions of British politics, even in those that are influenced by radical Marxist and feminist ideas. This is despite the attention given to this issue in other disciplines.

One of the paradoxes is that the relatively underdeveloped analysis of the politics of racism in Britain is not so evident in the US, where social scientists working on racial questions from a number of disciplinary backgrounds have provided a more detailed historical account of race-related political issues. The experience of the race riots during the 1960s, the civil rights movement, black power movements, and the emergence of a black political élite have all been issues of concern not only for political scientists, but also for sociologists and economists. Additionally there are now numerous historical and contemporary case studies of the political context of racism and racial ideologies which have done much to illuminate the understanding of the political dilemmas faced by American blacks.

Manning Marable (1981) explains this emphasis on the politics of racism on a number of factors, but he draws particular attention to the role of black intellectuals and radical white intellectuals who have stressed in their work the importance of politics in determining the social and economic position of blacks in American society. Additionally he cites the experience of the riots of the 1960s as an important source of research on political power and powerlessness in relation to racism. A number of other studies of the American situation have highlighted similar processes, albeit from divergent analytical perspectives (Preston *et al.*, 1982; McAdam, 1982).

It is also worth mentioning that a number of the writers on race issues in Britain have been American, most notably Ira Katznelson, Donley Studlar, David Kirp and Anthony Messina (Katznelson, 1976; Studlar, 1978 and 1980; Kirp, 1979; Messina, 1985, 1987 and 1989). They have used their experience of events in America to analyse the British experience, and sometimes to theorise about the similarities and differences between the two situations. The work of Katznelson provides examples of the kind of comparisons that can be made between the British and the American situation, as well as a powerful analysis of the role of the interplay between politics and social change in the formation of racialised politics (Katznelson, 1976: xxii–xxiv).

Critiques of the race relations problematic

The other main conceptual framework which should be looked at is Marxism. Marxist discussion of the interrelationship of class relations and forms of social differentiation based on racial and ethnic categories has become intense since the 1970s. This explosion of Marxist debate on this issue certainly contradicts the oft-cited argument that the preferred response of Marxism to non-class forms of social division is either silence or an attempt to force a complex reality into narrow and deterministic models. But what advances have been made through these debates? To what extent have the problems encountered been due to a failure to move beyond economistic interpretations of class?

The early 1980s saw the emergence of a number of substantial criticisms of the research agenda on race relations, written largely from a Marxist perspective. Such criticisms were influenced by both theoretical and political considerations, and they helped to stimulate new areas of debate which to some extent continue to this day.

A number of key questions dominated the debates. First, there is the issue of Marx's and Engels' views on the subject, or rather their supposed failure to analyse it systematically. Second, there is the problem of how Marxist concepts of class can help us understand the dynamics of societies that are structured by racial and ethnic categorisation. Third, there is the question of how recent Marxist debates on ideology, hegemony and over-determination can help us understand the development of racism as an important ideological force in contemporary societies. Fourth, there is the question of how the important debates about the class position of women and about sexism interlink with the analysis of race. Finally, a lively discussion has taken place on the alleged Eurocentric bias of Marxist theory.

The starting point of the majority of recent Marxist studies of the dynamics of race and class is that classical Marxism contains no systematic treatment of this question. It has been pointed out, for example, that although the works of Marx and Engels contain a number of scattered references to the pertinence of racial and ethnic relations in certain social formations, for example the reference to race as an economic factor of slavery in the US, they contain little historical or theoretical reflection on the role of such processes in the capitalist mode of production as a whole. Perhaps even more damaging, a number of critics have argued that several statements on race by Marx and Engels reveal traces of the dominant racial stereotypes of their time and an uncritical usage of racist imagery (Robinson, 1983). Additionally, a number of critics of Marxism have argued that the reliance by Marxists on the concept of class has precluded them from analysing racial and ethnic phenomena in their own right, short of subsuming them under wider social relations or treating them as a kind of superstructural phenomenon (Parkin, 1979; Banton, 1983).

In the writings of Marx and Engels references to racial and ethnic divisions, along with related issues of religious differences, regional identity and nationality, are organised around two central themes. The first is the question of internal divisions within the working class. A good example of this strand is the question of the Irish workers who migrated to England and Scotland in search of employment. Both Marx and Engels commented at various points in their work on the impact of this division upon the consciousness of the English working class and the manner in which it was perpetuated. The second theme is the issue of the nation and the national question. Marx and Engels drew frequent attention to the significance of national identities and their interrelationship with class relations. For example they initially highlighted the effect that the development of Irish nationalism had on the consciousness of the English proletariat. Later they came to perceive the development of a nationalist movement in Ireland as essential to the emergence of a strong labour movement in England. Their historical works are suffused with references to the emergence, development or demise of nationalities. The analysis provided is by no means as detailed as it could have been, but it does allow us to question the notion that Marx and Engels were silent on forms of extra-class differentiation, and it provides a basis for later attempts by Marxists to analyse the impact of nationalism and racism within the working class.

Early Marxist work on racial and ethnic divisions concentrated particularly on race and class as modes of exploitation. Oliver Cox's *Caste, Class and Race* (1948) is an early example of this focus. Cox was primarily interested in the historical economic interests which produce racist exploitation and ideologies and he explained racial inequality as an outcome of the interest of the capitalist class in super-exploiting sections of the working class. Since he saw class divisions as the fundamental source of exploitation in society, the main thrust of his work was to conceptualise racial exploitation as a special form of class exploitation. This model was subsequently to exercise a deep influence on the work of Marxist writers on race in the US, and to a more limited extent in European and other societies.

New life was breathed into this question during the 1960s, particularly as a result of the regeneration of Marxist debates on class and historical materialism which sought to transcend economic reductionism, and partly through increasing political awareness that contemporary racial inequalities were being reproduced in a complex manner which could not be reduced to economistic notions of class. This rethinking of class theory and the historical context of race/class relations is evident in new research on slavery in the US, studies of racism and labour market segmentation, the analysis of state racism in South Africa and the large body of work on the economics of migrant labour.

Out of this large body of research and historical writing since the 1960s a number of main themes have emerged. These have centred on: (1) the question of the autonomy of racism from class relations; (2) the role of the state and political institutions in relation to racial and ethnic issues; (3) the impact of racism on the structure of the working class and dynamics of class struggle and political organisation; (4) the

processes through which racist ideologies are produced and reproduced.

The question of autonomy in relation to race and class introduced
into this field theoretical problems which had been posed through the
analysis of class formation and the capitalist state by radical and neo-
Marxist writers. The focus of these writers has been particularly on
the interplay between class forces and political strategies (Jessop,
1982; Evans *et al.*, 1985; Alford and Friedland, 1985; Dunleavy and
O'Leary, 1987), but in recent years some attempt has been made to
utilise the insights of these studies to analyse the politics of racism in
Britain and elsewhere.

One of the first attempts to provide a theoretical critique of the
approaches of both Banton and Rex is to be found in the work of
Robert Miles since the early 1980s. The starting point of Miles's
critique was his opposition to the existence of a sociology of race, and
his view that the object of analysis should be racism, which he viewed
as integral to the process of capital accumulation (Miles, 1982, 1986).
His analysis was first articulated in *Racism and Migrant Labour* and it
is perhaps the most sustained attempt to include the study of racism
within the mainstream of Marxist social theory. His empirical
research has focused specifically on the situation in Britain and the
rest of Europe, and has looked at the role of political, class and
ideological relationships in shaping our understanding of racial
conflict and change in these societies.

For Miles the idea of race refers to a human construct, an ideology
with regulatory power within society. Analytically race constitutes a
paper tiger (Miles, 1988) that may be a common term of reference
within everyday discourse, but which presents a serious theoretical
problem. It is here that Miles diverges from what he sees as the race
relations problematic. While Rex is concerned with models of social
action (that is, for Rex it is enough that race is utilised in everyday
discourse as a basis for social action) Miles is concerned with the
analytical and objective status of race as a basis of action (Miles,
1982: 42). Race is thus an ideological effect, a mask which hides real
economic relationships (Miles, 1984). Thus the forms of class
consciousness which are legitimate for Miles must ultimately be
reduced to economic relations which are hidden within the regulatory process of racialisation.

For Miles the process of racialisation is interrelated with the
conditions of migrant labourers. Its effects are the result of the

contradiction between 'on the one hand the need of the capitalist world economy for the mobility of human beings, and on the other, the drawing of territorial boundaries and the construction of citizenship as a legal category which sets boundaries for human mobility' (Miles, 1988: 438). Within the British setting this ideological work conducted primarily by the state acts as a means of crisis management and results in racialising fragments of the working class. Race politics are thus confined to the forces of regulation. For Miles the construction of political identities which utilise racial consciousness plays no part in the development of progressive politics.

While Miles's work does have limitations, he raises some important questions about the nature of political action within communities of migrant labour. The most important of these is the degree to which black and minority politics are really distillations of class conflict. If this is true any movements away from class-based political action (that is movements towards any notions of black community politics) are doomed to failure (Miles, 1988, 1989). If one takes this argument further, class-based political action is ultimately in opposition to any sort of sustained political organisation around a notion of race. For Miles the politics of race is narrowly confined to the struggle against racism. This is neatly captured in the way he uses Hall's (1980: 341) statement on the relationship between class and race. He concludes that it is not race but racism which can be the modality in which class is lived and fought through (Miles, 1988: 447).

Another influential critique of the sociology of race in the early 1980s emanated from the Centre for Contemporary Cultural Studies (CCCS) in Birmingham. The work of the CCCS Race and Politics Group during this period was particularly concerned with the changing nature of the politics of race during the 1970s and the development of new forms of racial ideology. The theoretical approach of the group was influenced by the work of Stuart Hall (1980) in particular. They were critical of the arguments of both the sociologists of race and of Miles.

The work of the group resulted in the publication of *The Empire Strikes Back* (CCCS, 1982). This volume attracted widespread attention at the time and it still remains a point of reference in current debates. Two of the contributors to this volume have subsequently attempted to develop substantive studies derived from it (Gilroy, 1987; Solomos, 1988). A major concern of the group was the need to analyse the complex processes by which race is constructed as a social and political relation. They emphasised that the race concept is not simply confined to a process of regulation operated by the state but that the meaning of race as a social construction is contested and fought over. In this sense they viewed race as an open political construction where the political meaning of terms like black are struggled over. Collective identities spoken through race, community and locality are, for all their spontaneity, powerful means to coordinate action and create solidarity.

Within this model of political action a multiplicity of political identities can be held. An inclusive notion of black identity can prevail and at the same time allow heterogeneity of national and cultural origins within this constituency (Gilroy, 1987: 236). For Gilroy the crucial question here is the extent to which notions of race can be reforged into a political movement of opposition. He holds little hope that this process can be developed within the arena of representative democracy. Instead he views as the way forward pressure group strategies which have evolved out of community struggles and which utilise a specifically black political vernacular.

A number of studies emanating from the US during the early 1980s also took as their starting point the interrelationship between relations of politics, power and racism. The most influential of these was a study by Michael Omi and Howard Winant of the processes of 'race formation' in the US. They placed particular emphasis on the role of political and legal relations in defining the existence of racial categories and defining the social meanings of notions such as racial inequality, racism and ethnicity (Omi and Winant, 1986).

This theme has been taken up in studies of the situation of ethnic minorities in Europe in recent years. Such studies have looked particularly at the processes by which minority communities and migrant workers are often excluded from equal access to political institutions and are denied basic social and economic rights. It is interesting to note in this context that in countries such as Germany and France a key point in recent political conflicts has been the question of whether migrant workers should be given greater political rights.

In Britain, where the position of black minorities is somewhat different than in the rest of Europe, a key concern of a number of recent studies of the politics of race in Britain has been the need to develop a conception of racialisation as a process which has specific effects on politics and ideology. Aspects of this process include the impact of racist ideologies and nationalist discourses, antiracist discourses, and black political action on political institutions and forms of political mobilisation.

It is within this context that the concepts of racial categorisation and racialisation have been used to refer to what Robert Miles calls 'those instances where social relations between people have been structured by the signification of human biological characteristics in such a way as to define and construct differentiated social collectivities' (Miles, 1989). A number of writers have attempted to use these concepts to analyse the processes by which race has been socially and politically constructed in specific historical, political and institutional contexts.

Good examples of such studies include attempts to analyse critically the role of race relations legislation, the emergence of black minority representation in political institutions and the development of public policies dealing with specific aspects of racial inequality in areas such as employment and housing. The premise of such studies is that the processes by which race is given particular meanings are variable across and within national boundaries and are shaped by political, legal and socio-economic environments. Comparative studies of immigration policies in Europe have, for example, shown that the drafting of legislation to control the arrival of specific groups of migrants was often the subject of intense political and ideological controversy.

Culture, community and identity

The debates of the 1980s are still going on, and they continue to influence research agendas. But in the past few years we have also seen the emergence of new perspectives which go beyond the terms of these debates. New contributions engage in one way or another, for example, with the arguments of poststructuralism and postmodernism and the need to avoid uniform and homogeneous conceptualisations of racism.

Although not yet part of the agenda of mainstream research on race relations, a range of studies of racialised discourses in the mass media, literature, art and other cultural forms have begun to be produced. A growing body of work has been produced on the use of race as a symbol in various areas of cultural expression and experience. Reacting against what they see as the lack of an account of cultural forms of racial discourse, a number of writers have sought to develop a more rounded picture of contemporary racial imagery by looking at the role of literature, the popular media and other cultural forms in representing changing images of race and ethnicity.

As David Goldberg has pointed out, 'the presumption of a single monolithic racism is being displaced by a mapping of the multifarious historical formulations of *racisms*' (Goldberg, 1990). In this context it is perhaps not surprising that a key concern of many recent texts in this field is to explore the interconnections between race and nationhood, patriotism and nationalism rather than analyse ideas about biological inferiority. Clear examples of this trend are the growing number of studies which have looked at the role of political interventions in shaping racial relations in specific national settings. This has led to growing interest in the development of racist ideologies and the various forms such ideologies have taken at different stages of development. Although this issue has not received much attention among scholars in the past, the renewed interest in the analysis of culture and discourse has helped to overcome this neglect and questions have begun to be asked about the historical, cultural, literary and philosophical roots of ideologies of race. Specifically, questions are being asked about the role that ideological relations can play in providing a basis for the articulation of racist discourses and practices.

The role of the press and other popular media in shaping social images about racial and ethnic minorities has been a particular focus. A number of detailed studies have, for example, looked at how press coverage of racial questions can help to construct images of racial minorities as outsiders and as a threat to social cohesion. One interesting example of this process was the furore about Salman Rushdie's *The Satanic Verses* and the response of some Muslim political leaders and community organisations to its publication. The attempt by some Muslim community leaders to use the affair as a means of political mobilisation received wide coverage in the media and led to a wide-ranging debate about the future of race relations in British society. Sections of the press used the events surrounding the affair to question the possibility of a peaceful transition towards a multi-racial society. Hostile media coverage thus served to reinforce the view that minorities who do not share the dominant political values of British society pose a threat to social stability and cohesion. The affair also gave added impetus to debates about the multiple cultural and political identities that have been included in the broad categorisation of 'black and ethnic minority communities'. This is an issue to which we shall return in chapter 10.

Another focus has been the role of race and ethnicity as symbols in a variety of cultural forms, including literature and the cinema. This has traditionally been a neglected area of research but in recent years this has been remedied by the publication of a number of important studies of race, culture and identity. Originating largely from the US such studies have looked at a number of areas, including literature, the cinema and other popular cultural forms. They have sought to show that within contemporary societies our understanding of race, and the articulation of racist ideologies, cannot be reduced to economic, political or class relations.

This type of approach is in fact more evident outside sociology. The work of literary and cultural theorists in the US and Britain has in recent years begun to explore seriously the question of race and racism, and has led to a flowering of studies which use the debates around poststructuralism and postmodernism as a way of approaching the complex forms of racialised identities in colonial and postcolonial societies (Gates, 1986, 1988; Goldberg, 1990).

Perhaps as a result of broader transformations in social theory this area of research has developed rapidly in recent years. Apart from studies of contemporary trends there has also been a growth of interest in historical research on the origins of ideas about race and in the dynamics of race, class and gender during the colonial period. This has been reflected in important and valuable accounts of the changing usage of racial symbols during the past few centuries and in accounts of the experiences of colonialism and their impact on our understanding of race and culture. The work of Gayatri Spivak has helped to highlight, for example, the complex processes of racial and gender identification experienced by the colonised during the colonial and postcolonial periods (Spivak, 1987). Other studies have sought to show that the oppressed themselves have produced their own discourses about race and identity in the context of their own experiences of domination and exclusion (Bhabha, 1990; Young, 1990).

What kind of alternative?

Given the critical tone of the above discussion of existing approaches to the study of race and racism in contemporary Britain, the question arises as to what kind of alternative analysis will be offered in this book. There are, in fact, two basic elements which make up the distinctive contribution offered here to the study of the politics of racism. The first is an insistence on the need to look at the impact of racism on politics and ideology in contemporary Britain beyond the scope of conventional politics. The second is a detailed analysis of the impact of racist ideologies and nationalist discourses, anti-racist discourses, and black political action on political institutions and forms of political mobilisation. Since the 1950s political discourses on race and nation have become a central component of British political culture, a phenomenon which can only be partially understood if one looks merely at the role of extreme right-wing groups or the ideologies of the new right. Much more central, and of vital importance for future political change, are the complex interrelationships of power which are represented through the political language of race.

It is not the aim of this book to provide a detailed analysis of all the issues that will be raised, since the main channel for a historical and multidimensional conception of the politics of racism must be a critical and more reflexive debate among scholars, researchers and practitioners. There are areas of the political analysis of racism which have still to be analysed and yet others that need to be understood more fully. But such work must be part of a longer-term project which aims to comprehend the 'concrete historical work which racism accomplishes under specific historical conditions – as a set of economic, political and ideological practices' (Hall, 1980: 338–42).

Although much of the recent work on the politics of racism can be seen as a contribution to such an understanding, there are a number of areas which need to be analysed more fully, including (a) the politicisation of racism from the postwar conjuncture to the growth of Powellism and the institutionalisation of racist discourse; (b) the growth of popular racism and its relationship to the broader economic and legitimation crisis of the British state; (c) the role of black politics in redefining the terms of political discourse about race; (d) the politics of policing and disorderly protest in relation to black communities and their environment.

A number of recent studies have addressed these issues in some form or other. Robert Miles and Annie Phizacklea, for example, have attempted to analyse the racialisation of British political culture since 1945 as an outcome of the complex intermingling of economic, political and ideological relations (Miles and Phizacklea, 1984). Zig Layton-Henry has provided a detailed narrative history of the politics of race, particularly in relation to party politics and electoral strategies (Layton-Henry, 1984). Gary Freeman has analysed the differences in the responses of the British and French labour movements to immigration through an intricate account of shifting political ideologies and economic conditions (Freeman, 1979). A number of recent studies have analysed the role of black political mobilisation through the mainstream political parties and in relation to specific policy issues (Fitzgerald, 1984; Anwar, 1986; Jacobs, 1986). More provocatively, and perhaps too abstractly, some authors have talked of the emergence of a new racism, which is defined by the way it mobilises notions of culture and nation to construct a definition of the British nation which excludes those of a different cultural, ethnic or racial background from the national collectivity (Barker, 1981; CCCS Race and Politics Group, 1982; Reeves, 1983; Miles and Phizacklea, 1984; Gilroy,1987).

The narrow focus of these studies, however, has meant that they have not addressed two core questions. The first focuses on the general characteristics of racism in British society and asks: How do political structures and institutions in Britain function in relation to race and in what ways do they produce/reproduce or help overcome racism? The second points to a related but more concrete set of concerns about how racism is formed and transformed historically, asking: How does racism shape the ways in which class, gender and other social relations are actually experienced and how do they structure political action?

The chapters that follow detail some of the major perspectives which have been used to account for the racialisation of British politics and evaluate them against each other on the basis of these two fundamental questions. This leads on to a critical analysis of the racialisation of politics at specific points in British history and the substantive content of state interventions to manage race relations in contemporary Britain.

Summary and conclusion

The past four decades have seen important developments in the study of racial and ethnic issues in British society. What is also clear is that over this period the politics of race and racism have undergone numerous transformations, some of which have hardly begun to be discussed. No one theoretical perspective is dominant at the present time. Indeed little of the mainstream research in this field is theoretically informed in any substantial way. There is a need for greater theoretical clarity on key concepts and a broadening of the research agenda to cover issues that have been neglected, such as the politics of culture and identity. But in this sense Banton may well be right in his contention that different theoretical paradigms may be able to contribute their own distinctive accounts of the processes which involve the attribution of specific meanings to racial situations (Banton, 1991).

Yet, it is clear that we are a long way from resolving many of the theoretical problems which have preoccupied many writers in recent years. It has to be admitted as well that there are real problems in trying to make sense of the constructions of race that are to be found in particular discursive fields. This is something I have discussed elsewhere in relation to my research on the changing dynamics of race and politics in Birmingham (Back and Solomos, 1992c).

What is interesting is that although many writers argue against the use of race as an analytic category in social analysis their own accounts are persistently bedevilled by the paradox that ideas about race continue to pervade social, political and cultural relations. The problem which has preoccupied many writers has been how to establish the epistemological validity and causal power of racialisation and race formation without endorsing everyday ideological discourse. A number of writers have attempted to use these concepts to analyse the processes by which race has been socially and politically constructed in specific historical, political and institutional contexts. A key concern of these studies is the need to develop a dialectical view of racialisation as a process which has specific effects on politics and ideology. Aspects of this process include the impact of racist ideologies and nationalist discourses, anti-racist discourses, and black political action on political institutions and forms of political mobilisation.

The study of race and racism has clear political consequences, whether intended or unintended. Any analysis of this issue must therefore have a clear theoretical understanding of the questions to be asked, methods to be used, and the political climate within which the research is to be carried out. This is precisely what this chapter has attempted to do. But many of the questions it has raised will perhaps become clearer after reading the subsequent chapters, and so we shall return to them for further reflection in the concluding chapters.

2 Historical Background and Context

Introduction

This chapter covers an issue which is addressed inadequately in many texts about race and racism in contemporary British society, namely the role that earlier processes of migration and settlement played in shaping our understanding of this issue. The focus is specifically on the interplay of debates about race and immigration from the late nineteenth century and into the early part of this century. This is necessary because it is impossible to comprehend fully the politicisation of racial questions in Britain since 1945 without a historical perspective, despite the tendency of many recent studies to ignore this dimension.

In particular we shall examine three dimensions of this historical background: (a) the history and political response to Irish migration; (b) the politics of Jewish immigration; and (c) the history of the migration of black and other colonial peoples to Britain, particularly in the early twentieth century. These three aspects link up directly with the politics of race and immigration since 1945. All three aspects are deserving of more detailed analysis, and some important work on the history of these issues has already been carried out. An interesting overview of the major migratory processes since the nineteenth century can be found in Colin Holmes's *John Bull's Island*, which covers the history of immigration and British politics from the late nineteenth century to the 1970s (Holmes, 1988). The history of black settlement in Britain is analysed in some detail in Peter Fryer's *Staying Power*, which contains a wealth of original sources (Fryer, 1984).

Additionally there are clearly other aspects which are being addressed in the growing and rich literature on the history of immigration and on the social and political processes which have shaped the construction of 'Britishness' over the past two centuries (Holmes, 1988; Samuel, 1989a; Colley, 1992). Recent research on these and related questions has highlighted the historically contingent and contradictory forces which have shaped popular notions of 'Britishness' and 'Englishness', and their interactions with the role of race and empire in British political life (Rich, 1986).

The historical context of racism in Britain

In terms of the arguments developed in the previous chapter, an understanding of the processes which produce and reproduce social distinctions based on racial and ethnic divisions requires an analysis of both the historical context and contemporary social relations. Only by analysing the way in which history overlaps the present is it possible to understand the continuities and discontinuities between contemporary racial ideologies and previous forms.

There is by now a rich comparative literature on the complex forms which racial ideologies and structures have taken in different societies over time and space (Greenberg, 1980; Fredrickson, 1981; Wolf, 1982). This body of work includes studies of the development of racial ideologies and institutions in the US and South Africa, the two situations that have attracted most attention over the years. But increasingly attention is turning to the history of racial categorisation in other societies, and comparative research is being broadened to include the situation in societies such as Britain.

Yet it is clear that much of the analysis of race relations in Britain since 1945 has been dominated by perspectives which lack a historical and comparative dimension. There are, of course, some notable exceptions to this trend, and a number of useful monographs have analysed the complex history of racial thought, of immigration and of anti-Semitic and other racist political trends in Britain (Holmes, 1978 and 1979; Lunn, 1980; Fryer, 1984). Such studies have highlighted two interrelated issues. First, the complex variety of migratory processes which have occurred at various times in British history. Second, a number of studies have looked at aspects of the continuities and discontinuities between the political and social responses to these waves of immigration.

As argued in Chapter 1, however, the relative neglect of racial and ethnic issues in the study of British politics has had a negative effect on the development of a detailed political analysis of migration and racial categorisation. Thus while in the past decade there has been a renewed interest in analysing contemporary political conflicts over race, particularly in the aftermath of the urban unrest during the 1980s, this has not resulted in rigorous attempts to analyse the main trends in the historical development of racism in Britain.

Anglo-Saxons and Celts

The story of Irish emigration to Britain and the political responses to it represents an important, but often ignored, aspect of the historical background to contemporary debates about race and immigration. While an Irish presence in Britain can be traced back over several centuries, the issue of Irish immigration is usually considered separately from other migrations since, in the words of James Walvin, it is seen as a special case (Walvin, 1984: 48–60). More recently, however, the theoretical work of Bob Miles on migrants has served to emphasise the historical importance of Irish immigration and its relevance to any rounded political analysis of this issue (Miles, 1982: 121–50). A number of detailed historical studies of migration from Ireland to Britain and responses to it have helped to focus more attention on this question (Gilley, 1978 and 1980; Curtis, 1984; Swift and Gilley, 1985).

The history of Irish emigration to Britain can be traced back to the late eighteenth and early nineteenth centuries (Hechter, 1975), a period of important economic and social changes in both Ireland and Britain. During this time the emigration of Irish labour to Britain seems to have been largely determined by the uneven interdependence between the two societies and the pace of economic and social transformation within them. The genesis of Irish immigration was therefore connected with a period of rapid economic change, urbanisation and class formation within British society. According to the account developed by Miles it was precisely this process of rapid social change that led to the demand for labour and a search for new sources of labour (Miles, 1982: 121–50).

At the same time in Ireland a process of land consolidation was occurring in the north and east as part of the process of development of capitalist agriculture (Hechter, 1975; Redford, 1976). The objective was to produce grain, meat and dairy products as commodities for exchange in Britain and the result for sections of the Irish population in these regions was dispossession and ejection from the land. In the south and west, which were dominated by small peasant landowners or small tenant producers, a process of extensive subdivision of plots was underway in a context where the population was increasing and the potato had been introduced as the main crop and means of subsistence. The consequent freeing of sections of the population from the land coincided with attempts to establish capitalist industrial production within Ireland, especially around Belfast, where a demand for labour was developing. Following the Act of Union and the subsequent abolition of protective tariffs in Ireland, the development of capitalist agriculture was intensified while the flow of cheap manufactured goods from Britain stemmed the rise of industrial production within Ireland (Miles, 1982; Swift and Gilley, 1985).

During this early period Irish migration to Britain tended to be seasonal, especially on the part of small peasant producers who sought a cash income to meet increasing rent demands. The potato was planted early in the year and then the men of the family unit migrated to Britain to sell their labour to British farmers, especially during harvesting (Jackson, 1963; Lees, 1979). In 1841 approximately 60 000 seasonal migrants came to Britain from Ireland but the numbers declined from the 1850s, although demand for their labour power remained high in certain areas. However seasonal migration was only a serious option for those who retained access to land in Ireland. Thus, in combination with a growing demand for semi- and unskilled wage labour in British urban areas, a second consequence was the development of an emigration from Ireland which resulted in settlement in Britain.

The appearance of potato blight in 1845, and the resulting starvation, intensified a migration that was therefore already well-established (Jackson, 1963: 7–9). The 1841 census indicated that there were more than 289 404 Irish people living in England and Wales and 126 321 in Scotland. By the 1851 census, largely as a consequence of the famine, the Irish population increased to 519 959 in England and Wales and 207 367 in Scotland. The peak was evident in the 1861 Census which gave the total Irish-born population resident in England and Wales as 601 634, although in Scotland it had declined somewhat to 204 083. After this there was a slow decline. In 1901 the Irish-born population was 426 565 in England and Wales, and 205 064 in Scotland (Holmes, 1988: 20–1). As a proportion of the total population the 1851 figures comprised 2.9 per cent for England and Wales and 7.2 per cent for Scotland (Jackson, 1963: 11).

In England the main areas of Irish settlement were London and Lancashire, with smaller concentrations in the West Midlands and Yorkshire (Jackson, 1963; Lees, 1979; Gilley, 1980; Waller, 1981; Miles, 1982; Swift and Gilley, 1985). In Scotland the main areas of settlement were in various parts of the west, particularly around Glasgow. This migration and settlement led to the formation of distinct communities, identifiable by cultural differences, notably religion (O Tuathaigh, 1985).

In purely numerical terms the number of Irish immigrants to Britain over the past two centuries has been far in excess of any other immigration. Yet, as a number of studies have shown, there has been little direct state intervention to regulate this migration and settlement, particularly when compared with the response to later Jewish and black migrations to Britain. Part of the explanation for this relative absence of state regulation of Irish immigration lies in the fact that in 1800 the Act of Union incorporated Ireland into the United Kingdom. In practice, and then in law, therefore, the population of Ireland has been incorporated into a larger political unit within which it had the status of common citizenship and within which it circulated in response to economic and political circumstances, within constraints imposed by the British state (Hechter, 1975; Miles, 1982).

This situation was maintained even after the formation of the Republic of Ireland in 1922 because citizens of the Irish Republic retained the right to enter freely and settle in Britain. Even after the Irish Republic left the Commonwealth in 1947 the British Nationality Act accorded citizens of the Republic the unique status of being free to enter, settle, work and vote in Britain (Evans, 1983: 61). Though there seems to have been some Cabinet opposition to the continuation of this status during the 1950s (DO 35/5219, 1957), there was no change in the policy of non-intervention in relation to Irish immigration.

This laissez-faire approach to Irish immigration did not mean there was no hostile political. There is in fact a long history of anti-Irish stereotypes and images in British culture (Curtis, 1968, 1971; Lebow, 1976; Dangerfield, 1976). At various times during the nineteenth century there was a hostile response to Irish migrants and this was helped by popular images which stereotyped them in terms of their Catholicism as well as their supposed biological inferiority (Gilley, 1978; Miles, 1982: 135–45; O Tuathaigh, 1985: 20–3). There was also widespread use of violence against Irish migrants (Waller, 1981; Millward, 1985; Gallagher, 1985).

The widespread nature of anti-Irish images in popular culture during the late nineteenth century has been illustrated in studies of working class and élite cultures. Holmes for example argues that in towns such as Liverpool 'a particularly fierce anti-Irish sentiment existed which was capable of combining various complementary strands of antipathy and susceptible to political exploitation' (Holmes, 1988: 60). Drawing on a study of popular images of the Irish in Victorian England, Curtis argued that not only were such images widespread among the working class but that 'many educated Victorians actually believed in the existence of a wide racial and cultural gap between themselves and Irish Celts' (Curtis, 1968: 121). Some aspects of these images were to persist well into the twentieth century.

It is important to note one final point about such beliefs and we shall return to it in later chapters. Images of the racial or cultural inferiority of the Irish were based not only on particular ideological constructions of the Irish but on a self-definition of Englishness or Anglo-Saxon culture in terms of particular racial and cultural attributes. In later years such images of the uniqueness and purity of Englishness were to prove to be equally important in the political debates about black migration and settlement (Reeves, 1983; Rich, 1986).

Political and ideological responses to Jewish immigration

From the late nineteenth century a significant factor in the politics of immigration was the arrival of large numbers of largely Jewish immigrants from Eastern Europe. The political and ideological responses to this immigration have often been compared to the post-1945 politics of black immigration. This interest in comparing the two periods is partly the result of the relative importance of political debates about immigration during these two periods. It is also because the Aliens Order of 1905 was a radical departure from previous policies on immigration and formed the foundation for subsequent legislation on this issue until after the Second World War (Garrard, 1971; Gainer, 1972; Gartner, 1973; Holmes, 1979).

The context of the politicisation of Jewish immigration during the late Victorian and Edwardian periods was the arrival of a new group of Jewish settlers from Eastern Europe, but as Lebzelter has pointed out it was the response of broad sections of British political opinion to these new arrivals that provides the key to understanding this process. She argues that:

> In the 1880s and 1890s as well as in the post-war period, anti-Semitism in England served as an explanatory model to account for objective problems – unemployment and poverty in the first instance, opposition against British authority in the Empire in the second – by attributing them to the outsider, the Jew (Lebzelter, 1981: 102).

As an illustration of how this process worked she gives the example of how in the context of economic crisis and high unemployment the slogan 'England for the English' became popular with both Conservatives and trade union leaders (ibid.: 90).

What is interesting in this context is that the level of political opposition to Jewish immigration was not simply related to the number of migrants. The pressure to restrict Jewish immigration contrasts sharply with the continuing and unrestricted entry of Irish migrants into Britain, who represented a numerically much larger group. In the late nineteenth century there were approximately 60 000 Jewish people living in Britain, more than half having been born in Britain. The majority of this population were shopkeepers and merchants, but a smaller proportion constituted a part of the capitalist class and another section were artisans of various kinds (Lipman, 1954: 27–9, 79–81). Between 1870 and 1914 some 120 000 Jewish people migrated to and settled in Britain (Gartner, 1973: 30) and by 1914 the Jewish population had grown to about 300 000 persons (Pollins, 1982: 130). This was relatively small when compared to the size of the Irish community, but from the 1880s to the First World War and afterwards Jewish immigration remained a bitterly controversial issue (Lee, 1980; Kennedy and Nicholls, 1981).

The political debates and state actions in response to this immigration were partly influenced by the processes of social and economic change of the particular localities of Jewish settlement. For example in the East End of London the political debates about Jewish immigration were structured by the context of competition for jobs, housing and amenities. Gainer argues that:

'Immigrant' and 'Jew' became synonymous terms because of the extraordinary concern for the social problems of the East End of London which emerged roughly at the time of the first great wave of immigration (Gainer, 1972: 3).

Holmes (1979) has shown that this wider social context was an important element in trade union agitation for immigration controls. These demands were recognised in resolutions passed at Trade Union Congresses in 1892, 1894 and 1895, although that section strongly in favour of restrictions on entry was small and weak (Garrard, 1971: 71, 174) because the economic consequences of Jewish immigration were experienced by only certain sections of the working class. But the more significant reflection of this opposition was evident in Parliament because a small number of Conservative MPs took up the issue in order to attract working class votes. Their support for restrictions on entry was logically and politically consistent with Conservative demands for state intervention for, for example, the protection of domestic industry (Gainer, 1972: 144; Pollins, 1982: 140). The Liberal Party, on the other hand, remained opposed to restrictive legislation because of its support for free trade and therefore the free movement of human beings as well as commodities (Garrard, 1971: 90).

Parliamentary support for immigration controls was linked with extra-Parliamentary action. In 1901 a Conservative MP for an East London constituency formed the British Brothers League to agitate against Jewish immigration and settlement. It organised mass protest rallies and attained a membership of around 45 000 people (Gainer, 1972: 60–73; Holmes, 1979: 89–97). The activities of the British Brothers League gave wider public prominence to the demand for control by Parliament, and agitation within Parliament made Jewish immigration a national political issue. The ideological form in which the political issue was expressed, and the motivation for some of the agitation, was explicitly racist (Gainer, 1972: 113) and articulated with nationalism (Garrard, 1971: 56).

The progress of the demand for restrictive legislation by Parliament is well documented (Garrard, 1971; Gainer, 1972; Alderman, 1983: 66-85). Demands for legislation were first raised in 1887 but could not be realised until the election of a Conservative government . But even after this happened in 1895, political circumstances obstructed their realisation until 1905 when the Aliens Order was passed. The legislation applied to the entry into Britain of all non-United Kingdom subjects, or those otherwise defined as 'aliens'. The most important provisions of the legislation were, first, that aliens could be refused permission to enter Britain if they did not have, or did not have the means to obtain, the means of subsistence in adequate sanitary conditions; and, second, that an alien could be expelled from Britain without trial or appeal if he or she was found to be receiving poor relief within a year of entering Britain, and if he or she was found guilty of vagrancy or was found to be living in insanitary conditions due to overcrowding. Other provisions of the order were that the home secretary was given the power to expel 'undesirable' immigrants, and that an immigrant refused permission to enter Britain could appeal to an immigration board. But the order also embodied in law the provision that an immigrant could not be refused permission to enter Britain where it could be shown that he or she was the subject of political or religious persecution (Gainer, 1972: 190; Macdonald, 1983: 8; Bevan, 1986: 71–2).

Soon after the Aliens Order became law the Conservative government was replaced by a Liberal government which, although it failed to repeal the legislation, implemented it in a non-restrictive manner. Until 1914 approximately 4–5000 Jews entered Britain annually (Lebzelter, 1978: 9). But it was the outbreak of war which initiated further legislation on immigration. The Aliens Restriction Act, 1914 passed through Parliament in a single day and gave the government considerable power to control immigration through Orders in Council, the justification for such powers being couched in terms of national security in circumstances of war. The legislation empowered the government to decide who could be prohibited from entering Britain, who could be deported and who could be subject to restrictions on where they lived and travelled.

After the end of the war the Aliens Restriction (Amendment) Act 1919 repealed the 1905 legislation and extended the 1914 Act for one year, despite the fact that the original justification for the Act no longer applied. In the following year a new Aliens Order was passed and thereafter the Acts of 1914 were renewed annually under the Expiring Laws Continuance Acts. Under the Aliens Order 1920 immigration officers could refuse entry to an alien who was considered unable to provide for his or her own support and they were also given increased powers to deal with aliens who had evaded immigration control. Aliens had to register their address and any change thereof. The Home Secretary gained the power to deport any alien whose presence was not considered to be 'conducive to the public good'. Finally, if an alien wished to work in Britain he or she could only do so following the issuing to an employer of a permit by the Ministry of Labour, the permit being issued only when it was shown that no British labour was available (Evans, 1983: 10–12; Macdonald, 1983: 8–9; Gordon, 1985: 9–11; Bevan, 1986: 72–4).

It is important to note that it was partly within the terms of this legislation that the British state responded to the growing numbers of Jewish and other refugees fleeing from Germany following the installation of a fascist government (Hirschfeld, 1984; Berghahn, 1984; Holmes, 1988). It is also important to recall that the substance of that legislation was that aliens considered to be without the means to support themselves could be refused permission to enter Britain, while poverty was not sufficient grounds to refuse entry to those claiming to be fleeing religious or political persecution.

Events demonstrated that other circumstances were cited as reasons for denying entry to Britain to political refugees. Throughout the period 1933–1939, the British government asserted that Britain was not suitable for immigration because of its large population and high level of unemployment, and therefore the admission of Jewish (and other) refugees from Germany could only be on a limited scale (Sherman, 1973: 259). During this time about 55 000 refugees from Germany, Austria and Czechoslovakia were admitted to Britain (Sherman, 1973: 271). But despite evidence of the consequences of events in Germany on the Jewish community there was a political reluctance to act decisively to help Jewish refugees because of widespread anti-Semitism within British society.

Race and labour in the early twentieth century

The historical presence of black communities within Britain can be traced back over several centuries. Black communities and individuals were a feature of British society and culture for centuries before the arrival of Asian and Afro-Caribbean immigrants after 1945. By the end of the nineteenth century black seamen had settled in Liverpool, London, Cardiff, Bristol and other port towns.

This is not the place to go into the details of this history, which has recently been the subject of a number of important and insightful studies (Walvin, 1973; Shyllon, 1974; Fryer, 1984; Ramdin, 1987). But we should look at some aspects of the politics of black migration and settlement in Britain in the early twentieth century, since it was during this period that the terms of political debate and domestic ideologies and policies towards 'coloured workers' and their communities began to be formed.

Indeed it was during this period that the issue of racial difference began to play a central role in the politics of immigration. This was the case despite the relatively small size of the black population and the fact that they possessed the formal right to citizenship. According to Harris (1988) a central theme in debates about the black communities during the interwar period related to the supposed social problems which their presence gave rise to:

> Social decay was supposed to be connected with the presence of a 'Negro' population of Somalis, Arabs, West Indians, West Africans and so on who constituted an almost insignificant percentage of the population of the sea-port towns (1988: 18).

Such issues were to become a more central feature of political debate from 1945, yet it is clear that their origins can be traced, to some extent, to the interwar years and the commonly held image of black communities in the port towns and beyond.

Part of the history of the interwar years period is being uncovered by the research of scholars such as Fryer, Rich and Harris, and by the increased interest in the history of the black presence in British society (Walvin, 1984; Ramdin, 1987). Much more research needs to be done, but its importance for any rounded analysis of the politics of race and racism in British political life is already clear.

Yet the preoccupation of the bulk of studies in this field remains with the period since 1945 and is stubbornly ahistorical, even when written from a radical perspective. This means that many important connections and continuities in the history of race and racism in British society are hardly discussed (Cohen, 1988).

Let us take an example of the consequences of such an approach, and its limitations. The preceding section was concerned with the policy of the British state towards the entry into Britain of people who were, by law, aliens, that is non-British citizens. Yet it is also clear that the legislation effected by the state was also used to deal with, and contained provisions concerning, certain categories of British subjects, specifically seamen recruited in different parts of the Empire, particularly from India and the Caribbean. Despite being British subjects, Indian seamen (widely known as lascars) had been subject to discriminatory treatment by the state since the nineteenth century, if not before, partly in order to limit their settlement in Britain when the passage that they had worked terminated in Britain.

An Act of 1813 required the East India Company to provide subsistence for Indian sailors in Britain until they returned to India, while an Act of 1823 stipulated that Indian seamen were not British subjects and prohibited them from becoming British subjects. These powers were consolidated in the Merchant Shipping Act 1894 which set out articles of agreement to be signed by Asian seamen and masters binding the former to return to their country of origin and giving the Secretary of State the power to repatriate those who attempted to become resident in Britain (Hepple, 1968: 42-4; Joshua and Wallace, 1983: 14–16; Gordon, 1985: 5–6). These attempts were only partially successful, as the continuing presence of Asian and Caribbean people in British seaports proved (Fryer, 1984: 294–5; Visram, 1986: 34–54; Ramdin, 1987).

After 1918 the British state reinforced discriminatory practices and made further efforts to prevent British subjects considered to be of a different race from settling in Britain. This occurred in the context of the ending of the First World War, during which time there had been an increase in the number of British subjects from the Empire employed as seamen. Concerning discriminatory practices, Section 5 (2) of the Aliens Restriction (Amendment) Act 1919 legalised different rates of pay for British subjects employed as seamen according to their race (Hepple, 1968: 44–5; Joshua and Wallace, 1983: 16). Additionally there was a slump in employment in the shipping industry after 1918 and the relevant trade unions campaigned to restrict employment to 'white' seamen. In the resulting competition for work, Indian, Chinese and Caribbean seamen resident in Britain became the victims of racist violence in Cardiff, Liverpool and Glasgow (May and Cohen, 1974; Evans, 1980, 1985; Jenkinson, 1985). In Cardiff the police sought to 'repatriate' these seamen (Evans, 1985: 73–4). The Home Office pointed out that they were British subjects and therefore were not subject to enforced expulsion from Britain, but arrangements were made for the return of as many seamen as might be 'persuaded' to go. This initiative by the state was largely unsuccessful (Joshua and Wallace, 1983: 31–2).

Subsequently a further initiative was taken using Article 11 of the Aliens Order 1920. By refering to this Article the Special Restrictions (Coloured Alien Seamen) Order 1925 was drafted (Hepple, 1968: 45; Joshua and Wallace, 1983: 32–5; Gordon, 1985: 7: Evans, 1985: 80–1; Rich, 1986: 122–30). The Order formally applied to colonial seamen (who had previously been entitled to sign off from a ship in a British port and to seek residence there) who did not possess satisfactory documentary evidence of being British subjects. These seamen were required to obtain the permission of an immigration officer to land and were subject to removal from Britain. In practice the police, the Aliens Department and immigration officers forced 'coloured' British subjects possessing the required documentation to register under the Order, an action that deprived them of the legal status of British subjects and thereby rendered them subject to the powers of the Alien Restriction (Amendment) Act 1919 and the Aliens Order 1920 – including the requirement that they register with the police, to whom they were required to report any change of address – and to the possibility of deportation. Joshua and Wallace comment that:

> The Order was specifically designed to restrict the entry and settlement of black colonial British citizens. But, because the Conservative government did not wish to undermine the notion of a British subject which was at the heart of the Empire, the Order could achieve its ends through a series of legalistic contortions and double standards (1983: 32).

The concern of the state, both at the local and national level, was multi-faceted. It was responding to local racist agitation and violence against those defined as 'coloured' seamen, action that was grounded in the inability of the economic system to provide full employment (Lunn, 1985). But it was also grounded in a wider, racist concern that followed from the settlement of these seamen in Britain, specifically the growth of a population that resulted from sexual relations between these seamen and indigenous women (Rich, 1986: 120–44; Ramdin, 1987).

In the same way as after 1945, the two most common responses to black immigration and settlement were reflected in political debates about the need to control the arrival of this group of migrants and in calls for the repatriation of those who had already settled in Britain. Partly through the violent conflicts which occurred with some regularity in some of the port towns, but largely through the mobilisation of images of the black communities as a source of social problems, even the relatively small-scale black settlements that took shape in the interwar period were perceived as 'alien' and a possible threat to the British way of life.

Summary and conclusion

In the light of the story told in this chapter it becomes difficult to sustain the notion that the politicisation of immigration and racial issues is somehow a unique feature of political life since 1945. By the Second World War there was already a long historical experience of political debate and mobilisation around issues of ethnicity, race and religion. The complex history of these processes has, indeed, only barely been touched upon in this chapter.

In part the response of the state and political institutions to Irish, Jewish and black colonial and other immigrants before 1945 was the product of the specific social, economic and political conditions prevalent at the time. Yet the experience of the past four decades cannot be completely separated from this longer historical experience of racial and ethnic categorisation. Indeed it can be argued that we can best understand aspects of the more contemporary experience of racism in Britain if we look back at this historical background and compare the processes through which racialised political action developed in different periods. This is a point to which we shall return once we have analysed the history of race and immigration since 1945.

3 The Politics of Race and Immigration since 1945

Introduction

The story of the politics of immigration from the nineteenth century onwards told in the previous chapter has shown us that immigration and race were contested issues long before the arrival of large numbers of black colonial immigrants from 1945. We have seen that the response of political institutions to the arrival of Irish, Jewish and black immigrants was complex and not uniform. The response to Irish migrants, despite a degree of opposition and some violent confrontation was markedly different from the attempts to exclude and control Jewish and black migrants. There was also a more limited political mobilisation in defence of the interests of these groups.

In this chapter we shall look at the history of ideological and political responses to the arrival and settlement of black immigrants from 1945 onwards. Of course migrants from a variety of racial and ethnic backgrounds have continued to arrive and settle in Britain, and it is important in any rounded account of migrant labour to look at their experiences also (Holmes, 1988). For the purposes of this study, however, we shall now concentrate on the politics of black immigration and settlement since 1945.

This period has attracted the attention of most researchers on racial issues in Britain, and there is by now a voluminous literature on most aspects of this phenomenon. Looking specifically at the politics literature, two main themes have been highlighted above all else. First, a number of studies have sought to analyse how the question of immigration per se has become inextricably linked to black immigration, that is the arrival of migrants from the new Commonwealth and Pakistan (Katznelson, 1976; Freeman, 1979; Layton-Henry, 1984). This body of work has looked particularly at the political debates about black immigration and the role of changing political ideologies in the construction of racial issues.

Second, other research has shown how successive governments have attempted to regulate and eventually halt the arrival of black immigrants through immigration legislation and other means (Sivanandan, 1982; Macdonald, 1983; Miles and Phizacklea, 1984).

According to this body of work arguments about the supposed problems created by the arrival of too many black immigrants have been used to legitimise legislative measures which have had the effect of institutionalising controls on black immigrants, thereby excluding potential immigrants on the basis of the colour of their skin.

Both these interpretations have been the subject of much controversy and debate, to which we shall refer in the course of this chapter. The main task, however, will be to analyse and explain the political and ideological responses to the arrival of immigrants from the West Indies, India, Pakistan and other new Commonwealth countries. The first section provides a critical review of the development of political opinions and policy responses immediately after the war. We then move on to assess the impact of state intervention on the patterns of black immigration, and to look at how immigration became a focus of political discourse and conflict from the 1940s to the 1990s.

The tensions evident in political debates about immigration since 1945 are ones to which we shall return in Chapters 8 and 10. There we shall explore the various ways in which political mobilisation around racial symbols took place, both in the form of racist political actions and in the political mobilisation of the black communities themselves. For the moment we shall concentrate on the processes of political debate and decision making.

The post-1945 conjuncture and European migration

During the Second World War black settlement in Britain became an issue in a number of related but distinct ways. As a result of the war black workers and soldiers arrived from the colonies to fight in the British army or to help with the war effort (Richmond, 1954; Sherwood, 1984). Additionally, black American soldiers also arrived and attracted a variety of responses (Smith, 1987). At the time there was concern about two issues. First, the social effect of the arrival of new groups of black workers and soldiers on the older black seaport settlements. Second, there was increased concern that the arrival of new black immigrants could lead to conflict and the institutionalisation of a 'colour bar' in a number of towns.

Despite evidence of increased concern about black immigration both during and immediately after the war, the debate about immigration did not focus primarily on the arrival of black colonial migrants. Despite the arrival of the SS *Empire Windrush* in 1948 with some 400 British subjects from the Caribbean there was no large scale immigration from the colonies and dominions at this stage – most of the migrants arriving in Britain from 1945 to 1954 were from other European countries. Between 1945 and 1951 between 70 000 and 100 000 Irish people entered Britain. Although some concern was expressed later about the entry of Irish migrants, there was surprisingly little debate about this issue at this stage (PREM 11/1409, 1956; Jackson, 1963; Holmes, 1988; Kay and Miles, 1992).

The Labour government was instrumental in encouraging the settlement of Polish soldiers and their families in Britain (Zubrzycki, 1956: 36; Lunn, 1980). In 1940 the exiled Polish government and armed forces (a total of 30 500 persons) were allowed to enter Britain. Additionally the Polish Second Corps, which joined the British Command in 1942, was brought to Britain in 1946, followed by families and dependants of members of the Polish armed forces. The latter were subsequently absorbed into the Polish Resettlement Corps and those who were unwilling to return to Poland were given the option of settling in Britain. It has been estimated that in 1949 the resident Polish population in Britain consisted of 91 400 members the Polish Resettlement Corps, 31 800 dependants of Polish ex-servicemen, 2 400 relatives and 2 300 additional ex-members of the Polish armed forces. These groups totalled 127 900 persons, to which one can add 29 400 European volunteer workers of Polish origin (Zubrzycki, 1956: 62).

The other significant group of migrants encouraged by the government was recruited by the state specifically to resolve labour shortages in certain sectors of the economy. On the European mainland there were several camps for displaced persons or political refugees who were unable or did not wish to return to their country of birth following the redrawing of political boundaries after the defeat of Germany, and the Labour government decided to send out Ministry of Labour officials to recruit some as workers. The occupants of these camps were or had been, in law, nationals of other countries and were therefore aliens as far as the British state was concerned. But the procedures for admission under the Aliens Order 1920, concerned as they were with the admission of single persons, were not appropriate for what was to become a considerable migration. The result was, in the British context, a unique scheme, the British state undertaking to meet all the costs of recruitment, transport and repatriation on behalf of those capitalists short of labour power. In a number of respects this action anticipated the contract migrant labour system set up by a number of Western European states in the 1950s and 1960s (Castles and Kosack, 1985; Castles *et al.*, 1984; Miles, 1986). The total cost of the scheme up to October 1948 was £2.75 million (Tannahill, 1958: 56).

Those displaced persons who came to Britain were required to sign a contract, the terms of which stated that they would accept work selected by the Minister of Labour and that they could only change that employment with the permission of the Ministry of Labour. Therefore they became European Volunteer Workers (EVWs). Following health checks they were admitted initially for one year, an extension being dependent upon the individual complying with the conditions of the contract and behaving 'as a worthy member of the British community' (Tannahill, 1958: 123–8). Many of those recruited were not initially eligible to bring their dependants with them, although most of those who eventually settled in Britain were subsequently joined by their families. The conditions of placement of EVWs in employment varied but usually included the requirements that no British labour was available, that in the event of redundancy EVWs would be the first to be made unemployed, that EVWs should join the appropriate trade union and that they should receive the same wages and conditions as British workers (Tannahill, 1958: 57).

EVWs were recruited during 1947 and 1948 under a number of different schemes, the most important being the Balt Cygnet and Westward Ho schemes. In total 74 511 persons (17 422 women and 57 089 men) were recruited by those two schemes. Most originated from Estonia, Latvia, Lithuania, Poland and Yugoslavia. In addition 8 397 Ukrainian prisoners of war were brought to Britain for political reasons in 1947 and it was subsequently decided to treat them as EVWs. Under the North Sea and Blue Danube schemes 12 000 German and Austrian women were recruited on a distinct temporary contract for two years, most returning to Germany and Austria upon the termination of the contract. Under a similar arrangement 5 000 Italians of both sexes were also recruited (Tannahill, 1958: 5–6, 30–3). Although, approximately 85 000 refugees were recruited as workers for employment in the late 1940s, this total was lower than that originally envisaged. For example it was anticipated that 100 000 workers would be recruited in 1948 alone.

The encouragement given to these two groups of migrants to settle in Britain contrasted with the concern of the government with the social and political consequences of the relatively small scale migration from the colonies during this period. What recent research has made clear is that even at this early stage black migration and settlement was politically perceived in a different way from European migration. Privately the government was considering the most desirable method of discouraging or preventing the arrival of 'coloured' British citizens from the colonies.

Migration, colonial labour and the state: 1945–62

At the end of the Second World War the British state had legislative powers in the form of the Aliens legislation to control the entry into Britain and access to the labour market of non-British subjects. However the vast majority of British subjects in the colonies and dominions retained a legal right to enter and settle in Britain. This legal right was confirmed by the British Nationality Act of 1948 which, in response to the granting of independence to India, made a formal distinction between British subjects who were citizens of the United Kingdom and its colonies and those who were Common-wealth citizens, both categories of people having the right to enter, settle and work in Britain (Evans, 1983: 59–62; Bevan, 1986: 112–13). Additionally citizens of the Republic of Ireland retained the right of unrestricted entry and settlement. Despite this the state encouraged the use of immigrants from Europe to meet the demand for labour. Some British subjects from the colonies did arrive during this period, particularly from the West Indies, but almost as soon as they began to arrive they were perceived as a problem.

The relatively liberal attitude towards the arrival of European workers contrasted sharply with the fears expressed about the social and racial problems which were seen as being related to the arrival of 'coloured' colonial workers, even though they were British subjects. Both the Labour governments of 1945–51 and the Conservative governments of the 1950s considered various ways of stopping or reducing the number of black migrants arriving and settling in Britain (Joshi and Carter, 1984; Carter, Harris and Joshi, 1987; Dean, 1987). It was during this time that the terms of political debate about 'coloured' immigration were established, leading to a close association between race and immigration in both policy debates and in popular political and media discourses.

Contrary to the arguments of some scholars it seems quite inappropriate to view this period as an 'age of innocence' and lack of concern about black immigration into Britain (Rose *et al.*, 1969; Patterson, 1969; Deakin, 1970). Throughout the period an increasingly racialised debate about immigration took place, focusing on the supposed 'social problems' of having too many black immigrants and the question of how they could be stopped from entering given their legal rights following the 1948 British Nationality Act.

Although much publicity was given to the arrival of 417 Jamaicans on the *Empire Windrush* in May 1948, and the subsequent arrivals of large groups of West Indian workers, the focus on 'coloured' immigration helped to obscure the fact that the majority of immigrants continued to come from the Irish Republic, from 'white' Commonwealth countries and other European countries (Patterson, 1969: chapter 1; Miles and Phizacklea, 1984: 45–8). The number of West Indian immigrants, and later on the number of immigrants from India and Pakistan, has been shown to have been an issue of debate within the Cabinet during the period 1950–5, when various measures to control black immigration and to dissuade black workers from coming to Britain were considered. On the basis of a careful analysis of Cabinet and ministerial debates about immigration from the colonies, a recent study has concluded that from 1948 to 1962 the state was involved in complex political and ideological racialisation of immigration policy (Carter, Harris and Joshi, 1987).

The period between the 1948 Nationality Act and the 1962 Commonwealth Immigrants Act is frequently characterised as one in which the principle of free entry of British subjects into the UK was only relinquished with great reluctance and after considerable official debate. This was not the case. On the contrary the debate was never about principle. Labour and Conservative governments had by 1952 instituted a number of covert, and sometimes illegal, administrative measures to discourage black immigration (Carter, Harris and Joshi, 1987).

Throughout the 1950s the debate about immigration in Parliament and the media focused on the need to control black immigration. Although both in public debate and in private policy discussions attention was sometimes focused on the behaviour of 'undesirable' black immigrants, such as those involved in crime or prostitution, the terms of political debate throughout the 1950s were about the desirability of letting into Britain a sizeable number of West Indian or Asian migrants. The 1958 riots in Notting Hill and Nottingham may have helped further to politicise this process (Miles, 1984; Pilkington, 1988), but it is clear that both before and after the riots the question of control was being integrated into the policy agenda.

With the growing emphasis on the control of 'coloured' immigration the terms of ideological and policy debates about the future of black immigration turned on two themes which were to prove influential later on. First, a vigorous debate took place in and out of Parliament about the possibility of revising the 1948 Nationality Act so as to limit the number of black workers who could come and settle in the UK. The terms of this debate were by no means fixed purely by political party ideologies, and there was opposition from both Conservative and Labour politicians to the call for controls and the abandonment of the free entry principle. Second, a parallel debate developed about the problems caused by 'too many coloured immigrants' in relation to housing, employment and crime. This second theme became particularly important from 1956–8 and in the aftermath of the 1958 riots (*Hansard*, vol. 596, 1958, cols 1552–97).

By linking immigration to the social aspects of the 'colour problem' a theme was established which was later to prove influential in shaping both the immigration control legislation and the Race Relations Acts. This was the argument that it was necessary to use direct state intervention to halt the 'gathering momentum' of black immigration and to resolve the social 'problems' perceived as linked to it.

Controls on 'coloured' immigration had been discussed as early as the late 1940s, and were discussed seriously again in 1954 and 1955. A number of arguments were used in opposition to such controls, and it was not until 1961 that a bill to control Commonwealth immigration was introduced by the government. The reasons for the reluctance to introduce controls remains to some extent a matter of speculation, although the release of government documents for the early 1950s has shed some light on this non-decision making process (Joshi and Carter, 1984: 55–63; Rich, 1986: chapter 7). But at least part of the reluctance to introduce controls seemed to result from a concern about whether legislation which excluded black people could be implemented without causing embarrassment to Britain's position as head of the Commonwealth and Colonies, the fear that it would divide public opinion, and a doubt about the legality of controls based on colour in both British and international law (Deakin, 1968: 26–30; Miles and Phizacklea, 1984: chapter 2).

What is clear, however, is that the late 1940s to the late 1950s was not a period of laissez faire in relation to black immigration. Rather it was one of intense debate within government departments and in public circles about the impact of black immigration on housing, the welfare state, crime and other social problems. It is important to note, however, that these debates were not purely about the supposed characteristics of black immigrants. They were also about the effect of black immigration on the 'racial character of the British people' and on the national identity. Harris (1988) makes this point clear when he argues that the debates about black immigration during the 1950s reinforced a racialised construction of Britishness which excluded or included people on the grounds of race defined by colour:

> When individuals like the Marquis of Salisbury spoke of maintaining the English way of life, they were not simply referring to economic or regional folk patterns, but explicitly to the preservation of 'the racial character of the English people'. We have developing here a process of subjectification grounded in a racialised construction of 'British' Subject which excludes and includes people on the basis of 'race'/skin colour (Harris, 1988: 53).

This process was still in its early stages during this period, but it is impossible to understand the legislation passed to control black immigration during the 1960s and 1970s without referring to the genesis and articulation of political discourse about black immigration during the period from 1945 to 1962.

Immigration and racialised politics

The 1958 race riots in Nottingham and Notting Hill are commonly seen as an important watershed in the development of racialised politics in Britain. It is certainly true that the events in these two localities helped to bring to national prominence issues which had previously been discussed only locally or within government departments.

The riots themselves consisted of attacks by whites on blacks but this did not prevent them from being used as examples of the dangers of unrestricted immigration. By the time of the 1958 riots, however, the mobilisation of opinion in and out of Parliament in favour of controls was well advanced, and the disturbances in Nottingham and Notting Hill were used by the pro-immigration controls lobby to support calls for the exclusion or even the repatriation of 'undesirable immigrants'. They were also used in support of the argument that black immigration was a threat to the rule of law in the inner cities and endangered the 'English way of life'. Lord Salisbury used the riots to justify his claim that controls should be imposed on black immigration, and he argued that 'he was extremely apprehensive of the economic and social results, for Europeans and African alike, that were likely to flow from an unrestricted immigration of men and women of the African race into Britain' (*The Guardian*, 3 September 1958).

Between these events and the introduction of the Commonwealth Immigrants Bill in 1961 a number of important debates on immigration control took place in parliament and at party conferences (Patterson, 1969; Freeman, 1979: 49–52; Miles, 1984). In Parliament a number of Conservative MPs, including Cyril Osborne, organised a campaign in favour of immigration controls, though they made their case against 'coloured' immigrants largely through coded language. The Labour Party, along with the Liberals, generally argued against controls, though this was by no means the case for all Labour MPs and local councillors (Reeves, 1983: chapter 7; Layton-Henry, 1984: 31–43).

Outside Parliament there was widespread coverage in both the popular and serious newspapers of stories relating to race and immigration issues. There was a flowering of popular debate about housing and social conditions in areas of black settlement, about aspects of employment and competition for jobs, and a resurgence of extreme right-wing groups which sought to use immigration as a basis for political mobilisation. The interplay between these processes produced a wide variety of stereotypes and popular images about black people. In September 1958 *The Times* reported that in the areas affected by the riots:

here are three main causes of resentment against coloured inhabitants of the district. They are alleged to do no work and to collect a rich sum from the Assistance Board. They are said to find housing when white residents cannot. And they are charged with all kinds of misbehaviour, especially sexual (*The Times*, 3 September 1958).

It was precisely around such concerns that right-wing extremist groups focused much of their propaganda during and after the riots. There was no need in this context for such beliefs to be substantiated by evidence, but it proved equally difficult to counteract such stereotypes. This weakened the attempts to resist the pressures for immigration controls.

The ambiguities in the pressure for controls became even more pronounced during the early 1960s, the period of the passage of the first legislative measures controlling the immigration of citizens of the United Kingdom and colonies, the 1962 Commonwealth Immigrants Act. It is to this period that we now turn.

Immigration controls and state racism

In the previous section it was argued that the racialisation of the immigration issue during the 1950s formed the basis for the move towards the control of black immigration, an objective which was first implemented through the 1962 Commonwealth Immigrants Act. Part of the dilemma faced by the Conservative government of the time was how to legitimise a policy which aimed to control black immigration as a more universal measure. William Deedes, who was a Minister without Portfolio at the time, recalls that

The Bill's real purpose was to restrict the influx of coloured immigrants. We were reluctant to say as much openly. So the restrictions were applied to coloured and white citizens in all Commonwealth countries – though everybody recognised that immigration from Canada, Australia and New Zealand formed no part of the problem (Deedes, 1968: 10).

The racialisation of the immigration issue was in other words done through coded language: commonwealth immigrants were seen as a 'problem', but race itself was not always mentioned as the central issue. The politicisation of such terms was later to lead to a situation where, despite the continuing scale of white immigration, all immigrants were perceived as black and immigration became a coded term for talking about racial questions.

Two competing models have been used to explain the move towards immigration controls. Some scholars have seen this shift as a response by the state to the pressure of popular opinion against black immigration (Foot, 1965; Rose *et al.*, 1969). This is also the main line of argument used by some of the main political figures involved in the crucial debates about control of black immigration (Butler, 1971; Macmillan, 1973). Yet others have argued that the state was responding to the economic interests of the capitalist class, which required the adoption of a migrant labour system which undermined the right of black workers to migrate and settle freely in the UK (Sivanandan, 1982: 101–26).

Both explanations have been widely used in the extensive literature on the politics of immigration, but as we have indicated already it seems inadequate to view the role of the state as purely responsive, whether to popular opinion or to economic interests. Throughout the period 1948–62 the state was actively involved in monitoring and regulating the arrival of black workers, and it helped to articulate a definition of the immigration question which was suffused with racialised categories. Additionally, as recent research seems to indicate, the Conservative government came close to agreeing on a policy of controls on black immigration in 1955-56 (Carter, Harris and Joshi, 1987).

The genesis of the demand for the control of black immigration during the early 1950s matured during the period 1955–62 into a concerted campaign within the Cabinet, Parliament, the media and political parties in favour of action to 'curb the dangers of unrestricted immigration'. This in turn led to the policy debate which developed in the period leading up to the introduction of the Commonwealth Immigrants Bill in 1961 about the formulation of legislation which could exclude black labour from entry and settlement. This process can hardly be interpreted as a move from laissez faire to state intervention, since the state and its institutions were already heavily involved in defining the terms of the debate about the problems caused by black immigration.

The 1962 Commonwealth Immigrants Act

The acceptance of the need to extend administrative controls on black immigration into legislative action was formally announced in October 1961, when the Conservative government announced the introduction of the Commonwealth Immigrants Bill. The controls introduced by the Bill were legitimised by arguments about the need for a halt to black immigration because of the limited ability of the host society to assimilate 'coloured immigrants'. Even though some MPs and commentators were reluctant to accept that the Bill was simply a way of dealing with the immigration of 'coloured workers', the Labour Party and sections of the media identified the Bill as a response to crude racist pressures. Hugh Gaitskell, as Leader of the Labour Party, led a particularly strong attack on the Bill in Parliament and its crude amalgamation of immigration with race (Patterson, 1969: 17–20; *IRR Newsletter*: May 1962). But despite strong criticism from the Labour Party and sections of the press, the collective pressures against the entry of black British succeeded when the Commonwealth Immigrants Act became law in 1962.

Since it was the outcome of the sustained political campaign against black immigration, it is not surprising that despite claims to the contrary, the main clauses of the Act sought to control the entry of black Commonwealth citizens into Britain. The Act introduced a distinction between citizens of Britain and its colonies and citizens of independent Commonwealth counties. All holders of Commonwealth passports were subject to immigration control except those who were (a) born in Britain; (b) held British passports issued by the British government; or (c) persons included in the passport of one of the persons excluded from immigration control under (a) or (b) (Macdonald, 1983: 10–12). Other Commonwealth citizens had to obtain a Ministry of Labour employment voucher in order to be able to enter Britain. The Act initially provided for three types of vouchers:

- Category A: Commonwealth citizens who had a specific job to come to in Britain.
- Category B: applicants who had a recognised skill or qualification which was in short supply in Britain.
- Category C: all other applicants, priority treatment being given to those who had served in the British forces during the war.

The creation of these different categories was legitimised in coded terms as a way of controlling the number of immigrants entering the country, but it was clear in both the parliamentary and the media debates about the Bill that it was widely seen as a piece of legislation specifically aimed at black migrants. In this sense the Act can be seen as the climax of the campaign for the control of black immigration which was launched from both within and outside government during the 1950s.

Public debate about the Act reflected a variety of views and was by no means all in favour of it. In fact a number of lead articles in the press during 1961–2, along with sections of the Labour Party, expressed opposition to the racist thinking behind the Act. Concern was also expressed about the possible consequences of the passage of the Act for Britain's standing in the black Commonwealth countries (Deakin, 1968).

The changing terms of political debate

Almost as soon as the Act became law there was widespread debate about its effectiveness. From 1963 to 1972, when the voucher system was abolished, there was pressure to cut back the number of vouchers allocated, and this was reflected in a fall from a level of 30 130 vouchers in 1963 to 2 290 in 1972. Significantly, no controls were imposed on the entry of citizens of the Irish Republic into Britain. Nevertheless opponents of immigration were quick to call for even tighter controls, and in the political climate of the mid 1960s their voices were a major influence on the terms of political debate about race and immigration.

The opposition of the Labour Party to the Act was not sustained. When Harold Wilson took office as Labour Prime Minister in 1964 he announced that the Commonwealth Immigrants Act would be maintained. In 1965 the government issued a white paper on *Immigration from the Commonwealth* which called for controls to be maintained in an even stricter form, along with measures to promote the integration of immigrants. The white paper represented a shift in the direction of what some have called a 'Little England' policy (Rose *et al.*: 229) and signalled a convergence of the policies of the Conservative and Labour Parties in favour of immigration controls (Wilson, 1971).

This was to be exemplified by the nature of the political debate about race and immigration from 1964 to 1970, when the Labour Party was in power. Three events that represent good examples of this debate are the controversies over the electoral contest in Smethwick in 1964, the immigration of East African Asians during 1968–9 and the political turmoil caused by Enoch Powell's intervention in this debate from 1968 onwards.

Smethwick and immigration

The impact of events in Smethwick during 1964 on national political debates about race and immigration is sometimes forgotten. Yet it is no exaggeration to say that the political turmoil around the issue of immigration in Smethwick and the surrounding area had a deep impact on both the local and national political scene. Popular debate and media coverage were aroused by the contest between the Labour candidate, Patrick Gordon Walker, who was widely seen as a liberal on immigration, and the Conservative Peter Griffiths who fought the election largely on the basis of defending the interests of the local white majority against the 'influx of immigrants' (Foot, 1965; Deakin, 1972). In the volatile political climate of the time one of the slogans commonly heard during the election campaign was 'If you want a nigger for a neighbour vote Labour', and Griffiths was later to defend the use of this slogan as 'a manifestation of popular feeling' about immigration in the area, and refused to condemn those who used it (*The Times*, 1968: 139; Griffiths, 1966).

The debate about the implications of Griffiths' victory in Smethwick continued on for some time and was influential on both the Labour Party (*The Economist*, 7 August,1965; Deakin, 1965; Wilson, 1971; Crossman, 1975) and the Conservative Party (Berkeley, 1977; Layton-Henry, 1980). In the West Midlands region in particular the events in Smethwick helped to shift political debate and attitudes in both major parties towards a stance which emphasised their support for strict controls on black immigration (Lenton, *et al.*, 1966; Deakin, 1972).

East African Asians

One of the features of the 1962 Act was that citizens of the United Kingdom living in independent Commonwealth countries were exempt from control provided they had a British passport. This included a large number of European settlers as well as a sizeable number of East African Asians in Kenya and Uganda. From 1965 to 1967 a steady flow of this group began to arrive in Britain and when sections of the media and MPs started to call for action to be taken to stop their arrival a heated political debate ensued in late 1967 and early 1968.

This debate reached its climax in February 1968. As noted above, between 1963 and 1965 the Labour Party had moved towards acceptance of the need for firm immigration controls and so it came as no surprise when it responded to this political campaign by introducing the second Commonwealth Immigrants Act in early 1968. This Act sought to control the flow of East African Asians by bringing them under immigration control. Under the new law any citizen of Britain or its colonies who held a passport issued by the British government would be subject to immigration control unless they or at least one parent or grandparent was born, adopted, naturalised or registered in Britain as a citizen of Britain or its colonies.

The political context in which the Act was passed made it difficult to argue that it was non-racial, as to some extent had been claimed by the Conservative government which had passed the 1962 Act. *The Times* contrasted the behaviour of the Labour government to the attitude of the Labour opposition in 1962 and went so far as to call the Act a 'colour bar' and 'probably the most shameful measure that the Labour members have ever been asked by their whip to support' (*The Times*, 27 February 1968).

The transformation of the political climate between 1962 and 1968 was, however, clear enough for all to see in the Parliamentary debates about the 1968 Act. Given the highly politicised nature of the debate around the Act and the defensive stance taken by the government, only a few MPs and newspaper commentators saw fit to question the racism which underlay the legislation (Freeman, 1979: 56; Miles and Phizacklea, 1984: 59–67). In the period between the 1968 Act and the 1970 election, which saw the return of a Conservative government, there was further racialisation of the immigration issue. Even though it was difficult to see how immigration could be cut even further than the controls imposed by the 1962 and 1968 Acts, it was precisely during the period 1968–70 that immigration and race relations became issues of partisan political debate on a larger scale than before.

Powellism and political debate

During this period the Labour government was forced onto the defensive by Enoch Powell's famous 'rivers of blood' speech in Birmingham in April 1968, which helped to popularise the racial message that even tighter controls on immigration were not enough to deal with the 'race problem'. In this speech, and in a succession of others over the next few years, Powell sought to warn of what he saw as (a) the dangers of immigration leading to a 'total transformation to which there is no parallel in a thousand years of British history' and (b) the longer term danger of increasing racial tensions manifesting themselves in Britain on the American model. In the most infamous section of his speech Powell said:

> As I look ahead, I am filled with foreboding. Like the Roman, I seem to see 'the River Tiber foaming with much blood'. The tragic and intractable phenomenon which we watch with horror on the other side of the Atlantic, but which there is interwoven with the history and existence of the States itself, is coming upon us here by our own volition and our own neglect (*The Observer*, 21 April 1968).

According to Powell's argument the long-term solution to the immigration issue went beyond immigration controls and was likely to involve the repatriation of immigrants already settled in Britain. Such a line of argument helped to push political debate beyond controls as such and established repatriation as part of the political agenda. Indeed in the same speech Powell used all his rhetorical powers to construct an image of white Britons increasingly becoming isolated and 'strangers' in their 'own country':

> They found their wives unable to obtain hospital beds in childbirth, their children unable to obtain school places, their homes and neighbourhoods changed beyond recognition, their plans and prospects for the future defeated (ibid.)

Against this background Powell was able to argue that it was the failure of successive governments to act decisively to halt immigration in the 1950s that had led to a situation where more drastic measures were required to 'solve' the problem.

The furore caused by the speech was such that Powell was forced out of the shadow cabinet. There was extensive media coverage of the issues he raised throughout 1968 and 1969 and in the period leading up to the 1970 general election (*IRR Newsletter*, April/May 1968 and April 1969). It also acted as a focus for those calling not only for tighter controls on black immigration but for action to facilitate the repatriation of those black immigrants already settled.

Institutionalising immigration controls

Within the political climate created by Powell's interventions and the ensuing political debates, the continued arrival of the dependants of Commonwealth migrants already settled in Britain helped to keep the numbers game alive, leading to increasing calls in and out of Parliament and in the media for more action to halt immigration and to deal with the problems that were popularly seen as associated with it. The combined effect of those two pressures, and the use of immigration as an electoral issue, opened up the possibility of further legislative measures.

In 1969 the Labour government introduced the Immigration Appeals Act, which was officially based on the report of the Committee on Immigration Appeals headed by Sir Roy Wilson (Macdonald, 1983: 269). This report accepted the need for restrictions on immigration, but argued that a system of appeal ensured that the restrictions were applied fairly. Although this Act is sometimes interpreted as a positive measure, it institutionalised a process of deportation for those breaking conditions attached to entry. It also legitimised restrictions on the right of entry of those who were legally entitled to settle in Britain through the obligation that dependants seeking settlement in Britain had to be in possession of an entry certificate. Such certificates had to applied for at an interview at the nearest British High Commission. Applicants had to prove their claimed relationship to the person legally resident in Britain, and if they were unable to do so they could be denied entry. It is under this system that many recent controversial cases have arisen (Moore and Wallace, 1975; CRE, 1985b).

The marked shift of the Labour Party towards the idea of firm immigration controls was part of a wider political process which led to the introduction of the 1971 Immigration Act by the Conservative government. During the 1970 election campaign the Conservative Party had promised that there would 'be no further large-scale permanent immigration'. When the Immigration Bill was introduced in February 1971 it was legitimised on this basis, but as a number of speakers pointed out during the debates on the Bill it was difficult to see how it would actually reduce further the number of primary immigrants. In essence the 1971 Act qualified the notion of citizenship by differentiating between citizens of Britain and its colonies who were patrial and therefore had the right of abode in Britain, and non-patrials who did not. The most important categories of patrials were:

- Citizens of Britain and its colonies who had the citizenship by birth, adoption, naturalisation or registration in Britain or who were born of parents, one of whom had British citizenship by birth, or one of whose grandparents had such citizenship.
- Citizens of Britain and its colonies who had at any time settled in Britain and who had been ordinarily resident in Britain for five years or more.

Under the Act all aliens and Commonwealth citizens who were not patrials needed permission to enter Britain. Whilst before, Commonwealth citizens entering under the voucher system could settle in Britain, after the 1971 Act came into force they entered on the basis of work permits. They thus became subject to control by annual work permit, and therefore to the non-renewal of the permit. This change of status has been defined by some scholars as a move towards the migrant worker system of other European countries, with Commonwealth workers who were not patrials (and by definition almost certainly black) reduced to the effective status of short-term contract workers rather than settlers (Castles and Kosack, 1985; Sivanandan, 1982: 108–12).

During the Parliamentary debates on the 1971 Immigration Act the amalgamation of immigration with race became an issue of dispute between the Conservative and Labour parties. Although during the late 1960s the Labour Party effectively accommodated itself to a 'White Britain Policy', in 1971 it felt moved to question the treatment of Commonwealth immigrants along the same lines as aliens and the overtly racial criteria which underlay the notion of partiality. Despite the fact that the new Act was rightly seen as racist because it allowed potentially millions of white Commonwealth citizens to enter under the patriality clause and settle in Britain, a right denied to almost all non-white Commonwealth citizens, successive immigration rules issued by the Home Secretary to supplement the 1971 Act have emphasised the intention of the Act to keep out black Commonwealth citizens as opposed to whites (Macdonald, 1983: 25–30). With the exception of the Ugandan Asians who were expelled by Idi Amin in 1972, and some of whom were allowed to settle in Britain during 1972–3, this policy has been consistently pursued ever since. Additionally such measures have emphasised the essentially sexist nature of immigration controls (WING, 1985).

The decade between 1961 and 1971 had seen the introduction of three major pieces of legislation aimed largely at excluding black immigrants. The 1971 Act eventually took away the right of black Commonwealth immigrants to settle, and thus represented an important step in the institutionalisation of racist immigration controls.

Immigration and race since 1979

The amalgam of immigration controls and race relations policies as a solution to the problem was fostered under the Labour administrations from 1974–9. But in the lead up to the 1979 election sections of the Conservative Party, including its leader Margaret Thatcher, chose to emphasise the dangers posed to British social and cultural values by the black communities already settled here. Thatcher's intentions on this issue was part of a wider campaign to use race as a symbol for the neo-Conservative ideology of Thatcher's wing of the party (Barker, 1981). Even though the political language used still referred to immigrants, the main reference point of this campaign were the black communities already settled in Britain. Immigration control remained an issue of public and policy debate, particularly in relation to dependants and the marriage partners of those settled legally (Gordon, 1985).

The policies pursued by the Conservative government since 1979 represent a further stage in the development of immigration policy. This has involved two main policy changes. First, a number of changes to the immigration rules issued under the 1971 Immigration Act have been introduced with the explicit intention of tightening controls even further. Second, the 1981 British Nationality Act was passed under the first Thatcher administration and came into force in 1983. Debates in Parliament on both these issues give a clue to the attempt by the government to further circumvent the rights of those black Commonwealth citizens with a legal right to enter Britain and to construct the question of nationality along racial lines (*Hansard*, vol. 5, 1981: cols 765–1193; *Hansard*, vol. 31, 1982, cols 692–761; *Hansard*, vol. 34, 1982, cols 355–439; *Hansard*, vol. 37, 1983, cols 178–280; *Hansard* vol. 83, 1985, cols 893–989).

The main legislative action of the post 1979 Conservative administrations, the 1981 British Nationality Act, is a case in point. The government argued that in introducing the bill it was rationalising both existing nationality and immigration legislation in order to create a British citizenship which automatically gives the right of abode in Britain. It did this by dividing the existing category of Citizen of the United Kingdom and Commonwealth into three categories; British citizens; British Dependent Territories citizens; British Overseas citizens. Although the government argued that the Act would make immigration control less arbitrary, public and Parliamentary responses criticised it for reinforcing racial discrimination (Layton-Henry, 1984: 157–9). Indeed the category of 'British Overseas citizens' effectively excludes British citizens of (mostly) Asian origin from the right of abode in Britain. In this sense it seems correct to argue that the 1981 Act 'enshrines the existing racially discriminatory provisions of immigration law under the new clothing of British citizenship and the right of abode' (Macdonald, 1983: 69).

A government document prepared for the OECD conference on immigration policy states the broad policy objectives in traditional terms, but links them closely to other areas of concern:

In recent decades, the basis of policy in the United Kingdom has been the need to control primary immigration – that is, new heads of households who are most likely to enter the job market. The United Kingdom is one of the most densely populated countries in Europe. In terms of housing, education, social services and, of course, jobs, the country could not support all those who would like to come here. Firm immigration control is therefore essential, in order to provide the conditions necessary for developing and maintaining good community relations (OECD, 1986: 1).

In practice, therefore, the strategy pursued since 1979 has continued to legitimate the supposed link between firm controls and good community relations. The signs are that this amalgam will continue to guide the thinking of the mainstream of the Conservative Party.

At the same time the government has steadfastly refused to strengthen the 1976 Race Relations Act or to adopt a more positive approach against discrimination and racism. Even after the Scarman Report of 1981 called for a coordinated government-led policy against racial disadvantage, a call repeated a number of times since by Lord Scarman and others, the response of the various agencies of the state has been at best limited. Rather it has continued to emphasise the need for tight immigration controls because 'of the strain that the admission of a substantial number of immigrants can place on existing resources and services' (Leon Brittan, *Hansard*, vol. 83, 1985, col. 893).

The logic of this approach is to displace conflicts and strains in race relations on the black communities as a whole or specific sections of them. This in turn has allowed the idea of blacks being the 'enemy within' and a threat to social stability to become more deeply rooted.

If the main rationalisation of the immigration laws and the race relations acts was the objective of producing an atmosphere for the development of 'good race relations' and integration, it needs to be said that they failed to depoliticise the question of black immigration. The racialisation of British politics proceeded apace during the 1970s and took on new forms in relation to specific issues or groups, for example education, the police, young blacks and urban policy (CCCS, 1982; Miles and Phizacklea, 1984; Jacobs, 1986). The restrictions imposed by the 1971 Immigration Act, and the successive immigration rules issued under this Act have seemingly fulfilled the ostensible objective of post-1962 policies, which has been to control primary immigration and restrict secondary immigration, but the politicisation of race has continued during this time.

What examination can be given to this racialisation of political discourses in the context of firm immigration controls? A number of issues are involved and not all of these can be analysed in this chapter, but at least two are worth noting. First, debates about immigration and race have taken place within a broader context of social, political and economic change which has influenced the ways in which such debates have developed. The rapid transformation of many inner city localities over the last two decades, particularly in relation to the economic and social infrastructure, has provided fertile ground for the racialisation of issues such as employment, housing, education and law and order (Hall *et al.*, 1978; Phizacklea and Miles, 1980: 42–68; Solomos, 1986). This racialisation process has moved public and political debate beyond the question of immigration per se, with the focus moving towards the identification and resolution of specific social problems linked to race. But the link with the immigration question is maintained at another level, because it is the size of the black population, whether in the schools or the unemployment queue, which is identified as the source of the problem (Macdonald, 1983; Castles *et al.*, 1984).

Second, the continuing racialisation of British politics in the context of firm immigration highlights the way in which political language is often a way of emphasising what one wants to believe and avoiding what one does not wish to face (Edelman, 1977; Katznelson, 1986). Thus, although calls for more controls on immigration are often laced with references to the number of immigrants or to the large numbers who could potentially arrive and 'swamp' British culture, such statements are not necessarily based on 'the facts' in any recognised sense. Rather references to statistics and reports are often highly selective and emphasise symbolic fears about the present or future. Good examples of this process are the debates which occurred during the mid 1970s about the Hawley Report on immigration from the Indian sub-continent (1976) and the Select Committee on Race Relations and Immigration report, *Immigration* (1978). In both cases the debates about these reports in Parliament, the media and in other contexts focused on the dangers of 'massive' numbers of immigrants arriving and the possible social and political consequences; and this despite the fact that firm controls on immigration had been implemented during the 1960s (Freeman and Spencer, 1979). Perhaps a more recent phenomenon is the case of the visa controls introduced in 1986 for visitors from India, Pakistan, Bangladesh, Nigeria and Ghana on the basis of controlling the number of illegal immigrants from these countries. The fact that only 222 out of 452 000 visitors from the five countries absconded as illegal immigrants in 1985 did not prevent the symbolic use of visa controls as another means of holding the tide of immigration (*The Guardian*, 2 September 1986).

Another disturbing example of this tend to tighten controls was the way the government responded to the refugee crisis that followed the collapse of the former Yugoslavia. While other European countries took in sizeable numbers of refugees from Bosnia during 1992 the British government introduced restrictions on the number of people it would accept as legitimate refugees. It defended this position on the basis of the argument that only a limited number of refugees could be allowed to enter the country. Despite protests from a number of pressure groups, and criticism by other countries, the Major administration refused to change its stance on this issue.

The agitation of right-wing extremist groups and sections of the Conservative Party in favour of stricter immigration controls and repatriation came into focus in the late 1970s and 1980s as much on the supposed dangers of this 'alien wedge' as on the arrival of new immigrants. The symbolism of the language used by Enoch Powell in 1968–9 to warn of the dangers of immigration was reworked in the late 1970s around the issue of the 'enemy within', who was in many cases no longer an immigrant but had been born and bred in Brixton, Handsworth, Liverpool and other urban localities. The generation and amplification of the mugging issue in the early 1970s, confrontations between the police and young blacks, and the identification of young blacks as an alienated group within the black communities and British society generally, helped to construct a new racialised discourse about black youth (Solomos, 1988). Increasingly this group was identified as drifting into either criminal activities or radical political activities which brought them into direct contact, and hence conflict, with the police. Just as in the 1950s and 1960s the numbers game mobilised a conception of the problem which focused on the need to keep black immigrants out, now the language of political debate seemed to shift towards the view that black youth was a kind of social time-bomb which could help undermine the social fabric of the immigration and race relations amalgam and possibly society as a whole.

Prospects for reform

The shift noted in the previous section from a preoccupation with immigration and the numbers game as such to the question of the 'enemy within' and related images of social disorder is an important development. At least in relation to the disorders experienced in 1981 and 1985, it highlights the complex processes through which racialised political discourses are working in contemporary Britain. But I should emphasise that I am far from suggesting that immigration will become less important as a political issue. Rather I see the growing use of political symbols which depict blacks as an 'enemy within' as inextricably linked with the history of state responses which we have analysed in this chapter. Indeed the post-1979 Conservative administrations have continued to mobilise the immigration question as a political symbol, and to legitimise the maintenance of racially specific controls as a necessary response to the fears of 'ordinary people' about too much immigration.

Since 1979, however, the Labour Party and the minority parties have shown some signs of questioning the basis of this approach (Fitzgerald and Layton-Henry, 1986). The Labour Party, which was responsible for the introduction of the 1968 Commonwealth Immigrants Act, has seemingly come round to the view that current immigration laws are racist, and it aims to introduce its own legislation when in power to ensure that controls are both non-racist and non-sexist. In a Parliamentary debate on immigration in July 1985 Gerald Kaufman affirmed that the intention of a future Labour administration would be to (a) maintain firm controls on immigration and (b) ensure that such controls were applied equally to all immigrants regardless of race (*Hansard*, vol. 83, 1985, cols 909–10). He accused the Conservatives of trying to identify immigration with race, when recent history questioned this assumption:

> Viewed objectively, immigration should be neither a problem nor an issue in Britain. Substantial primary immigration ended at least a decade and a half ago, and there is no prospect of it starting again. In most years there is a net emigration from the United Kingdom. In the year only 15.5 per cent of immigrants came from the West Indies, Africa and the Indian subcontinent – the areas from which, according to the government, there is the greatest pressure to migrate to the United Kingdom (ibid., col. 910).

This approach represents a marked shift from the actions of the Labour governments of 1964–70 and 1974–9, but it is difficult to say what is meant by 'non-racist' immigration controls and how a future Labour administration could effectively break away from the logic of politics since 1962 – which has been to turn black immigration into a problem. Certainly since the 1980s a strong black and anti-racist lobby has emerged within the Labour Party. This lobby is pressing the party for a firm commitment to implement the reforms (Fitzgerald and Layton-Henry, 1986: 110–14).

In the context of the current political climate, however, it is hard to see how a depoliticisation of questions around race and immigration can come about. Growing urban unrest and violence create a space for the Powellite imagery of a racial civil war to take root in the popular imagination, for the real fears of the white population to be deflected onto the 'enemy within'. Promises of a fundamental break from its past practice by the Labour Party have to be set against the wider political background. What would be the response of Labour to a successful campaign around immigration and race by the Conservatives? The signs are not promising. Whenever sections of the popular press accuse Labour of promising to open the flood gates to future primary immigration from black Commonwealth countries, as they do at election time, it is forced to take a strong stance against immigration. From 1974–9 the Labour government failed to take immigration out of politics and the 1979 election campaign suffered from the racist language used by the Conservatives. Its response to these pressures showed up the ambiguities in Labour thinking since the mid-1960s. Whether its responses in the future will be significantly different remains to be seen, but given the entrenched nature of racist immigration controls it is clearly going to require major structural changes to make the promises of reform a reality.

The above discussion has demonstrated that it is far too simplistic to see the state as a reactive instrument of either economic forces or popular pressures in relation to the control of immigration and the management of migrant labour. Rather, it has highlighted the social, economic, political and ideological contexts which have helped to shape state legislation in this field and to bring about the present articulation between racially exclusionary practices and social policies against discrimination.

In a broad sense the state interventions described above can be seen as making a contribution to the reproduction of the dominant social relations of contemporary Britain, particularly through the regulation of migrant workers and the reinforcement of racialised and ethnically based social divisions (Miles and Phizacklea, 1984). But such a generalisation does not capture the complexity of the role of the state in relation to immigration and other important issues on the political agenda of the period covered. Far from the state simply responding to outside pressures, it has been shown throughout this chapter that it played a central role in defining both the form and the content of policies and wider political agendas. Indeed the state and its agencies have become the locus of struggles over the form of the political regulation of immigration and the management of domestic race relations.

Summary and conclusion

The central conclusion to emerge from this chapter returns us to the question of the role that political institutions play in the regulation of the entry and incorporation of migrant labour. The story of post-1945 responses to immigration that we have covered in this chapter shows how popular responses and state policy-making have been shaped by specific contexts and political situations. The circumstances which bring about specific types of policy response are not given but are the product of struggles and contradictions, both within and outside state institutions. During the period covered in this chapter state responses to immigration have by no means been uniform, although there are trends that can be delineated.

We still need to know more about the dynamics and the limits of state intervention in this field if we are to understand how the interplay between immigration and the state has produced a situation whereby racist immigration controls have become institutionalised. In this chapter we have concentrated on the broad contours of political debate and policy change since 1945, but in Chapters 8, 9 and 10 we shall return to the dynamics of social change and racialised politics in the present.

Such an analysis will inevitably take us into debates about political practice, and beyond the confines of a narrow academic focus. In the context of virulent racism and calls for the repatriation of black citizens it is hardly possible to look at the history of immigration and race since 1945 without coming to terms with the practical impact of immigration controls on the everyday lives of black citizens.

But first we shall look at the other element of state intervention over the past two decades, namely, race relations legislation and anti-discrimination policies.

4   Race Relations Policies and the Political Process

Introduction

We have seen in the previous two chapters that the genesis, legislative implementation and institutionalisation of controls on black immigration was a complex process. Similarly the development of anti-discrimination legislation and policies aimed at promoting greater equality of opportunity for black British citizens has been a thoroughly contradictory process based as much on political expediency as on any commitment to justice and equality. The three major race relations acts passed since 1965, for example, have been highly controversial and have aroused the opposition of those who see them as an attempt to give favourable treatment to blacks over whites in the search for jobs, homes, and other goods. At times this kind of opposition has boiled over into open calls for the dismantling of the major institutions of what is sometimes called the race relations industry (Flew, 1984; Palmer, 1986).

This and the following chapter will explore the substantive transformation of the politics of race, from the expansion of state policies dealing with racial discrimination and other aspects of racial inequality during the mid 1960s to the contemporary forms of state intervention. This chapter will analyse the national processes involved in this transformation, while Chapter 5 will concentrate on the development of racialised political debates and practice at the local level. This division is not meant to suggest that there is a clearly defined separation of national and local political processes. Indeed it will be made clear throughout both chapters that there are many complex linkages between these levels and that it is to a certain extent impossible to understand one without some reference to the other. But for heuristic reasons it seems sensible to present the histories of state intervention at national and local levels as analytically distinct, albeit with important connections.

This chapter approaches the question of the political management of race by analysing the institutionalisation of the dual interventionist strategy adopted by both major political parties in the mid 1960s outlined in Chapter 3: the balance between controls on immigration and integrative measures aimed at improving race relations. It will analyse this process by (a) detailing the various legislative measures passed by successive governments since 1965, and (b) analysing the most important political events in this field from the early 1960s onwards. This will inevitably return us to the role of Enoch Powell in fashioning the racialisation of political debate from 1968 onwards, and the changing ideologies and practices of the Conservative and Labour parties. The account in this chapter of broad trends in state policies thus links up with the analysis in Chapters 9 and 10 of the dynamics of racist, anti-racist and black political mobilisation. It provides the essential historical background to the development of the movements and groupings discussed in those chapters.

Racism and racial discrimination

First of all, it might be useful to look at some of the differences between the concepts of racism and racial discrimination. Sometimes these two concepts become merged in practice, so that they have little apparent difference. For example Banton writes that since the International Convention on the Elimination of All Forms of Racial Discrimination was adopted by the General Assembly of the United Nations in 1965, the United Nations has in practice taken racism to mean almost the same thing as racial discrimination. However others wish to identify clear differences between racism and racial discrimination. One difference is that racism is conceived as pathological: 'When referring to racism, speakers and writers often employ medical metaphors, likening it to a virus, a disease, or some sickness that can be spread in the manner of an epidemic' (Banton, 1992: 70). Racial discrimination, on the other hand, is more normal, 'in the sense that crime, deplorable as it may be, is a normal feature of all kinds of human society' (Banton, 1992: 70).

Some see racism as an ideology and racial discrimination as a practice, with corresponding differences in the necessary responses to them. If racism is an *ideology* then anti-racist movements must emphasise methods which counter ideologies, including the use of mass media and schooling. If racial discrimination is an *act* then anti-racists must emphasise methods ranging from collective action to legislation to fight such acts. Banton argues that in theory 'for every act of racial discrimination someone is responsible and should be brought to account' (Banton, 1992: 73). However in practice things are not quite this simple. Research evidence of the treatment of postwar black immigrants and their descendants shows that we should not only be concerned with *acts* of discrimination but with *processes* of discrimination. Processes are established, routine and subtle; only occasionally will an individual act of racial discrimination become visible within these processes, and only intermittently can one individual actor be identified as responsible for the exclusion of another from rightful opportunities. The denial of racial discrimination is common because, quite simply, it *can* be denied, due to the normality of its invisibility.

The operation of racial discrimination in employment can be drawn to public attention in a number of ways. Firstly, there can be action by anti-racists or those discriminated against, such as strikes or other collective action called over racist practices (for some examples, see Phizacklea and Miles, 1987: 118–20). Secondly, there can be discrimination testing by agencies such as the Commission for Racial Equality (CRE) or the Policy Studies Institute (PSI) in Britain, which have produced a number of notable demonstrations of the pervasiveness of discrimination (Daniel, 1968; McIntosh and Smith, 1974; Hubbuck and Carter, 1980). Thirdly, there can be research, usually carried out by academic researchers, into the operation of discrimination within social institutions.

Race relations legislation in context

The main objective of this chapter is to explain the genesis, development and contradictions of political strategies on race relations, as pursued by both Conservative and Labour administrations since 1965. But it will also attempt to show what the substantive achievements of these strategies were, both at a practical and a symbolic level. Thus as well as analysing the legislation implemented by the state over the past two and a half decades, it will look at the interplay between the stated objectives and the actual outcomes of the most important legislative measures.

From one perspective the various legislative measures passed by successive governments since 1965 are seen as largely symbolic or inadequate. Fully two decades after the first Race Relations Act was passed in 1965 there seems to be little evidence of significant advances against entrenched forms of racial inequality. A recurrent criticism of the attitude of central government departments in this field is that they have not shown a clear commitment to or allocated adequate resources to racial equality programmes (Jenkins and Solomos, 1989; McCrudden, 1988; McCrudden *et al.*, 1991).

By carefully analysing the interplay between stated objectives and substantive outcomes this chapter will highlight the problems that past policies have helped to reproduce as well as those that they have ameliorated. It will thus enable us to show the impact of state intervention over the last two decades on the reproduction and persistence of racial inequality, and to explore the possibilities for alternative political strategies which can tackle racism and racial inequality more effectively.

The key legislative measures we are concerned with are listed in Table 4.1, which also lists the various immigration control measures passed during this period, since in practice the two sets of legislation were inextricably linked.

The main justification for looking closely at these legislative measures is that since the early 1970s the debates and controversies that have surrounded them have served to illustrate the changing terms of political debate about the role of government in tackling racial inequalities.

Additionally, however, we shall seek to link aspects of this account to the dynamics of political conflicts and struggles about the politics

Table 4.1 *Legislation on immigration and race relations since 1962*

Year	Legislative measure
1962	Commonwealth Immigrants Act
1965	Race Relations Act
1966	Local Government Act
1968	Commonwealth Immigrants Act
1968	Race Relations Act
1969	Immigration Appeals Act
1971	Immigration Act
1976	Race Relations Act
1981	British Nationality Act
1988	Immigration Act

of race. We shall look at this issue in more detail in Chapters 8 to 10, but it would clearly be impossible to explain the genesis and development of state interventions without looking at the history of racist political mobilisation, black protest and changing racialised ideologies.

The origins of anti-discrimination legislation

From the 1950s the question of what to do to counter racial discrimination emerged as a major dilemma in debates about immigration and race relations. Even in the early stages of black immigration there was an awareness that in the longer term the question of racial discrimination was likely to become a volatile political issue. In the early stages of postwar black immigration political debates about race were centred upon the question of immigration controls. However, an underlying concern, even at that stage, was the question of future race relations. The notion that the arrival of too many black immigrants would lead to problems in relation to housing, employment and social services was already widely articulated (Patterson, 1969; Freeman, 1979).

In the context of the intense debate about immigration during the late 1950s, for example, the Labour Party set up a working party to look at the question of legislation to combat racial discrimination, and instructed it to make practical legislative proposals (*The Times*, 24 July 1958). Other discussions on this issue were encouraged through the efforts of politicians like Fenner Brockway and welfare groups which took a special interest in the position of the black communities either locally or nationally.

Two problems were usually seen as in need of urgent attention. First, the negative response of the majority white population to the competition of black workers in the housing and labour markets. In the context of particular localities, such as London, Birmingham and its surrounding area, and Wolverhampton, such competition was seen as creating the conditions for future conflict. Second, the frustration of black workers who felt themselves excluded from equal participation in British society by the development of a colour bar in the labour and housing markets, along with related processes of discrimination.

Both these issues were perceived as potential sources of conflict which the government had to manage and control through direct intervention. In the early stages, however, it was not totally clear what the best mechanisms for state intervention actually were.

The genesis of race relations policies

The first attempts to deal with potential racial conflict and tackle racial discrimination can be traced back to the 1960s, and took two basic forms. The first involved the setting up of welfare agencies to deal with the problems faced by black immigrants and to help the white communities understand the immigrants. The second stage of the policy response began with the passage of the 1965 and 1968 Race Relations Acts, and was premised on the notion that the state should attempt to ban discrimination on the basis of race, colour or ethnic origin through legal sanctions and public regulatory agencies charged with the task of promoting greater equality of opportunity (Rose *et al.*, 1969: 511–30).

This dual strategy was clearly articulated by the Labour government's 1965 white paper on *Immigration from the Commonwealth*, but it has its origins in the debates of the 1950s and the period leading up to the 1962 Commonwealth Immigrants Act. The notion that immigration was essentially an issue of race was consistent with the view that: (a) the growing number of black citizens resident in Britain was either actually or potentially the source of social problems and conflicts, and (b) that it was necessary for the state to introduce measures to promote the integration of immigrants into the wider society and its fundamental institutions.

The linking of immigration controls with integrative measures was a significant step since it signalled a move towards the management of domestic race relations as well as legitimising the institutionalisation of firm controls at the point of entry. In the same year as the white paper the Labour government passed the first Race Relations Act, which enunciated the principle of ending discrimination against black immigrants, and their descendants, on the grounds of race. Although fairly limited in its scope the Act was important in establishing the concern of the state with racial discrimination and as an affirmation of the broad objective of using legislative action to achieve 'good race relations' (Lester and Bindman, 1972: 107–49).

Much has been written about the inherent contradictions involved in balancing racially specific controls on immigration with measures against discriminatory practices. Yet since the 1960s the two sides of state intervention have been seen as inextricably linked. According to Roy Hattersley's famous formula, 'Integration without control is impossible, but control without integration is indefensible' (*Hansard*, vol. 709, cols 378–85). The rationale of this argument was never articulated clearly, but it was at least partly based on the idea that the fewer immigrants (particularly black ones) there were, the easier it would be to integrate them into the English way of life and its social cultural values.

During the tenure of Roy Jenkins as Home Secretary in the mid-1960s, this notion of integration was linked to the idea that unless the political institutions helped deal with the social problems of the immigrants and of the areas in which they lived there was the prospect of growing racial tension and violence on the American model. In this context concern was particularly focused on the second generation of young blacks, who were perceived as a potentially volatile group (Solomos, 1988: 53–87).

Given this perspective the Race Relations Acts of 1965 and 1968 were based on the twin assumptions of (a) setting up special bodies to deal with the problems faced by immigrants in relation to discrimination, social adjustment and welfare and (b) helping to educate the population as a whole about race relations, and hence minimising the risk of racialised conflict developing in Britain in the way it had done in the US.

The basis of these assumptions lay, as argued above, in the notion that too many black immigrants could result in racial conflict. Additionally, however, the numbers game was tied to the idea that the cultural differences between the immigrants and the host population were a potential source of conflict. From 1962 onwards both the Conservative and Labour Parties accepted the need for immigration restrictions to be balanced by measures to bring about integration in housing, education, employment and the social services.

Significantly however, successive governments did not seek to use mainstream government departments to tackle this issue. While the Home Office was directly responsible for the enforcement of strict immigration controls, the responsibility for enforcing the 1965 and 1968 Race Relations Acts was given to regulatory agencies and the judicial system. The 1965 Act set up the Race Relations Board, while the 1968 Act set up the Community Relations Commission and strengthened the powers of the Race Relations Board in dealing with complaints of discrimination (Abbott, 1971: chapters 9 and 10). From 1965 to 1975 successive governments left the issue of tackling racial discrimination to these bodies, and there was little direction or support provided by central government itself.

The 1976 Race Relations Act

Critics of the 1965 and 1968 Race Relations Acts pointed out that these early attempts to tackle racial discrimination were limited both in their intention and their impact. By the early 1970s critics of the 1960s legislation were calling for a new and more effective strategy to tackle racial discrimination, particularly in areas such as employment (Abbott, 1971; Lester and Bindman, 1972). At the same time research on aspects of racial discrimination by a number of bodies showed that high levels of discrimination persisted, and this was taken to imply that the efforts of successive governments from 1965 onwards had produced little or no change (Smith, 1977). More critical studies took their cue from this evidence to argue that race relations legislation, particularly when linked to discriminatory immigration controls, could be no more than a gesture or a symbolic political act which gave the impression that something was being done while in practice achieving very little (Moore, 1975; Sivanandan, 1982).

The debate about the effectiveness of the 1965 and 1968 Acts raged throughout the early seventies, and began to have an impact on the organisations charged with implementing the legislation. The Race Relations Board, for example, produced a critical analysis of the operation of race relations legislation which argued, among other things, that the 1968 Act was very limited in its effectiveness because of its concentration on individual forms of discrimination and the lack of resources for implementing the law fully. It also argued that racial discrimination was less a matter of active discrimination against individuals than the reproduction of 'situations in which equality of opportunity is consciously or unconsciously denied' (Race Relations Board, 1973). At the same time the Select Committee on Race Relations and Immigration launched a major investigation which produced a major report, *The Organisation of Race Relations Administration*, in 1975.

Though this report looked at the situation from an administrative angle, it helped put a number of arguments on the political agenda. The most important of these arguments were (a) the need to go beyond the narrow definition of discrimination used in the 1965 and 1968 Acts in order to include institutionalised or unintended forms of discrimination, (b) the need to strengthen the administrative structures and legal powers of the Race Relations Board in order to allow for a more effective implementation of anti-discrimination policies, including penalties for those found guilty of discrimination and (c) the need for a more interventionist stance from central government departments, particularly the Home Office, to buttress the role of race relations institutions (Select Committee, 1975: vii).

Taken together these assumptions were seen to support the need for stronger action by government to promote equal opportunity because 'there is a growing lack of confidence in the effectiveness of government action and, in the case of some groups such as young West Indians, this lack of confidence can turn into hostile resentment' (Select Committee, 1975: xvi–xix). In addition they were seen as supporting the need for more efficient social policies on race in order to achieve the original aim announced by Roy Jenkins during the 1960s: namely, the achievement of a genuinely integrated society where there was 'equal opportunity, accompanied by cultural diversity in an atmosphere of mutual tolerance'.

More fundamentally perhaps, the evidence that went into these reports had a major impact on the white paper on *Racial Discrimination*, which was published in September 1975. This accepted the relative failure of past policies to achieve fundamental changes, the need for stronger legislation and the need for a 'coherent and coordinated policy over a large field of influence involving many government Departments, local authorities, the existing and future statutory bodies concerned with the subject and, indeed, many individuals in positions of responsibility and influence' (Home Office, 1975: 5). It also accepted the need for a broader governmental role in tackling those 'more complex situations of accumulated disadvantages and of the effects of past discrimination'. The rationale for this emphasis, according to the white paper, was the recognition by the government that the majority of the black population was 'here to stay' and that policies had to be based on recognition of this fundamental principle.

In this sense the white paper was a departure from the policies pursued by successive administrations from the 1960s onwards. However although the role of government and a political commitment to racial equality was prioritised there was no detailed analysis of how to link the legal and administrative framework with active political involvement by the Home Office and other government departments in the promotion of racial equality. More fundamentally, while this strategy was recognised as involving major expenditure implications, as well as a reassessment of priorities in existing programmes, no attempt was made to assess what these were, or to examine how the government's own contribution to the new strategy was going to be implemented.

In the ensuing legislative proposals therefore the emphasis was placed on changing the legislative and administrative framework, while the wider changes promised in the Select Committee report and the white paper were put to one side. Against this background the 1976 Race Relations Act 'represented a strengthening and extension of existing anti-discrimination policy rather than a new and unfamiliar policy' (Nixon, 1982: 366).

The most important innovations were (a) an extension of the objectives of the law to cover not only intentional discrimination but racial disadvantage brought about by systemic racism, (b) reorganisation of the Race Relations Board and the Community Relations Commission into a joint agency, the Commission for Racial Equality (CRE) and (c) a different procedure for the handling of individual complaints about discrimination, which in the case of employment cases were to be handled directly by the industrial tribunals rather than processed through the CRE (McCrudden, 1982: 336–48; Lustgarten, 1980).

The first innovation was intended to overcome the problem of proving the existence of institutional filter processes that were biased against minority workers. While *direct discrimination* was defined by the 1976 Act quite straightforwardly as arising 'where a person treats another person less favourably on racial grounds than he treats, or would treat, someone else', it also put on the statute book the category of *indirect discrimination*. This was defined as consisting of treatment which may be described as equal in a formal sense as between different racial groups, but discriminatory in its effect on one particular racial group. An example of what could be defined as

indirect discrimination is the application of conditions and requirements for jobs which may mean that:

(a) the proportion of persons of a racial group who can comply
with these is considerably smaller than the proportion of persons
not of that racial group who can comply with them;
(b) they are to the detriment of the persons who cannot comply
with them;
(c) that they are not justifiable irrespective of the colour, race,
nationality or ethnic or national origins of the person to whom they
are applied (Home Office, 1977: 4–5).

The introduction of the concept of indirect discrimination into race
relations legislation was partly based on the American experience of
affirmative action against institutionalised forms of racism, which
was widely commented upon during the immediate period leading up
to the 1976 Act (Abbott, 1971; Lester and Bindman, 1972). Indeed,
according to one account, both the American programmes based on
the Civil Rights Act of 1964 and the post-1976 British concern with
indirect discrimination were attempts 'to circumvent the problems of
proof of intentional discrimination, to go beyond its individualised
nature, and to provide a basis for intervening against the present
effects of past and other types of institutional discrimination'
(McCrudden, 1983: 56).

The second innovation, the setting up of the CRE, resulted from
the experience of the organisational management of anti-discrimination policies during the period 1965–75. The setting up of an agency
that combined roles previously held by the Community Relations
Commission and the Race Relations Board was seen as paving the
way for a more coherent implementation of the law and the
promotion of equality of opportunity and good race relations.

The CRE was seen as having three main duties: (a) to work toward
the elimination of discrimination, (b) to promote equality of
opportunity and good race relations and (c) to keep under review
the working of the Act and draw up proposals for amending it. Under
the first two headings the CRE was empowered to carry out formal
investigations into organisations where it believed unlawful discrimination was taking place, to help individual complainants in cases of
discrimination and to issue codes of practice containing guidance
about the elimination of discrimination in the field of employment or

for the promotion of equality of opportunity. In addition the CRE was to carry out promotional work aimed at bringing about changes in both the attitudes and behaviour of employers toward minorities.

As mentioned above, the third major innovation introduced by the 1976 Act was to allow individuals direct access to courts or industrial tribunals to obtain redress in respect of complaints under the Act. Although the CRE could offer individuals assistance in carrying through their complaint, direct access to industrial tribunals was seen as providing a stronger basis for a legal strategy against discrimination in employment to complement the work of the CRE. This viewpoint was also supported by reference to the need to treat cases of race discrimination in the same manner as cases of sex discrimination or complaints of unfair dismissal.

From policy to practice

Given these stated objectives, and the government's promise of an effective race relations policy, it may at first sight seem surprising that since the 1976 Act came into force much of the discussion has focused on the disjuncture between its objectives and its actual impact. Even Lord Scarman's sober report on urban unrest during 1981 pointed out that policies had failed to make a major impact on the roots of racial disadvantage (Scarman, 1981: para 2.38).

Offe (1984: 144) has pointed out that 'the increasingly visible conflict between the promise and the experience, form and content, of state policies' can result in increased conflict and disenchantment. Broadly speaking, this is what seems to have happened. While the Act seemed to promise radical changes, the translation of broad objectives into practice has not been easy.

Detailed evidence about the workings of the 1976 Act has only recently begun to emerge, though it has been the focus of much critical comment from an early stage (Home Affairs Committee, 1981b). It does seem, however, that the translation into practice of the initiatives introduced by the Act has at best been achieved in only a limited sense. Almost all the academic research that has been done on the effectiveness of the 1976 Act has pointed to three ways in which policies have proved to be ineffective in tackling racial inequality. First, the machinery set up to implement the Act has not functioned effectively. Second, the policies have not produced the intended results. Third, the policies have failed to meet the expectations of the black communities (Jenkins and Solomos, 1989; McCrudden *et al.*, 1991).

For example, recent evidence indicates that both formal investigations and individual complaints procedures have had only a limited impact on discriminatory practices in areas such as employment or housing, and that the CRE has encountered severe problems in exercising its powers in such a way as to challenge entrenched processes of discrimination (Brown and Gay, 1985; McCrudden, 1987; McCrudden *et al.*, 1991). The Home Affairs Committee's investigation of the CRE in 1981 highlighted a number of organisational problems which hampered its formal investigations in the early stages of the Commission's work (Home Affairs Committee, 1981b: xxiii–xxxiii) There is also clear evidence, however, that the ambiguous nature of the law has acted as a brake on its ability to carry out investigations successfully or speedily (Applebey and Ellis, 1984). By 1983 the formal investigation procedure was so unworkable that the CRE itself proposed a sharpening of its investigative powers in order to reduce delays (CRE, 1983 and 1985a). The CRE has itself acknowledged that despite the relatively sizeable number of formal investigations, their impact on discriminatory processes has been limited at best.

The picture in relation to individual complaints is by no means clear due to the lack of a critical analysis of the various stages of the complaints process, but research evidence suggests that there has been a very low level of success in proving discrimination. The CRE can claim a certain amount of success in that most successful cases were supported by the CRE. But these successful cases can only amount to a small proportion of the reported cases of discrimination, let alone those cases that go unreported.

Overall it seems clear that black workers have remained in a relatively restricted spectrum of occupational areas, are overrepresented in low-paid and insecure jobs, or are working antisocial hours in unhealthy or dangerous environments. Although by the 1970s Afro-Caribbean and Asian people were employed in a broader range of occupations than before, these were still jobs that were deemed fit for ethnic minority workers rather than white workers (Brown, 1992: 52). In 1984 the Policy Studies Institute published a major survey on the state of black people in Britain, covering housing, education and employment and showing that black people were still generally employed below their qualification and skill level, earn less than white workers in comparable job levels and were still concentrated in the same industries as they were 25 years earlier (Brown, 1984).

On top of this black people have a higher unemployment rate, which increases faster than that of the white population. Particularly badly hit are ethnic minority young people, or the second generation descendants of immigrants. A review of the statistical evidence reported:

> While employment prospects are discouraging for all young people, the evidence . . . shows that black youth unemployment has reached astronomical proportions in some areas. The differential unemployment rates between blacks and whites are in fact generally greater for this age group than for any other. When account is taken of the fact that black people are far more likely to go into further education than whites, we can see that young black people in the 1980s are facing a desperate situation (Newnham, 1986: 17).

However, simple statistics of inequality in employment do not by themselves demonstrate the operation of racial discrimination. The denial of racism draws on a number of alternative explanations for the persistence of inequalities of opportunity for the descendants of black immigrants. In societies like Britain, where most postwar immigrants have citizenship and civil rights and face no legal barriers to employment opportunity, there are a whole range of forces which could still conceivably lead to the perpetuation of inequality amongst immigrant groups and ethnic minorities long after the first generations have become settled and consolidated. These could be factors such as the persistence of language and cultural differences, the existence of identity problems amongst the second generation, the educational attainment of the descendants of immigrants, the geographical areas they settled in, the particular occupational and industrial sectors the first immigrants originally found work in, and their own aspirations, preferences and choices.

Proposals for reform

During the 1980s and and early 1990s a number of bodies, including the CRE, lobbied for a major reorganisation of the administration of race relations policies and for a stronger central government lead. Lord Scarman's report on urban unrest and numerous other reports have argued for a major radical programme of action to tackle the root causes of racial inequality (Benyon and Solomos, 1987).

The CRE itself has joined the voices calling for a more positive stance from the government. The CRE's proposals for change, which were first made in draft form in 1983 and have been on the table since 1985, recommended a number of basic changes to strengthen the implementation process, including (a) a clarification of the meaning of both direct and indirect discrimination to take account of the complex situation on the ground (b) the setting up of specialist tribunals to deal with discrimination cases, these tribunals having the power to order changes to prevent a recurrence of discrimination (c) clarification of the procedures for formal investigations in order to prevent delaying tactics by employers or other bodies; (d) a redefinition of the law to allow for more effective positive actions to redress the effects of past and present discrimination and (e) a strengthening of the sanctions against those found to be unlawfully discriminating.

Such changes were seen by the CRE and by academic researchers as a way of overcoming some of the most well known limitations of the 1976 Act, and of reinforcing the political commitment of central government to racial equality. Additionally they were seen as a way of showing the black communities that the CRE was able to distance itself from the government and propose changes which were not necessarily popular with ministers and officials.

Such calls have remained unheeded. Yet, as the CRE has recently stated, levels of discrimination in employment, housing and other areas remain alarmingly high, and there is no sign that the government is willing to strengthen the legislation so as to make it effective (CRE, Annual Report for 1987).

In the absence of a strong lead from central government the CRE has attempted to innovate within the terms of its powers. One of the major innovations introduced by the CRE during the early 1980s was a code of practice for the elimination of discrimination in employment, which came into force in April 1984. First published in draft form in early 1982 the code went through a number of stages of discussion and redrafting before the government formally laid it before Parliament in April 1983. Since April 1984 the Code has been admissible in evidence at tribunals, and if they think a provision in it is relevant to the proceedings they can take it into account when determining the question (Home Office, 1977: 39). The CRE considered that the code 'will do much to advance the cause of racial equality at work' (CRE, Annual Report for 1983: 15), particularly when combined with the operation of formal investigations and the individual complaints process. Yet its own survey of employers' responses to the code revealed that many employers were still unaware of its existence (CRE, Annual Report for 1987: 8).

As the CRE itself seems to be aware, however, such changes only touch the tip of the iceberg. It recently stated that 'the scale and persistence of discrimination are insupportable in any civilised society' (CRE, Annual Report for 1987: 8). The dilemma it faces, however, is that there seems little room for radical change in the present climate of political opinion.

Summary and conclusion

By the very nature of the political debates about race and immigration over the past two decades it is clear that the development of race relations policies has formed part of a wider political process. The central element of that process has been the political and media debates about the impact of black immigration on various aspects of British society. This has meant that major policy initiatives have been largely the result of attempts by successive governments to meet the demands of those calling for action to tackle racial discrimination and to respond to those who oppose such intervention. The end result seems to be an unhappy compromise which pleases few and angers many for a variety of reasons.

Given this context it is difficult to be optimistic about the prospects of radical change within the constraints of the existing legislation. It is now over a decade since the 1976 Race Relations Act came into force, and there is little ground for arguing that it has achieved in practice the kind of radical changes which it promised. The failure of successive administrations to respond positively to calls for more powers for the Commission for Racial Equality and to remedy the weaknesses of the 1976 Act has led to increased cynicism about the willingness of the state to include the question of racial inequality as a central element of the policy agenda.

Moreover, over the past decade the new orthodoxies on social and economic policy advocated by the new right have attempted to undermine the case for any major intervention by the state and the efficacy of legislative measures against racial inequality. While such ideas have not yet attracted the kind of support that the views of liberal market economists such as Thomas Sowell have in the US (Sowell, 1981), there are signs that such ideas are gaining some currency in the work of the new right think tanks. Perhaps such ideas are more likely to find a hearing in the present political climate than the calls for stronger legislation and increased central government intervention in this area. The consequences of such a development remain to be seen.

5 Urban Politics and Racial Inequality

Introduction

In previous chapters we have noted that the politicisation of the public debate about race and immigration in Britain has been partly determined by local political processes. As was shown in Chapters 3 and 4 a number of local authorities, pressure groups and individuals have raised the question of the impact of immigration on their specific localities. Moreover, throughout the 1950s and 1960s the local political élite in areas such as London, Birmingham, Wolverhampton and other localities had to come to terms with the increasingly multi-racial composition of their localities.

This chapter takes this account a step further by examining the history of the local politics of race through (a) an analysis of the impact of local conditions and processes on the racialisation of the political agenda and (b) a critical review of legislative and political interventions which have sought to structure race relations at the local level. The main focus of this chapter is therefore on the dynamics of the incorporation of race into the local political agenda. This allows us to link up with the questions raised at the end of Chapter 4 about the changing context of state intervention in this area and the prospects for transforming existing patterns of racial inequality in British society through political intervention both nationally and locally.

Concepts and models of local politics

Since the early 1980s a wide-ranging theoretical debate about local politics and institutions has taken place, which has successfully sought to develop a more dynamic and critical perspective on various aspects of this subject (Dunleavy, 1980; Saunders, 1981; Gregory and Urry, 1985; Thrift and Williams, 1987). The main features of this debate have been (a) a concern to include wider questions about power and society in the study of urban politics, (b) attempts to develop a dynamic analysis of the processes of policy change and formation at the local level and (c) a focus on the role of conflict and controversy in the shaping of local policy agendas.

In particular a number of writers have argued that many of the crucial features of contemporary class and social relations in advanced capitalist societies cannot be fully understood without reference to the local and spatial context. Studies in both Britain and the US have emphasised the massive impact of changes in the political economies, populations and spatial organisation of urban localities (Katznelson, 1982; Thrift and Williams, 1987). Dearlove (1973) argues that far from being neutral arbiters between competing interests local authorities are actively engaged in resisting, obstructing and excluding certain groups from decision making. From this perspective the role of local authorities is intrinsically one of making political choices and the management of conflictual pressures and interests.

What is notable about this literature, however, from the perspective of this book is that, in Britain at least, issues of race and ethnicity have been largely left off the agenda. A few writers have begun to acknowledge the significance of racial themes in urban politics, and have attempted to integrate this issue as an important dimension of contemporary British politics. Stoker, for example, has argued that 'we need to address more systematically the structures of inequality and the history of powerlessness which can lead to the exclusion and non-mobilisation of the working class, women, ethnic minorities and other deprived groups within local politics' (Stoker, 1988: 242). There are also signs that the increasing awareness of gender and other non-class specific forms of social categorisation is resulting in an increasing interest in the local processes of racial categorisation and exclusion. But these developments are still at a relatively early stage, and it is true to say that the local dimension of the politics of racism remains sadly neglected.

Race and local politics in historical perspective

During the controversy over her much discussed swamping statement in 1978 Margaret Thatcher made it quite clear that she was on the side of those who saw black immigrants as swamping British society. When in February 1979 she was asked if she had modified her view on this issue she forcefully restated her basic theme:

> Some people have felt swamped by immigrants. They've seen the whole character of their neighbourhood change. . . . Of course people can feel that they are being swamped. Small minorities can be absorbed – they can be assets to the majority community – but once a minority in a neighbourhood gets very large, people do feel swamped. They feel their whole way of life has been changed (*The Observer*, 25 February 1979)

This statement highlights the important role that images of community and neighbourhood play in the political debates about race in British society, and the role that they can play as symbols for the changing terms of debate on this question. This was referred to in the course of the discussion of the politics of race and immigration in Chapter 3. In this chapter we shall analyse the development of political debates and policy change at the local level in more detail, concentrating particularly on the two decades since 1970.

Since the early 1980s much of the public attention on and media discussion of the local politics of race has focused on the experiences of a number of local authorities which have introduced radical policy changes in relation to racial inequality. The most notable cases have been the now abolished Greater London Council, the Inner London Education Authority and a number of left-wing London boroughs, including Lambeth, Brent, Hackney and Haringey. Nationally a number of other local authorities, including Manchester, Birmingham and Bradford, have attracted attention when they have adopted comprehensive policy statements on racial equality and equal opportunity generally.

In this climate it is easy to lose historical perspective. It is all too easy to forget that as late as the 1970s a common complaint of activists and community groups was that local authorities had failed to develop an adequate policy response to the increasingly multiracial composition of their populations. Indeed during the 1970s the characteristic form of political intervention at the local level to deal with race issues was still limited in many cases to limited support for Community Relations Councils, financial aid to community groups and the distribution of central government funds made available through Section 11 of the 1966 Local government Act and the Urban Programme.

During the 1960s the characteristic form of political intervention at the local level to deal with race issues involved a complex interaction between central government, local authorities and voluntary agencies. From as early as the 1950s, as we saw in Chapters 3 and 4, the emergent social policy response to black immigration involved a two pronged strategy aimed at (a) providing newly arrived immigrants with special help in relation to housing, employment, social problems and cultural adjustment and (b) helping the host community to understand the immigrants and overcome its prejudices.

At the local level this strategy built upon the work of special officers appointed in a number of cities to help immigrants cope with their special problems, and the work of local agencies which had helped to define the policy response to black immigrants in areas such as London, Nottingham and Birmingham. In some areas this led to the formation of voluntary committees which consisted of representatives of statutory and voluntary social services, interested groups and individuals and trade unions. These committees played a particularly important role in areas of the country where race and related issues had already become politicised and aroused the interest of local politicians, the press and voluntary agencies.

Processes of racialisation

Since the early 1960s the racialisation of local politics has undergone a number of transformations. The processes which have resulted in the racialisation of local politics are complex, and to some extent they have been determined by the specific histories of particular localities. Broadly speaking, however, they can be divided into three stages. These stages themselves correspond to the transformations in the politics of immigration and race that have taken place from the 1960s onwards.

During the early 1960s and 1970s the local political context of race was a central theme in debates about immigration, particularly in parts of the West Midlands. Additionally, as was shown in Chapter 4, the direct and indirect impact of racist political mobilisation in Birmingham and the Black Country played an important part during the early 1960s in pushing the racialisation of political debate to a new level. Indeed the election of Peter Griffiths in Smethwick in 1964 was an important symbolic event, since it helped to shape the terms of political debate on immigration and entrench the consensus that black immigrants were a problem that had to be dealt with through the enforcement of strict immigration controls and ameliorative race relations policies.

It is clear from a number of local community studies that local authorities in areas such as London, Birmingham, Bristol, Wolverhampton and other inner city areas had developed ad-hoc initiatives about racial issues from the 1960s onwards. In a number of authorities this led to the development of policies about such issues as education, social services and housing. This was often linked to the formation of voluntary committees which consisted of representatives of statutory and voluntary social services, immigrant organisations and interested groups and individuals and trade unions. These committees played a particularly important role in areas of the country where race and related issues had already become politicised and had aroused the interest of local politicians, the press and voluntary agencies. From the late 1960s such committees began to receive the support of the Community Relations Commission and became known by the generic term of Community Relations Councils (Hill and Issacharoff, 1971; Gay and Young, 1988).

The main distinguishing feature of the earliest stages of racialised politics at the local level was the use of race as a symbol of the changing nature of local social and economic conditions. The manifest concerns expressed in the local press and in the pronouncements of local politicians were concentrated on such issues as housing, employment and the social problems which were popularly perceived as linked to immigration.

In conjunction with the emergence of race as a local political issue a steady stream of studies looked at various aspects of race relations and conflicts in particular cities or localities (Rex and Moore, 1967; Richmond, 1973; Lawrence, 1974; Katznelson,1976; Rex and Tomlinson, 1979). The work of John Rex and his associates during the 1960s and 1970s on the position of black minorities in Birmingham represents one of the major trends in this body of work. One of the issues analysed in this research was the role of local and national political processes in structuring the incorporation of black minorities in Birmingham into the institutions of the welfare state and into the employment and housing markets. For example Rex and Moore

(1967) analysed the interplay between race and housing in an inner urban area of Birmingham, Sparkbrook, that had a significant black population. Their central concern was to analyse the reasons for the concentration of Asian and West Indian immigrants in this declining area. But a central part of their research focused on the role of the policies practised by Birmingham's Housing Department and their impact on the incorporation of immigrant communities into the housing market. In a second research project, carried out in the early 1970s, Rex and Tomlinson (1979) analysed the position of the black underclass in the Handsworth area of the city. Once again the central concern of this project was to analyse the social position of the black communities in Handsworth, but Rex and Tomlinson did analyse the role of local and national political processes in determining this position. Additionally they looked in some detail at the political groups that developed within the Asian and West Indian communities in the area. They analysed the history of such groups and their interaction with local political institutions.

Other studies have been concerned with aspects of the incorporation of black and ethnic minorities into the local political system. Important studies from this perspective have looked at the role of racial and ethnic politics in the political life of cities such as Nottingham, Birmingham and Bristol since the 1950s. The works by Nicholas Deakin (1972), David Beetham (1970), Ken Newton (1976), and Ira Katznelson (1976) are the best known examples of this type of work. More recently important studies have been carried out by Gideon Ben-Tovim and his associates (1986) in Liverpool and Wolverhampton and by Anthony Messina (1989) in Ealing.

The main themes in this body of work have been the impact of race on both local and national politics, the role of the media, the response of local authorities to the race question and the racialisation of electoral politics. An interesting example of this type of analysis is the study by Susan Smith (1989) of the politics of racial segregation in British society. Smith's account of the political processes of racialisation and segregation explores the diverse political, social and economic dimensions of racial relations in contemporary Britain. Her account of this process emphasises the need to situate the analysis of the local politics of race within an understanding of how racialisation of residential space within urban localities has come about, and how the local and national political system has responded to this process.

Models of policy change

Most studies of the local politics of race have, however, not been concerned with these broader questions about the dynamics of local political power and change, but with the policies and agendas which have been associated with particular local authorities, and with the specifics of the implementation of particular policies.

A good example of this trend can be found in the work of Ken Young and his associate (Young and Connelly, 1981, 1984; Young, 1985). The main focus of this body of work has been on (a) the context and environment of policy change and (b) the implementation of policy change through particular initiatives and policies. In particular the emphasis has been on the assumptions used by policy makers to develop and implement policy change. According to this framework most of the changes in this area had been unplanned and unintended, and had resulted from the diverse impact of pressures for change both at the local level and from the impact on local authorities of the urban unrest of 1981 and subsequently (Young, 1985: 287).

Young and Connelly (1981) looked particularly at two aspects of policy change in a number of local authorities. First, the environment of policy change, and the variety and local political actors that make up this environment. Second, the content of the policy changes which local authorities have actually adopted and the processes by which they have sought to implement change. From this study Young and Connelly constructed a model which distinguished between four different types of local authority responses to racial issues:

1. Pioneers: innovative authorities that created a new machinery of policy making and implementation on racial issues.
2. Learners: authorities that accepted the need for change, and learned from the experience of the pioneers.
3. Waverers: authorities that issued formal statements but did little to put them into practice.
4. Resisters: authorities that did not accept the need for specific policies on racial issues (Young and Connelly, 1981: 6–7)

This model has influenced much of the debate about the local politics of race, and has helped to sharpen the interest of researchers in the analysis of the actual processes of policy making and diffusion in local multiracial settings.

A somewhat different framework of analysis has been offered by Herman Ouseley, who has worked at various levels of local government during the past two decades and who has specialised in equal opportunity issues. In Ouseley's account of policy development in this field the central role is occupied by the actions of black communities, local black politicians and administrators and by the political debates surrounding the 1981 and 1985 riots (Ouseley, 1981, 1984). From his own extensive experience of work in a variety of local government contexts he argues that the key to change in the practices of local authorities lies in the combination of pressure from both within and outside the institutions of local politics and policy making.

From this perspective, in order to understand the changing role that local authorities are playing in relation to racial issues it is necessary to look at such factors as the role of black community groups, the voluntary sector, black political leadership, the role of community relations councils as well as shifts in local and central government policies (Ouseley, 1982).

Policy change and conflict

At various stages since the mid 1960s a number of legislative measures have sought to give central Government a degree of influence in shaping the response of local authorities to race issues. The main measures are detailed in Table 5.1.

The two measures introduced during the 1960s seemed to have a rather limited impact on policy development within local authorities. Both Section 11 of the 1966 Local Government Act and the 1969

Table 5.1 *Legislative measures and the local politics of race*

Year	Legislative measure
1966	Local Government Act
1969	Local Government Grants (Social Need) Act
1976	Race Relations Act
1978	Inner Urban Areas Act

Local Government Grants (Social Need) Act had their origins in the intense debates about race and immigration which raged throughout the 1960s (Edwards and Batley, 1978). They were thus measures that were largely aimed at providing financial support from central government for those localities with particularly large black populations.

Section 11 of the 1966 Local Government Act was the result of the widespread debate during the mid-1960s about the impact of immigration on particular localities and was intended as a way of distributing central government money to local authorities in order to help meet the special needs of ethnic minority groups in relation to education and social welfare (*Hansard*, vol. 729, 1966 cols 1331–8). Substantial sums have been provided to a number of local authorities, though there has been some controversy about the direct impact of these monies on the needs of minority communities.

The 1969 Local Government Grants (Social Need) Act implemented the urban programme, announced by the government in May 1968. This was to some extent a direct response by the Labour government to the rivers of blood speech made by Enoch Powell in April 1968 (Edwards and Batley, 1978; Higgins *et al.*, 1983). It was meant to provide special help to areas where social deprivation was pervasive, including the special needs of ethnic minorities. Unlike Section 11 the urban programme was not presented as being concerned only with racial deprivation, but in practice many of the projects funded through it have had a strong emphasis on this issue.

These two initiatives were the first of a number of initiatives aimed at providing central government support to local attempts to tackle urban deprivation in multi-racial settings (Jacobs, 1986). The story of these policies would take us beyond the bounds of this volume (but see the papers in Ball and Solomos, 1990), though two points need to be emphasised in connection with their impact on the urban politics of racial inequality. First, the scale of these initiatives and the resources allocated to them did not in any way match the interventions by the federal government in the US during the same period. Given the extent of the deprivation they were supposed to tackle, both Section 11 and the urban programme were largely symbolic measures rather than national programmes of action. Second, during the 1960s and early 1970s local authorities themselves showed little interest in developing policies in this area. Although some local authorities were beginning to give some recognition to the existence of racial inequality, this rarely went beyond limited support for the work of Community Relations Councils and the allocation of grants to some local community groups (Ouseley, 1981).

By the mid-1970s the general picture was one of a limited or non-existent response by most local authorities to the question of racial inequality. This was why, during the passage of the 1976 Race Relations Act through Parliament, a Labour back-bencher, Fred Willey, argued forcefully that an amendment should be included about the role of local authorities in the promotion of better race relations. Although Willey's amendment was initially opposed by the government it was eventually included as Section 71 of the Race Relations Act, and it consisted of the following general injunction:

> Without prejudice to their obligation to comply with any other provision of this Act, it shall be the duty of every local authority to make appropriate arrangements with a view to securing that their functions are carried out with regard to the need: (a) to eliminate unlawful racial discrimination; and (b) to promote equality of opportunity, and good relations, between persons of different racial groups (Race Relations Act, 1976).

Thus Section 71 of the Act placed a particular onus on local authorities to eliminate unlawful racial discrimination and promote equality of opportunity between persons of different racial groups. This statutory provision did not seem to have an immediate effect on the policies or practices of the majority of local authorities, although a few did take up the opportunity offered by the Act to consolidate their efforts in this area (Young and Connelly, 1981). Additionally the CRE attempted from an early stage in its existence to encourage local authorities to develop better practices and to learn from the experiences of the more innovative ones.

Whatever the limitations of Section 71 in the late 1970s, in the aftermath of the urban unrest in Bristol, London and Liverpool during 1980–1 a growing number of local authorities started to develop policies on racial discrimination. As Ouseley (1984) has noted, the unrest does seem to have forced local authorities to respond to the demands of their local black communities for action on racial discrimination in employment, service delivery and housing. At the same time, although the impact of Section 71 remains unclear, it seems to have provided the basis for promoting policy change within the existing structure of local government (Young and Connelly, 1981; Young, 1989).

Pressures for change and their impact

A combination of factors seems to have prompted rapid policy change. First, bolstered by the urban unrest that was much in evidence during the 1980s, local black politicians and groups sought to include racial inequality on the local political agenda. Second, a number of left-wing local authorities sought to use the issue of equal opportunity as a mechanism for widening their basis of support among ethnic minorities and other constituencies (Stoker, 1988: 207–8). Third, the failure of central government to respond to calls for radical reform was seen as a sign that relatively little change could be expected as a result of the actions of central government.

The result of these pressures was reflected in three main policy changes. The first addressed the central question of who gets what, and the emphasis has been on establishing equality of treatment and equality of outcome in the allocation process. Ethnic records have been introduced to monitor channels of access and allocation. For example, in relation to housing, authorities such as Hackney and Haringey have sought to monitor the allocation of local housing stock and the quality of distribution, and to change procedures that facilitated discretion and contributed to discriminatory outcomes.

The second addressed the question of the employment of black staff within local authorities. This has resulted in a number of authorities linking the question of allocative equality with representation of blacks and ethnic minorities on the staff of local government departments. Racially discriminatory outcomes, it was argued, were not solely the function of organisational procedures but also related to the under-representation or exclusion of blacks and ethnic minorities. Consequently targets have been established to increase the proportion of black and ethnic minority staff members.

Finally, a number of local authorities have introduced promotional measures that are intended to improve communications with, and awareness of, the difficulties faced by blacks and ethnic minorities. These include such measures as translation of policy documents into ethnic languages, race awareness and equal opportunity training, and more effective controls against racial harassment.

Resistance to change

During the early 1980s, at the height of local authority intervention in racial equality, much hope was placed on the role of local authorities as an agent of change, particularly in the context of the neglect of racial equality by the Thatcher administrations. Indeed one study of the local politics of race argued that the local political scene had 'provided important sites of struggle, particularly for local organisations committed to racial equality' (Ben-Tovim *et al.*, 1986: 169). Yet in recent years the experience of a number of local authorities seems to indicate that any gains in this area were both fragile and vulnerable to pressure from central government.

By the late 1980s, however, there were already signs that even previously radical local authorities were adopting a lower profile on issues concerned with racial equality. This seems to be partly the result of the increasingly negative public attention given to the policies and programmes pursued by a number of local authorities in London and other areas, such as Manchester and Sheffield. Additionally, the Labour Party has increasingly sought to distance itself from being directly identified with the activities of the more left-wing local authorities and to encourage them to give a lower profile to issues which are seen as controversial or as giving too much support to minority causes.

Perhaps one of the most widely publicised features of this retreat is the increasing attention given by the popular media to the activities of local authorities that have traditionally been seen as being at the forefront of race equality initiatives. It is perhaps a sign of the nature of the present political climate that increasingly it is not racism which is presented as the central problem but the work of the anti-racists. This is why anti-racism has come to occupy such a central position in debates about the local politics of race in Britain. It has become a catch-all phrase to which various meanings are attributed. It has also become the target of much critical debate and attack in a number of policy arenas. Indeed over the past few years there has been a noticeable trend to either dismiss the relevance of anti-racism or for the new right and the media to articulate an anti-anti-racist position, which sees the anti-racists as a bigger political threat than the racists.

In certain arenas, such as education and social welfare, the issue of anti-racism has become a source of conflict and resistance. This became evident in the late 1980s in particular when public and media debate about anti-racism and multi-culturalism reached a high point. This was represented in its most extreme form in the context of educational politics. It was during this time that the educational policies of a number of radical Labour LEAs attempting to implement anti-racist programmes came under close scrutiny. The controversy that surrounded the views of Bradford head teacher Ray Honeyford in the mid 1980s attracted both local and national political attention to the debate about the role and function of anti-racist policies in education. Honeyford's views on the politics of multicultural and anti-racist education policies, as expressed in the pages of the *Salisbury Review* and the press, led to a campaign by local parents and political activists to remove him from his post. His criticism of the radical initiatives of local authorities in this field centred particularly on (i) a wholesale questioning of the political ideologies that he saw as underlying such policies, and (ii) a rejection of multicultural education in favour of integration. At the same time other groups organised expressions of support for his views and sought to defend his right to express them. Although he eventually left his teaching job, under pressure from a number of sources, he has continued to act as a major critic of radical policies (Honeyford, 1988a). The ramifications of the Honeyford affair went far beyond the boundaries of Bradford (Murray, 1986; Honeyford, 1988b; Halstead, 1988). During 1986 another controversy developed around the attempts by Brent Council to sack another head teacher, Maureen McGoldrick, because of her alleged views about the policies Brent Council was pursuing in relation to anti-racist initiatives in education. There were numerous other, perhaps less publicised, cases about educational issues.

More recently the controversy over events at Burnage High School, in Manchester, has also highlighted the controversial nature of anti-racist education policies. The controversy started in September 1986 with the murder of Ahmed Iqbal Ullah, a Bangladeshi pupil, by a white pupil in the playground of Burnage. The events surrounding this incident, and the response of the local education authority to it, became part of a broader national debate about the politics of anti-racist education and this simmered on until 1990. It led to a major report by radical barrister Ian Macdonald that sought to place the events in Burnage in the broader context of the complexities of implementing anti-racist initiatives in education (Macdonald *et al.*, 1989; Ball and Solomos, 1990).

The experience of local authorities seems to mirror that of central government initiative, since there has been a gap between the promise embodied in policy statements and the actual achievements of policies. During the early 1980s authorities such as Lambeth and Hackney did make some progress in changing their employment practices and service delivery to reflect the multi-racial composition of their local populations. Initiatives in specific policy areas such as social services and housing have also been put into practice. In Hackney's case the combination of pressure from the local black communities and a formal investigation by the Commission for Racial Equality forced the council to rethink its housing policy and introduce major changes. During the early 1980s local authorities were also the site of important debates about the delivery of social services and education.

Other areas of controversy have included the role of positive action and contract compliance initiatives which have been placed on the political agenda by some local authorities. Both of these issues have led to lively debate and controversy in recent years.

Positive action and new initiatives

In everyday usage the notion of positive action has come to be associated with giving preferential treatment to black and ethnic minority groups, or with the imposition of quotas and positive discrimination (*Equal Opportunities Review*, 10, 1986: 6–10; Institute of Personnel Management, 1987). This perhaps explains why since the early 1980s it has been the subject of intense debate and has attracted regular media attention. Such conflict is perhaps not surprising. Terms such as equal opportunity, racial equality and related notions have gained wide currency over the past decade, but there is still much confusion about what each of them means and, perhaps more fundamentally, about what kind of objectives they are supposed to fulfil (Young, 1990). Even within the confines of this collection it should be clear that researchers and practitioners do not concur on what they mean by such terms as equality of opportunity and racial equality, or what they consider as evidence of a move towards the stated goals of policies. Some writers see the development of equal opportunity policies as the outcome of a process of political negotiation, pressure group politics and bureaucratic policy making (Ben-

Tovim *et al.*, 1986; Young and Connelly, 1981). Others have, however, emphasised the need to look beyond the stated objectives and public political negotiations and explore the ways in which deeply entrenched processes of discrimination may be resistant to legal and political interventions while inegalitarian social relations structure society as a whole (Smith, 1989). From this perspective promises of equal opportunity can easily become largely symbolic political actions which can do little to bring about real changes in discriminatory processes.

In Britain, unlike in the US, there is no intellectual and political tradition which gives support to the view that affirmative action is a legitimate policy tool in attempts to tackle the effects of past and present racial and other social inequalities. Rather the basis of successive policies on racial inequality since the 1960s have been held together by the notion that the main objective of state intervention in this field is (a) to secure free competition between individuals and (b) to eliminate barriers created by racial discrimination. These objectives have been pursued through the twin mechanisms of legislation aimed at outlawing discrimination and administrative intervention by quasi-governmental bodies such as the Commission for Racial Equality. Yet a wealth of official reports and academic research findings have shown that in practice the impact of public policy in this field has been limited even within the limits of this narrow definition of equal opportunity. Recent research on employment, for example, indicates that equal opportunity policies have had little effect on levels of discrimination in employment, though they have reduced its more direct forms. Similar arguments have been made about the impact of equal opportunity policies in the areas of housing and education (Brown and Gay, 1985; Jenkins and Solomos, 1989).

It is against this background of disappointment about the achievements of past policies that in the past few years we have seen a growing interest in the use of positive action measures as a way of improving the likelihood of race equality policies bringing about effective changes in the employment and service delivery practices of local authorities. In practice positive action, as practised in Britain during the 1980s and early 1990s, consisted mainly of the following two kinds of measures:

1. Efforts to remove discriminatory barriers to full equality of opportunity, such as rethinking job qualification requirements, placing job advertisements in the ethnic minority press;

2. Attempts to facilitate and encourage minority group participation in education and the labour force by means of additional education and training, the use of Section 11 of the 1966 Local Government Act to create new posts and related actions.

The general principle behind such measures is that action should be taken to overcome the effects of past discrimination in order to allow certain sections of the community to catch up with the experience of other employees or applicants, and to remove those barriers which have the effect of excluding some people from employment opportunities (*Equal Opportunities Review*, 14, 1987: 13–18). Part of the rationale of positive action is thus the argument that even if racial discrimination could be removed overnight, employment opportunities would not be immediately equally available to all members of the community. Further steps are needed to make up for the past disadvantages and discrimination experienced by minority groups. It is thus not meant to be a means of providing direct benefits to minority groups, but an opportunity to encourage the promotion of equal opportunity in a more effective manner. The Commission for Racial Equality's definition of positive action is clear on this point:

> Positive action is a series of measures by which people from particular racial groups are either encouraged to apply for jobs in which they have been under-represented or given training to help them develop their potential and so improve their chances in competing for particular work. The element of competition remains paramount. The Act does not provide for people to be taken on because they have a particular racial origin, except in very limited circumstances where racial group is a genuine occupational qualification (CRE, 1985c: iv).

It is within these limits that authorities such as Hackney, Lambeth, ILEA and others have attempted to develop positive action initiatives. As yet it is not clear how effective such initiatives have been. There is some preliminary evidence that some limited success has been achieved in relation to some of the broad objectives which guided the initiatives, particularly in relation to the development of training and the reform of recruitment procedures.

But what is also clear is that within the limits imposed by the 1976 Race Relations Act and the present political climate those local authorities that want to develop positive action strategies are forced to work within very narrow confines. These confines do allow some radical initiatives to be taken, but those authorities that have attempted to go down this path have found themselves criticised for going too far in the direction of positive discrimination. This can be illustrated more clearly if we look at the experience of perhaps the most radical form of positive action attempted so far, namely contract compliance.

Contract compliance as a strategy adopted by local authorities attempting to develop positive action programmes to promote racial equality is largely the product of developments during the 1980s, though it has a longer history in the US and in the context of Northern Ireland. Its main advocate during the early 1980s was the Greater London Council and the Inner London Education Authority, although the idea was also taken up by other left-wing local authorities in London and elsewhere (Hall, 1986; Carr, 1987; IPM, 1987). It attracted much attention in the early 1980s, and a number of local authorities saw it as a way in which effective reforms in this field could be institutionalised.

The first major initiative came in 1983, when the GLC/ILEA amended their code of practice on tenders and Contracts to include an equal opportunities clause. This required tendering companies to undertake to adhere to an equal opportunity policy and to develop strategies for implementing this policy. To implement this initiative the GLC/ILEA set up the Contract Compliance Equal Opportunities Unit to ensure that companies with which it was trading understood the equal opportunity policy and were prepared to put it into practice. Those companies that failed to comply with the policy were threatened with removal from the Council's list of approved contractors. Similar initiatives were made at around this time by a number of other local authorities.

Another, more recent, form of contract compliance is that of local labour contracts, which require companies in receipt of government grants to carry out capital works in inner city areas should undertaking to employ mainly or only labour from the local area, thus ensuring that at least some inner city residents benefit. Such initiatives have been developed in areas such as Birmingham and London in the aftermath of the urban unrest of 1981 and 1985. The unrest was seen as partly related to the employment situation in inner city areas and local labour contracts were seen as one kind of positive action that could help to remedy the situation (CRE, 1987b).

From an early stage contract compliance initiatives such as this proved to be controversial with some major employers and with the Thatcher government. Additionally they became a subject of controversy in the popular media and regularly attracted negative publicity. One famous example of this occurred in 1985 with the news that the GLC/ILEA had decided to ban Kit Kat bars from its schools. This was on the ground that the manufacturers of Kit Kats, Rowntree Mackintosh, had refused to supply information about how it complied with the Sex Discrimination and Race Relations Acts (*Equal Opportunities Review*, 8, 1986: 9–15). This case, along with some others, helped to politicise the issue of contract compliance and link it to the broader moral panic about the role of the 'loony left' in local government.

At the same time the government was attacking the use of contract compliance as yet another example of the work of 'loony left' local authorities, and as an attack on the workings of the market. Nicholas Ridley, then Minister for the Environment, expressed this view directly when he argued in October 1986 that:

> Conditions in contracts which have nothing to do with the contractor's ability to carry out work or supply goods ignore a local authority's duty to its rate-payers to obtain value for money, and are merely an attempt by some councils to impose their own social policies on firms who wish to carry out business with them. Such actions have no place in the contractual processes of local government, and early steps will be taken to stamp them out (*DoE Press Notice*, 21 October 1986).

This criticism of the role of contract compliance initiatives was maintained even after the abolition of the GLC, and in spite of the fact that only a small number of radical authorities were interested in implementing meaningful contract compliance programmes. Part of the reason for this may have been that contract compliance fell outside the government's avowed programme of rolling back the boundaries of the state and increasing the role of market forces. Perhaps the main reason, however, was official concern with the actions of radical left-wing local authorities in the area of race relations.

After the stormy debate during the early 1980s about contract compliance it came as no surprise when the 1988 Local Government Act sought to prohibit the form of contract compliance practised by some of the more radical local authorities. The Act prevents local authorities and other specified public bodies from taking account of non-commercial matters in drawing up approved lists of contractors, inviting tenders and making or terminating contracts (*Equal Opportunities Review*, 18, 1988: 31). However, during the passage of the bill through Parliament the legislation was amended to permit local authorities to operate a limited and defined form of contract vetting so as to carry out their duties under Section 71 of the 1976 Race Relations Act as long as they did not take into account non-commercial criteria (*Equal Opportunities Review*, 19, 1988: 24–7; *Equal Opportunities Review*, 24, 1989: 26–31).

It is too early to assess how this arrangement will work out in practice, though it will clearly reduce local authorities' room for manoeuvre in developing an active policy stance on contract compliance in relation to racial equality. This seems to fit in with the government's concern to make sure that local authorities do not get involved in implementing controversial social policies on issues such as race. But it is already clear that the Commission for Racial Equality and some of the radical local authorities are attempting to find a way of continuing a weak form of contract compliance under the terms laid out in the 1988 Local Government Act (*Equal Opportunities Review*, 28, 1989: 32–5). What this will achieve remains to be seen, but the signs are not at all promising.

Training and racial equality

Controversy has also surrounded the thorny question of what is sometimes called 'race awareness training' (RAT) as practised by some local authorities. Race-related training has grown at a fast rate since the 1980s, particularly in the aftermath of the growth of local race equality policies. Whether under the rubric of race awareness training or of equal opportunity training local authorities, employers and other agencies have introduced courses on race issues as part of their training activities (*Equal Opportunities Review*, 3, 1985: 8–14, 18,

1988: 34–5). Such courses have been around for some time in the US, but in the British context they are basically a phenomenon of the 1980s. They have been conceived as a means of informing decision makers, employers, employees and other important actors of (a) the problems facing black and ethnic minority communities and (b) challenging individual prejudices and values.

Such training programmes take a number of forms but they generally start from the basic assumption that an essential part of policies in this field should be to challenge and change racist attitudes. Following from the work of Judy Katz (1978), which argued that the root cause of racism was the inherent prejudice of white people combined with power, the proponents of RAT have argued that the development of initiatives to deal with racism needs:

1. To challenge the individual prejudice upon which racism is based.
2. To develop in the people who take part in such courses attitudes which challenge their racism.

The proponents of such training argue that by challenging racial prejudice they could help to change the institutional practices that have discriminated against black and ethnic minority communities. It was perhaps this claim, along with the promise of quick results, that helped to push many local authorities into introducing such courses in the early 1980s.

Yet what became clear from the earliest stages of the introduction of RAT was that the claims upon which it was based were by no means universally accepted. Indeed opposition came from a broad spectrum of political opinion, ranging from avowedly anti-racist groups and individuals to the spokespersons of the new right (Sivanandan, 1985; Palmer, 1986; Gilroy, 1987 and 1990b).

Criticisms from anti-racists centred particularly on the assumed link between changes in attitudes and changes in practice, the guilt complex upon which the courses relied and the determinism of seeing all white people as inherently racist. Sivanandan's critique of RAT argues, for example, that its proponents ignore the role of socio-economic, cultural and historical factors, and therefore construct a deterministic view of racism as an individual problem. He argues:

> Racism, according to RAT, has its roots in white culture, and white culture, unaffected by material conditions goes back to the

beginning of time. Hence, racism is part of the collective uncon-
scious, the pre-natal scream, original sin. . . . It is a circular
argument, bordering on the genetic, on biological determinism:
racism, in sum, is culture and culture is white and white is racist
(Sivanandan, 1985: 29).

For Sivanandan, and other critics, such an analysis of racism is at best
superficial and at worst counterproductive since it ignores the
material social and political conditions which help to reproduce
discrimination and racist ideas.

For the new right the imposition of RAT courses, along with
broader anti-racist initiatives, is seen as yet another example of
attempts by left-wing local authorities to restrict the freedom of the
individual to express certain opinions and to impose multi-cultural
values rather than traditional British ones (Palmer, 1986; Honeyford,
1988b). Along with sections of the popular media they have
attempted, with some popular success, to portray the role of RAT
courses as akin to a form of race brainwashing. Over the past few
years the actions of numerous local authorities, including Lambeth,
Haringey, Brent, Birmingham and Bradford, have attracted critical
comment from sections of the press and from new right commentators.

Part of the problem is that although in the early 1980s numerous
local authorities, along with the police and other bodies, included
forms of RAT as part of their policies on race there is surprisingly
little information about the actual impact of these courses on the
implementation of equal opportunity policies. Much attention has
been given to the publicity which RAT courses have received but we
still know relatively little about how such courses have affected
employment and service delivery practices. This lack of concrete
evidence about their effectiveness has in turn contributed to the
controversy which surrounds them.

Some local authorities have attempted to respond to the criticism
by locating race related training within a broader strategy for
achieving organisational change. According to Valerie Amos, who
was involved in the development of this approach in the London
Borough of Hackney, the objective of race-related training in this
context is to make clear to staff the objectives of the equal
opportunity policies and to allow them to gain the skills necessary
for implementing them. While she rejects the idea that training on its

own can be effective as a means of bringing about organisational change, she argues that it can play a role in developing the right conditions for the implementation of equal opportunity policies (CRE, 1987a; *Equal Opportunities Review*, 20, 1988: 26–7).

The future of such training is still a matter of debate and controversy within local authorities and it still attracts regular attention from the media. But what already seems clear is that the controversy surrounding the development of RAT courses has forced local authorities to rethink the kind of race related training that they should provide.

Changing forms of local governance

Far from encouraging new initiatives to tackle racial discrimination, legislation on local government by the Thatcher and Major administrations during the 1980s and early 1990s has been based on the principles that there will in future be a considerable reduction in (a) the role of local authorities as direct service providers in education, housing and related fields and (b) in the ability of local authorities to develop alternative policies and practices to those that are part of the national political agenda. Within this broad ideological framework the pursuit of egalitarian social objectives does not even make first base on the government's political agenda.

The government has, for example, set itself apart from local authorities in the development of inner city policy and local economic regeneration. This was a key theme in the aftermath of the 1987 general election when Margaret Thatcher undertook a short tour through Britain's inner cities with the aim of declaring her government's commitment to regenerating these areas (Robson, 1988). Throughout the late 1980s and early 1990s the question of the regeneration of depressed inner-city localities remained a key issue in political debates between the Labour and Conservative parties. Whether at the symbolic level, in terms of Thatcher's commitment to do something about 'those inner cities', or at a more practical policy level the question of urban policy remains at the heart of debates about the role of race in British society.

Despite such symbolic gestures it is now a considerable time since Lord Scarman called for urgent action to tackle racial discrimination and the social conditions which underlay the disorders in Brixton and elsewhere, and in the meantime there has been little evidence of positive changes for the populations of those areas. Whatever the merit of the particular programme proposed by Lord Scarman, and this has been the subject of some debate, the one consistent response that has been evident since 1981 has had little to do with the pursuit of social justice: rather than dealing with the root causes of racial disadvantage and urban unrest the government has chosen to give more resources, more training and more equipment to the police in order to control the symptoms of urban unrest. The government's overall objective has been to decrease public expenditure, for the sake of lower taxation, and to encourage an enterprise culture in the inner cities (see the various papers in Stewart and Stoker, 1989). In this context aid for the inner cities has been dwarfed by the financial cuts applied to inner city local authorities.

The present political climate gives little cause for optimism that a radical change in governmental priorities in this field is likely. During both the 1981 and 1985 outbreaks of urban unrest central government promised to help those inner city areas particularly hard hit by economic restructuring and urban decay. The impact of such promises in practice has, however, been limited and their role in promoting equal opportunity has been minimal to say the least (Benyon and Solomos, 1987; Robson, 1988).

Since 1989 the vociferous public debate about Salman Rushdie's *Satanic Verses*, and the subsequent public interest about the role of fundamentalism among sections of the Muslim communities in various localities, has added a new dimension to the local politics of race (Samad, 1992). The wider impact of the Rushdie affair on both the local and national politics of race will be addressed in Chapter 10, but the impact on local politics seems clear. First, there are already signs that the affair has given a new impetus to debates about issues such as immigration, integration and public order. Second, it is likely to have a direct impact on local politics, both in terms of formal and informal political processes. The high profile claimed by various local Muslim political activists in areas such as Bradford, Leicester, Birmingham and elsewhere suggests that the affair will have important reverberations both locally and nationally (Parekh, 1989; Banton, 1989).

What is clear already is that such controversies have helped to create a political climate which is much less friendly to the development of local initiatives than was the case in the early 1980s. But perhaps the most important constraint on the role that local authorities will be able to play in the promotion of racial equality is that within the present political climate there seems to be little room for positive initiatives on racial equality or to the political autonomy of local government.

At the same time the massive changes which have been introduced in relation to local government since the late 1980s emphasise the limits which central government can impose upon the autonomy of local authorities. Within this context it seems likely that local authorities will be (a) less willing to innovate in areas which are controversial and (b) less responsive to demands for more resources from previously excluded groups. There is increasing evidence that this process of marginalisation has already started, and the consequence of this can be seen in the disputed nature of race equality and anti-racist initiatives.

The increasing incorporation of black politicians and community groups into the local political system may have some impact on how far black interests will be ignored or put on the back burner. Already there is evidence that black politicians are beginning to exercise a degree of influence in a number of local authorities (Back and Solomos, 1992a and 1992c).

This does not mean, however, that the racialisation of local politics is completely in retreat. Rather, it seems likely that the politics of race will remain a central feature of the local political scene in many localities, but its impact on the policy agenda may be more limited. In making any assessment about the possibility of bringing about racial equality through local initiatives it is important to bear in mind both the fundamental changes in local government since the early 1980s and the legislative and political actions which the Thatcher and Major governments have taken to transform the operation of local government finance, housing and education. Such measures have already transformed the face of local government and are likely to have an even bigger impact during the rest of 1990s (Stewart and Stoker, 1989).

Summary and conclusion

The main question addressed in this chapter was: What has been the impact of local political processes on the politics of racism in contemporary Britain? It seems impossible, however, to generalise and say that there has been a uniform pattern of policy response in this field since the early 1960s because local political and policy responses have been conditioned by national and local determinants which have produced important variations in the form and content of local state interventions. While at a broad level the wider social, political and economic context has imposed constraints on the extent of policy change, it is impossible to ignore the role of local politicians, professionals and bureaucrats in defining policy objectives and priorities.

Perhaps the most important conclusion to emerge from this and the previous chapter is that since the early 1970s policy change in this area, whether at a national or local level, has been a complex process of responsive actions to pressures from both within and outside the main political institutions. The actual impact of these policies upon the extent of racism and discrimination in British society has been fairly limited, and in the early 1990s there was increasing resistance and opposition to anti-racist policies at the local level.

The politics of race may remain a central feature of the local political scene in many localities, but in making any assessment about the possibilities for bringing about greater racial equality through local initiatives it is important to bear in mind the fundamental changes which local politics has already undergone since the early 1980s, and the changes to still come.

6 Race, Policing and Disorder

Introduction

Some reference was made in the previous two chapters to the impact of two processes upon the politics of racialisation since the 1970s: the evident racialisation of policing, particularly in inner city areas, and the impact of the riots of 1980–1 and 1985 on the politics of race at both national and local levels. Even from these general references it should be clear that no account of the politics of race in contemporary Britain can ignore the role that policing has played in public debate about racial issues since the early 1970s. This chapter will explore this question in more detail. This will be followed in Chapter 7 by an analysis of the political impact of the outbreaks of urban unrest in the 1980s.

Race, crime and disorder

Ideologies linking immigrants with crime have a long history in British society. This is not to say that these ideologies have been constant throughout this history, or that they were monolithic. They have undergone numerous transformations over the years, and ideologies which link immigrants to crime have not been universally accepted even by those who opposed immigration. But it is certainly true that whether one looks at the Irish immigrants of the nineteenth century, Jewish immigrants in the period 1880–1914, or other significant groups of immigrants the issue of crime has been a common theme in the construction of ideologies and policies towards them (Garrard, 1971; Gainer, 1972; Holmes, 1978; Lunn, 1980).

Black seamen who settled in port towns such as Cardiff, Liverpool and London were similarly stereotyped. The areas in which they lived were seen as localities in which an immigrant presence combined with social deprivation and poverty to produce not only patterns of criminal behaviour but also social values outside the mainstream of the majority society. A number of studies of black communities during the early twentieth century have noted how important such images were in determining both the form and content of dominant ideologies of the 'Negro problem' within official circles and local voluntary associations (Little, 1947; Banton, 1955; Fryer, 1984).

An important early study of St Clair Drake provides a detailed account of the processes through which the Tiger Bay area of Cardiff was constructed in this manner. He shows how the inhabitants of the area were defined as a problem by outside institutions, and how the black inhabitants were seen as a specific problem group. Even though many of the Tiger Bay inhabitants expressed the view that 'the colour-bar is the problem; not the coloured people', the black inhabitants of the area were attributed with characteristics which helped to define them as the problem. Of the black population the younger generation of 'half-caste' children was seen as a particular problem group (Drake, 1954: 69–129).

Other studies have shown how the areas into which post-1945 black settlers moved rapidly became identified as localities with crime-related behaviour and other social problems, including decaying housing, lack of social amenities and low levels of community involvement (Carter, Harris and Joshi, 1987). In areas such as Notting Hill and Brixton in London, Handsworth and Balsall Heath in Birmingham and similar localities in other cities the question of rising crime and law and order became intimately identified with the broader question of the impact of black immigration on these areas. Questions about the involvement of specific groups of immigrants in criminal activities were asked both in and out of Parliament and became a topic for popular concern in the press (*The Times*, 28 March 1958). Such questions became even more pronounced during and after the 1958 riots in Notting Hill and Nottingham, which helped to politicise the issue of black immigration and to influence the direction of both local and central government policies. Indeed during the late 1950s and early 1960s the issue of immigration control was intimately tied to the question of the involvement of black immigrants in criminal activities. Even before the 1958 riots a number of pro-immigration-control MPs had attempted to politicise the issue of black crime (*Hansard*, vol. 578, 1957, cols 743–6; vol. 585, 1958, cols 1415–26). The political climate in the aftermath of the riots proved to be conducive to those ideologies which blamed the rising levels of 'racial tension' on the arrival of 'undesirables' from the colonies. At the 1958 Conservative Party Conference Norman Pannell moved a resolution calling for the deportation of such 'undesirables', whom he defined as those migrants who were not of good character, not in good health, or lacked sufficient means to avoid becoming a liability on public funds (*The Times*, 13 October 1958).

Along with the broader processes of racialisation, the 1960s saw a growing politicisation of this question and continuous attempts by the police and the government to deal with the danger of conflict between the police and black communities. The concerns at this stage were about the growing number of complaints of racial discrimination by the police against blacks, the future of younger blacks if their social and economic position deteriorated, and the fear that an American-type situation of racial violence and disorder could be reproduced in major cities. In July 1967 the Home Office issued to all Chief Constables a circular, *The Police and Coloured Communities*, which advised them to appoint, particularly in areas of black settlement, liaison officers whose task would be to develop better relations with black communities and educate the police themselves on the dilemmas of policing such areas. This was followed by a number of consultative meetings to discuss the policing of particular localities and to analyse the long-term prospects of future conflict between the police and black communities. From 1967 to 1970 a number of articles appeared in specialist journals which discussed the policing of multiracial localities, the specific problems faced by young blacks and accusa-tions of discriminatory behaviour by the police in relation to the black communities in parts of London, Birmingham and other localities.

The police themselves began to recognise, somewhat hesitantly, the need to develop an understanding of the context of policing in multiracial areas. In 1970 a conference of US and British specialists and practitioners was held under the auspices of the Ditchley Foundation to discuss police–community relations on both sides of the Atlantic (Clarke, 1970). Other meetings and seminars were also held to discuss this issue, and from 1970 onwards the annual Reports of the Commissioner of Police of the Metropolis contain some discussion of the specific issues related to the policing of multi-racial localities.

In this context an article written by Robert Mark, who was then Deputy Commissioner of the Metropolitan Police, provides an enlightening insight into the emergent ideology of the police on the question of race. While being quite clear that 'there is no evidence to show that migrants commit a disproportionate amount of crime', Mark argued that a minority become involved in frequent contact with the police. He linked this to two issues: (1) the involvement of a small number of immigrants in prostitution, gaming and the fringes of criminal activity, and (2) the involvement of other immigrants in public order offences, family disputes or noisy parties (Mark, 1970: 4–5). For Mark such situations of conflict were partly the result of the newness of the immigrants and their socio-economic position in British society, but also the result of the failure of the police and other institutions to deal with the 'special problems posed by migrants' (ibid.: 5). But he saw the situation as one which would not damage relations between the police and the immigrant communities on a permanent basis:

> Traditionally the protector of all groups and classes, irrespective of race, colour or creed, we believe that we, the police, have done no less than any other public service to promote the welfare and security of the migrant in his transition from his homeland to an alien highly industrial, urban society; and we are not unduly discouraged that we should be attacked and criticised by representatives, self-appointed or otherwise, of the very people that we are trying to help (ibid.)

The implicit optimism about the effectiveness of positive action by the police was not shared, as Mark points out, by a growing number of critics of the overall strategy and tactics of the police in policing multi-racial areas. In fact it was partly in response to increasingly trenchant criticism of their police role from both within and outside the black communities that the police began to develop and articulate an ideological legitimation for their policies in relation to black areas (Lambert, 1970; Humphry, 1972).

This debate was carried forward in the national media as well as in specialised race journals like *Race Today*, which was at the time published by the Institute of Race Relations. The public nature of the debate helped to politicise the question of race and policing to a new level during the early 1970s, particularly as pressure mounted from within the black communities for investigations into cases of harassment by the police, and for 'greater equality before the law' (Nandy, 1970; John, 1970; Hall *et al.*, 1978). It should also be remembered, of course, that it was during this period that the question of immigration and race came to occupy a central role in debates about domestic social policies at both national and local political levels. This broader process of racialisation helped to increase the impact of the policy debate about the interrelationship of crime and race, since this issue served to give further credence to the Powellite warnings that immigration was undermining the whole of the social fabric of inner city localities. The imagery of black involvement in criminal activities and in public order offences helped to fuel and give a new direction to the increasingly volatile public debate about race relations.

Alienated youth and ghetto life

Throughout the late 1960s fears about the increasing alienation of young blacks from the mainstream of British society were regularly expressed in the media and policy documents, and became a constant refrain in both academic and policy writings on the subject. But by the early 1970s it had become clear that this was not merely a passing phenomenon which would disappear with the integration of young blacks into the mainstream institutions of British society.

This was so for at least two major reasons. First, it became clear that the calls for action to help 'coloured school leavers' gain equality of opportunity in employment and other arenas did not necessarily result in the development of effective policy measures to put such calls into practice. Evidence of high levels of unemployment, low levels of attainment in schools and homelessness among young blacks continued to accumulate during the early 1970s. The evidence tended to show that, even in the space of a few years, the picture painted in *The Problems of Coloured School Leavers* in 1969 had been overtaken by events. Far from the positive measures which had been called for in this report, the net result of the intense debates during the 1970s seems to have been inaction and a deterioration of the socio-economic condition of young blacks.

Second, by the early 1970s it had also become clear that the condition of young blacks was rapidly becoming one of the central concerns within the black communities. In various forums, both local and national, black political activists were discussing issues such as education, employment and policing in relation to young blacks. They were also questioning the failure to take positive measures to tackle the root causes of racism and racial inequality. Such political debates from within the black communities helped to emphasise the centrality of this issue within the context of racialised political debates, and to force state institutions to review the nature of their interventions.

At a symbolic level the commitment to the principle of equal opportunity was still part of the climate of political opinion. The Conservative Home Secretary, Robert Carr, restated this commitment in the context of the debate on race relations issues at the 1973 Conservative Party Conference:

> Our principle is that there should be no second-class citizens in Britain. Everyone who was born here or has come here legally should be equal before the law and not only that but they should be treated equally in the practices of everyday life. I know we do not live up to that perfectly but that is our commitment and that is what my colleagues and I will do our best to achieve (*The Times*, 11 October 1973).

But such symbolic promises did not answer the fundamental question raised by the portrayal of young blacks, along with their parents, as second-class citizens: why and how were the inequalities and problems faced by the first generation of black immigrants being reproduced within the second generation? What were likely to be the medium- and long-term consequences of this process both for young blacks and for society as a whole? Symbolic promises of future action did not touch upon the substantive issues, but deflected attention onto the prospect of a better future.

The reality of the situation in the early 1970s, however, was made clear in a number of reports which highlighted the dismal prospects for young blacks and the potential of conflict with the police. In 1970 Gus John published his influential study of Handsworth called *Race and the Inner City*, and in the same year John Lambert published a study of *Crime, Police and Race Relations*. Both studies attracted attention because they came out at a time when the issues of relations between the black communities and the police and the involvement of young blacks in crime were topical and widely discussed in the press. From 1969 to 1973 a number of feature articles and reports in the press discussed various aspects of the growing tension between the police and the black communities, both at a national level and in relation to specific communities. The complaints against the police by the black communities themselves, which had been articulated as early as 1966 in Hunte's *Nigger Hunting in England*, reached new levels during the early 1970s and were rapidly becoming a political issue.

John's study of Handsworth was a particularly important document in this growing debate. Written by a black researcher who had spent some time living within the black community in Handsworth it highlights the question of policing and the position of young blacks as the core concerns of local residents. It was written at a time when the police were discussing their role in the policing of multi-racial inner city areas and formulating their ideologies and practices on this issue (Humphry, 1972). Additionally, media coverage at the time talked of the growing tensions between the police and black communities, and 1969–70 saw a number of minor street confrontations with the police in areas such as Notting Hill. John began his account of Handsworth with an analysis of the area and the contrasting perceptions offered by local residents of the postwar period. But the core of his report, and the issue which gave rise to a full debate in the press, is the description it offers of relations between the local black community, particularly younger blacks, and the police. John reports that one police official had pointed out to him that the 'growth of black crime' in the area was the work of a 'hard core' of forty or fifty youngsters (John, 1970: 20). But his own perceptions of the situation were more complex, and he summarised them as amounting to three main issues:

1. The prevalence of rumours, fears and explanations of black involvement in criminal activities.
2. A tendency by police to blame the 'hard core' of young blacks for 'giving the area a bad name'.
3. Deep resentment by older and younger blacks of their social position and the discrimination they had to endure.

Additionally he warned that there were signs of 'a massive breakdown in relations between the police and the black community', and that if nothing was done the situation was likely to lead to confrontations between black residents and the police and outbursts of urban unrest:

In my view trends in Handsworth are a portent for the future. A decaying area, full of stress and tension, which also happens to be racially mixed, is going to find it increasingly difficult to cope with the root problems because racial animosities and resentments have taken on an independent life of their own. The problem is not, and can never be, simply one of law and order (ibid.: 25).

It was this context, argued John, which explained why both young blacks and the police saw the situation in the area as one of open 'warfare' (ibid.: 28–9). Some aspects of John's account of relations between the police and the black community were criticised as overstated and impressionistic. Yet there is a certain symmetry between his account of the situation and that described later on in the 1970s by John Rex and Sally Tomlinson in their detailed empirical analysis of the political economy of race and class in Handsworth (Rex and Tomlinson, 1979). Additionally, other studies of the interplay between race and policing during the early 1970s indicated that the relationship between young blacks and the police was becoming an issue of public concern in other areas similar to Handsworth.

Evidence from black communities across the country highlighted three particularly contentious issues. First, complaints by young blacks that they were being categorised as a 'problem group' by the police, and that they were therefore more likely to be questioned or arrested. Second, allegations that the police used excessive physical violence in their dealings with black suspects. Finally, it was argued that such attitudes and forms of behaviour by the police were helping to fuel popular rumours about the involvement of young blacks in crime, and to drive a wedge between the police and the black communities.

Policing minority communities

Perhaps most significant in the context of my general argument is that the shifting emphasis on young blacks as a problem category for the police and for society as a whole was being framed increasingly around the question of police–community relations. The shift became particularly clear when (a) the question of policing was investigated by the Select Committee on Race Relations and Immigration during 1971–2, and (b) popular and media debate focused on the involvement of young blacks in forms of street crime popularly defined as mugging.

As argued above, the politicisation of the question of crime in
relation to young blacks is best seen within the broader context of
official and public concern with the interplay between ghetto life, the
social position of young blacks and criminal activities. The Select
Committee on Race Relations and Immigration's investigation of
Police/Immigrant Relations, which was carried out during 1971–2,
represents a useful starting point for understanding the concerns of
the state, the police and the black communities about policing and
law and order. The Committee took evidence from community
groups, police officials, local authorities and government departments on the causes of growing tension between the police and
sections of the black communities. Although the popular press and
John's report on Handsworth had shown that police on the ground
perceived a section of the black community as being disproportionately involved in criminal activities, the Committee concluded that
this claim was not supported by the evidence:

> The conclusions remain beyond doubt: coloured immigrants are no
> more involved in crime than others; nor are they generally more
> concerned in violence, prostitution and drugs. The West Indian
> crime rate is much the same as that of the indigenous population.
> The Asian crime rate is very much lower (Select Committee, 1972,
> Report: 71).

It did point out, however, that there was one major source of conflict
between the police and black communities: the explosive relations
between the younger generation of West Indians and the police. The
source of this conflict was seen as lying in a combination of factors,
most notably in the situation of young blacks themselves and the
attitude of the police (ibid.: 68–9).

The Committee considered that young West Indians were becoming
increasingly resentful of society and were expressing their anger and
frustration against the police because they were an obvious authority
symbol. It explained this situation as arising from three factors:

(1) pressures faced by young blacks in competing for jobs and
housing;
(2) the nature of West Indian family discipline, which although
'Victorian' for younger children did not extend to the West Indian
youngsters aged between 16 and 25; and

(3) conflict between the younger and older generations of West Indians (ibid.: 69).

The report did accept that there were problems of discrimination faced by young blacks, but significantly it did not prioritise these processes in its account of the growing tension between them and the police. It pointed out that much of the evidence presented by black community groups argued that there was a process of 'nigger hunting' and a tendency for 'the police to pick on black youths merely because they are black'. But it balanced this out by adding that the evidence of the Metropolitan Police showed that 'in London black youths are stopped and/or arrested proportionately no more than white youths'.

On the question of allegations that policemen were engaged in practices ranging from harassment, assault, wrongful arrest and detention to provocation, fabrication, planting of evidence and racial insults, the Committee was much more reticent to come to any conclusions. It accepted that much of the evidence submitted to it by the Community Relations Commission contained claims that such practices were common in many localities (Select Committee, 1972, Evidence: vol. II: 65–8; vol. III: 716–35; vol. III: 765–71). While accepting that these claims were believed by many black people, it found it impossible to 'prove or disprove' them, with the truth lying somewhere in between the claims of the police and their critics (Select Committee, 1972, Report: 20–1). Rather it saw these claims and counter-claims as the natural outcome of a lack of communication between the police and sections of black youth. This lack of communication helped to build stereotypes and reproduce situations of conflict. The Committee explained this process thus:

> There are examples throughout our evidence of the way in which a simple situation builds up to a confrontation. A policeman's mode of address is resented by a black youth sensitive to insult; the youth replies with what the policeman sees as insolence, often accompanied by gesticulation; the policeman counters with what the young sees as hostile formality. Neither understands the other's point of view; each sees the other as a threat. The youth says he is being picked on because he is black and the policeman is immediately in a dilemma. If he takes firm action he can be accused of racial bias by black people, if he doesn't he is open to the same accusation by white people (ibid.: 69).

The Committee recommended that a programme of action should be implemented to improve communication, including more training and schemes to improve relations with the black communities in 'problem areas' (ibid.: 92–5). It concluded that such a positive programme of action could ensure that better relations were reestablished between young blacks and the police:

> If the best examples of leadership in police and immigrant relations prevailed throughout forces in the United Kingdom, many of the difficulties we have dwelt upon would, within a reasonable space of time, diminish. In some places they could wither away (ibid.: 92)

From this perspective the situation in some localities, although explosive and dangerous, could be defused if the pressures which produced tension between young blacks and the police were dealt with.

This hope was to remain unfulfilled throughout the 1970s since the production of the Select Committee's report, *Police/Immigrant Relations*, coincided with a marked politicisation of debates about black youth, and police and crime during the period 1972–6. This politicisation, occurring as it did at a time of upheaval about race and immigration more generally, was reflected in frequent media reports, official documents and speeches by politicians, police officers and other opinion leaders. From the summer of 1972 it focused particularly on the supposed involvement of young blacks in mugging.

Mugging and street violence

The social construction of the question of mugging and black youth during the early 1970s represents perhaps the clearest example of how the politicisation of this issue came about. The genesis and development of official, police and media ideologies about mugging has been analysed and commented on from a number of angles and I do not want to retrace the steps of existing accounts. In this section I shall focus on one aspect of this phenomenon, namely the interplay during the early 1970s of images of black youth and mugging and the consequences of this process for policy and practice in relation to young blacks.

During the 1960s the political debate about the second generation of young blacks became synonymous with images of alienation, despair, a lack of equal opportunity and urban disorder. The concern by the early 1970s, as we have already seen in the previous section, was beginning to shift towards the involvement of young blacks in mugging and other forms of street crime. This shift reached its peak from 1972–6, when the moral panic about the mugging issue was at its height in both the press and in official discourses, reaching the point where Enoch Powell could publicly declare mugging to be essentially a black crime (*The Guardian*, 12 April 1976).

The history of the media and popular response to the mugging issue has been analysed in some detail by Hall *et al.* in *Policing the Crisis* (1978). The premise of this study is that the construction of black communities as social problems was the ideological bedrock upon which the black youth/urban deprivation/street crime model of mugging was constructed during the early seventies. Mugging as a political phenomenon, according to Hall *et al.*, became associated with black youth because they were seen as:

(a) a social group which suffered the most direct impact of the cycle of poverty, unemployment and social alienation which afflicted inner city areas; and
(b) suffering from the added disadvantage of belonging to a racial group with a 'weak' culture and high levels of social problems, such as broken families and lack of achievement in schools (Hall *et al*, 1978).

The power of these images, according to this study, derived partly from commonly held images of race and the inner cities, but also from the feelings of uncertainty which were developing within British society as a whole about the position of black communities and their role within the dominant institutions (ibid.: 346–9).

This contradictory response to the growth of permanent black communities in many inner city areas coincided with growing concern about inner city problems and the impact of multiple deprivation on the residents of localities with a combination of problems arising out of (a) the rising levels of crime and violence which afflicted particular areas of cities (b) the emergence of racial disadvantage and inequality as a particular aspect of the social conditions of inner city areas and (c) the development of ghetto areas with distinct cultural values and attitudes towards law and order and the police.

Such concerns about the changing character of the inner city areas were intrinsically imbued with racial overtones as well, since the localities defined as particularly problematic – in terms of poverty, poor housing, lack of jobs, broken families and crime – were those of high levels of black settlement. Problems of the inner city were therefore often synonymous with questions about race.

Hall *et al.* note, for example, that even in areas where young blacks were a small minority of the total youth population, the issue of crime on the streets became intimately tied up with the category of black youth. This ideological construction became possible because from the early 1970s onwards a dominant concern about the ghetto areas focused on the supposed drift of young blacks into a life of crime and poverty. According to Hall *et al.*:

> For all practical purposes, the terms mugging and black crime are now virtually synonymous. In the first mugging panic, as we have shown, though mugging was continually shadowed by the theme of race and crime, this link was rarely made explicit. This is no longer the case. The two are indissolubly linked: each term references the other in both the official and public consciousness (ibid.: 217).

This convergence of concerns about race, crime and the ghetto areas into the category of black youth thus involved a combination of images which linked particular areas to specific types of crime, and these crimes to a specific section of the local population. The definition of criminal areas in everyday police practices thus gained a clear racial dimension, which was in turn further accentuated by the wider social and economic processes which confined black communities to inner city localities and excluded them from equal participation in the labour market and in society more generally.

The politicisation of the mugging question occurred with reference to a number of issues which preoccupied both government agencies and the police. Chief among these were (a) a breakdown of consent to policing in certain areas (b) confrontations between the police and young blacks and (c) a concern that Britain was becoming a violent society. I shall comment on each of these themes in turn before moving to the broader question of the racialisation of crime and the threat of urban disorder.

A glimpse of the everyday confrontations and conflictual situations between the police and sections of the black community can be found in the evidence collected by the Select Committee during 1971–2 for its report, *Police/Immigrant Relations*, in the press coverage of this issue during the early 1970s and the activities of various groups within black communities which prioritised the issue of policing as a central complaint. But it was during 1972–6 that the issue of declining consent to policing and the development of volatile problem areas became a major theme in public debate about policing (Humphry, 1972; Alderson and Stead, 1973; Cain, 1973; Pulle, 1973). This was a theme also in the government's response to the Select Committee Report, which was published in October 1973. After noting that the question of policing black communities was not just a problem for the police, it went on to argue that:

> The police are of course only one element of the society which is confronted by this challenge. While part of the test is the extent to which coloured people are treated by the police on the same terms as white people, any failure of the rest of society, in employment, in housing and elsewhere, to accept coloured citizens on equal terms would undermine the efforts made by the police and leave them facing forms of discontent which spring from causes outside their control (Home Office, 1973: 5).

This image of wider forces at work to delegitimise the role of the police pervades the government's response, although it also makes the point that only a small minority of young blacks were opposed to the police, while the majority were law-abiding.

At a more popular level this issue of a lack of consent to the police role was mentioned regularly in press coverage in both the popular and the serious press. The imagery of American writings on the black ghettoes was transposed onto the British situation – with areas such as Brixton, Notting Hill and Handsworth being compared to the streets of Harlem, Watts and other ghettoes. The questions being asked amounted to: Why are young blacks being driven to crime? How can they be resocialised into the dominant values of society?

The issue of mugging was therefore intimately linked to wider conceptions about the social problems faced by young blacks in areas of the country that were popularly and officially identified as problem areas. During the early 1970s it also became clear that everyday confrontations about minor issues could easily escalate into open conflict and acts of collective protest on the streets. This phenomenon had already been noted in media coverage and in the Select Committee's 1971–2 report, but the level of tension mounted during the mid 1970s in a sequence of incidents which can now, with the benefit of hindsight, be seen as presaging the larger-scale disturbances during the 1980s. This included the widely reported confrontation in June 1973 between black youth, the police and the wider black community in Brockwell Park, in south London. One of the features of the reporting of this event centred on the image of the events as a race riot and as a sign of larger riots and disorders on the horizon. This theme became more pronounced once it was clear that the Brockwell Park incident was not merely an isolated incident, and that outbreaks of a similar kind were becoming part of the everyday experience of many inner city localities.

The immediate causes for such outbreaks were often small incidents which escalated through rumour and counter-rumour, leading to the arrival of more police and more young blacks to join in the fray. But the underlying conditions which helped to create the basis for such confrontations were a much more complex issue. As early as 1970 John's study of Handsworth had noted that 'the massive breakdown of relations between the police and the black community' held the potential for violent unrest. Attempting to describe black feelings about the local police he says:

> The police station in Thornhill Road is one of the buildings most dreaded and most hated by black Handsworth. It is commonplace to hear references made to 'the pigs at Thornhill Road', or 'Babylon House', or 'the place where the thugs hang out' (John, 1970: 22).

Attitudes such as this helped to create a climate of opinion in areas such as Handsworth where the actions of the police were being questioned and at times actively resisted by both young blacks and older members of the community. At the same time the police were adopting a belligerent attitude toward all forms of black cultural and social activity which could be described as either alien or deviant. Thus, from 1969 onwards there were numerous reports in the media of confrontations between the police and young blacks in places such as youth clubs, restaurants and other locations which had become identified as trouble spots or as places where criminal activities thrived. Notable examples include the confrontations at the Mangrove restaurant in Notting Hill and the Metro youth club in the same locality. Confrontations between young blacks and the police were also reported in places such as Brixton, Chapeltown in Leeds, Handsworth in Birmingham, Liverpool, and Moss Side in Manchester.

Such contrasts and conflicting interpretations of the relations between young blacks and the police were themselves a reflection of wider preoccupations about the future of race relations in the urban localities that were experiencing major transformations in their economic, social, political and cultural institutions (CCCS Race and Politics Group, 1982; Gilroy, 1987). During this time the racialisation of political debates about urban policy and social policy more generally was reaching new heights through the interventions of Enoch Powell and the articulation of public concern about the immigration of Ugandan Asians. It was also during this period that the imagery of violence and decay became synonymous with those inner city localities in which black migrants had settled and established themselves.

The politicisation of the mugging issue was part of a wider picture of societal concern about the growing problem of violence, disorder and a breakdown of law and order in British society. Although this phenomenon was not always linked to popular and official perceptions of race, crime and policing, the volatile racialisation of political debate during the early 1970s helped to bring the two issues together in popular discourse.

In an important debate on the Queen's Speech in Parliament at the height of the public debate about mugging, the linking of arguments about black crime to this wider concern became apparent. The debate was ostensibly on the general theme of social problems and was called by the Labour opposition. But as Shirley Williams pointed out in her opening remarks, this was one of the few sessions when the House of Commons had discussed in detail 'the future directions in which our society is moving', particularly the 'crisis in the cities' (*Hansard*, vol. 863, 1973, col. 315). For Williams the situation in many inner city localities was the most critical in over a century, particularly in relation to policing, social deprivation, housing, education and juvenile delinquency. The centrality of youth to this scenario was made clear by the remark that:

Young people, white and black, in increasing numbers (are) moving into cities such as Birmingham and London, often in desperate and futile pursuit of better pay, amenities and conditions. They have themselves become a large floating element among the homeless and . . . an element that is particularly disturbing to the police, because it is this reservoir of homeless youngsters who, unless emergency action is taken, will become the young criminals of the next decade (ibid., col. 320).

This theme was taken up throughout the debate by MPs from all political parties, and also by sections of the media covering this and other debates in Parliament during this period. Indeed the Home Secretary, Robert Carr, emphasised the importance of ensuring that law and order was maintained in the inner city localities, and that disadvantaged groups were not allowed to drift into a vicious circle of disadvantage, alienation, violence and crime (ibid., cols 327–9).

By the mid-1970s therefore, confrontations on the streets between the police and young blacks had become a central feature of the political agenda about race. Yet the consequences of this politicisation remained to be worked out in practice.

Racialisation and popular images

The question of the involvement of young blacks in mugging and other forms of street crime remains very much a current issue in political and policy debates. This can be seen partly in the regularity with which stories in the media about mugging refer either directly or in coded terms to the involvement of young blacks. But since the 1970s the issue of mugging per se has been outweighed by other preoccupations about black crime, which involve broader issues about race relations as well.

At least two processes seem to be at work. First, the growing politicisation of debates about the social and economic conditions within the black communities has broadened concern out from a preoccupation with young blacks as such to encompass the wider communities within which the younger generation live. In this sense debates about black crime signify concern about the crisis of the urban black colonies (Hall *et al.*, 1978: 338–9). Second, since the mid-1970s the question of black youth has become intimately tied to the broader issues of disorder and violent protest, particularly in localities of high levels of black settlement.

The period from 1974–8 saw a number of examples of the material importance of these shifts in political language. The most important were the attempts by Enoch Powell and other politicians to politicise the debate about black crime, and the occurrence of small-scale riots in areas such as Notting Hill in 1976 and 1977, and in other localities from 1977 onwards.

As we saw earlier the 1971–2 Select Committee Report, *Police/ Immigrant Relations*, had concluded that on balance 'coloured immigrants are not more involved in crime than others'. But it seems clear from John's research in Handsworth and from much of the evidence in the Report's appendices that a stereotype of areas of black settlement as criminal areas was already deeply entrenched in police mythology. The report itself notes that despite the lack of evidence to support a link between blacks and crime:

> There seems to be a fairly widespread feeling, shared, as we found in informal discussion, by some police officers, that immigrants commit more crime than the indigenous population (Select Committee, 1972, Report: 22).

The public debate about mugging helped to amplify and popularise the perception, and the issue of black crime was firmly placed on the political agenda. A number of stages in this process were particularly important.

First, the release in January 1975 by the Metropolitan Police of figures from a study of victims' descriptions of assailants in the Brixton area of London. This claimed to show that 79 per cent of robberies and 83 per cent of offences of theft from the person were carried out by black people. This study was widely reported in the media and helped to attract attention to the growing problem of black involvement in crime and the destabilising role of young disillusioned blacks.

Second, in May 1975 Judge Gwyn Morris jailed five young West Indians for mugging offences in south London. In sentencing them he commented:

> These attacks have become a monotonous feature in the suburbs of Brixton and Clapham, areas which within memory were peaceful,

safe, and agreeable places to live in. But immigration resettlement, which has occurred over the past 25 years has radically transformed that environment (*The Guardian*, 16 May 1975).

He went on to argue that youngsters such as them were collectively a frightening menace to society, and that they represented immense difficulties for those interested in the maintenance of law and order.

Third, and perhaps more important in terms of its public impact, Enoch Powell's speech of April 1976 about mugging being a 'racial phenomenon' helped to articulate a wider undercurrent of concern about the interrelationship between race and crime. Powell's speech was in turn linked to the evidence submitted by the Metropolitan Police in March 1976 to the Select Committee on Race Relations and Immigration, which was investigating the West Indian community. In its evidence to the 1972 Select Committee Report, *Police/Immigrant Relations*, the Metropolitan Police had not raised black crime as a major problem, but the intervening four years had obviously transformed their image of this issue. In the very first paragraph of its evidence the Metropolitan Police mentioned the 'uneasy nature of the relationship between police officers and young blacks' in some localities. Although the memorandum did not argue for a direct link between crime and race, and although it did mention the social disadvantages which were common in such areas, it went on to argue that:

It is not part of our position that there is a causal link between ethnic origin and crime. What our records do suggest is that London's black citizens, among whom those of West Indian origin predominate, are disproportionately involved in many forms of crime. But in view of their heavy concentration in areas of urban stress, which are themselves high crime areas, and in view of the disproportionate numbers of young people in the West Indian population, this pattern is not surprising (Select Committee, 1977, Evidence vol. 2: 182).

Whether surprising or not this analysis was to prove extremely controversial and it was directly criticised in the evidence submitted by the Community Relations Commission, to which the Metropolitan Police responded with additional evidence to support their claims. The public debate over these statistics helped to push black crime onto the political agenda in a way which gave legitimacy both to popular concern about crime on the streets and to the arguments of politicians such as Powell who called for 'repatriation' as the only solution to crime and disorder.

Policing and violent disorder

As argued above, the symbolic threat of violent disorder was a theme in official political language about young blacks from the late 1960s onwards. But in August 1976 it became a material reality on the streets of Notting Hill. During the annual carnival in the area a major confrontation took place between young blacks (and to some extent young whites) and the police. Although not on the same level as the events in St Paul's, Brixton, Toxteth, Handsworth and Tottenham during the 1980s the symbolic significance of this event was clear at the time and has been reiterated with some regularity ever since. For example, Kenneth Newman argued that the events at the 1976 Notting Hill Carnival were at the time a unique phenomenon and represented an important watershed in the severity of the public disorder dealt with by the police:

> In relation to public disorder, the major changes over the last decade can be easily followed. In 1976, following the riot at the Notting Hill Carnival, defensive shields were introduced; five years later, after petrol bombs were used, we added flameproof clothing and metal helmets; and last year, after the police were shot at, plastic baton rounds were deployed, but not used (Newman, 1986: 9).

The unstated issue which links all these events together was that the confrontations mentioned all involved young blacks in one way or another. Other less major confrontations also took place in November 1975 in Chapeltown (Leeds), and in other localities. During this period police activities under the 'sus' legislation, which allowed them to stop and search suspected criminals, often led to frequent instances of lower level confrontations between the police and young blacks. Additionally, the operations of the Special Patrol Group in mainly black multi-racial localities became a highly visible source of tension and at times violent confrontation (Demuth, 1978; Hall *et al.*, 1978;

AFFOR, 1978). More broadly the concern with the 'growing problem' of black crime helped to make the police on the ground suspect all black youngsters, the imagery of violent street crime combining with that of violent street disorders and confrontations to make every young black, or particularly groups of them (such as Rastafarians), a potential suspect in police eyes. They were suspect not only because of social perceptions about their involvement in street crime, but because they were black, because of the areas in which they lived, their style of dress and social contact and their leisure activities. This is certainly how an increasing number of younger blacks, along with their parents and independent research-ers, saw the situation in many inner city localities – particularly those that were seen as 'immigrant areas'.

It was because of this 'growing problem' that Robert Mark, the Metropolitan Police Commissioner, chose to highlight in his annual report for 1975, even before the Notting Hill disturbances, the fact that there was a tendency within black communities 'for groups of black people to react in violent opposition to police officers carrying out their lawful duties' (Report of the Commissioner of Police of the Metropolis for the year 1975, 1976: 12). This theme was taken up in articles in police journals and by official police documents during this period. The widely publicised Metropolitan Police evidence to the Select Committee investigation of the West Indian community revealed the official police wisdom and feeling on the subject when it noted that:

Recently there has been a growth in the tendency for members of London's West Indian communities to combine against police by interfering with police officers who are affecting the arrest of a black person or who are in some other way enforcing the law in situations which involve black people. In the last 12 months forty such incidents have been recorded. Each carries a potential for large scale disorder; despite the fact that very few situations actually escalate to the point where local police are unable to cope. Experience indicates that they are more likely to occur during the summer months and that the conflict is invariably with young West Indians. They can occur anywhere in the Metropolitan Police District, but are of course more likely in those areas which have a high proportion of West Indian settlers (Select Committee, 1977, Evidence, vol. 2: 178)

This perception was repeated across the country in the areas where growing tension and confrontations between young blacks and the police had become a major local issue. Within this context references to urban disorder and street violence became a synonym for confrontations between young blacks and the police.

During 1976 and 1977 other widely reported incidents helped to fuel public and policy debate about this issue. First, the killing of an Asian youth, Gurdip Singh Chaggar, in Southall during June 1976 sparked off criticism about the lack of concern shown by the police following racial attacks on young blacks in contrast with their preoccupation with black crime. Second, the 1976 Carnival violence was repeated again in 1977 and led to public concern about whether such outbreaks of violent disorder were becoming a regular feature of 'police–black youth' confrontations in inner city localities. Third, in August 1977 confrontations took place in the Ladywood area of Birmingham and the Lewisham area of London. Both these disturbances involved clashes between the National Front and anti-fascist groups, but it was the involvement of young blacks and the police that became the central issue.

It is clear that the response of the police in areas such as Notting Hill, Brixton, Handsworth and Moss Side further accentuated the stereotype of young blacks (or at least a section of them) as members of a criminal subculture. Everyday contact between young blacks and the police was interpreted through police ideologies as involving a clash between the cultural values of the majority community and those of the minority communities. Such notions were supported by notions about the localities in which the black communities tended to be concentrated ('criminal areas') and the socio-economic conditions, such as poverty and unemployment, which confronted young blacks in inner city localities, indicating that the source of the problem lay in the culture and attitudes of young blacks, with racism and discrimination seen as playing only subsidiary roles.

The situation in Handsworth during the late 1970s is an example of the impact of such debates on particular localities. The police in the Handsworth area had for a long time been at the forefront of initiatives which aimed to improve relations between young blacks and the police. In the evidence submitted by the Birmingham Police to the Select Committee investigation, *Police/Immigration Relations*, the police had noted that they did not believe an 'isolated police effort' could deal with the young unemployed West Indians of Handsworth,

and they recommended an 'integrated social resources' approach
(Select Committee, 1972, Evidence, vol. 2: 446–7). Yet the area
became known as Birmingham's 'angry suburb', and as an area with
a massive potential for disorder and conflict. In a series of articles
during May 1976 on Handsworth the *Birmingham Evening Mail*
analysed the tensions below the surface of the area, the plight of
unemployed young blacks, and the everyday tensions between young
blacks and the police. A year later, in the aftermath of the 'Ladywood
riots', *The Observer* provided the following vivid description of one
confrontation between young blacks and the police:

> Birmingham's Soho Road at half-past nine last Monday night:
> fluid groups of edgy young blacks on the pavements. A blue-and-
> white police Allegro cruises over the traffic lights. With a sudden
> jagged movement, a group hurls bricks, sticks and bottles at the
> car, crunching into the windows and bonking on the metalwork.
> . . . Missiles clatter on shop doors and one shatters plate glass. The
> car slews to a stop and half a dozen youths bombard it from 15 feet.
> 'Babylon' yells a voice, and the blacks dart outwards, sprinting
> around corners as a police squad with riot shields and the
> occasional dustbin lid moves to the stranded panda car (21 August
> 1977).

At the same time the local press in Birmingham was full of stories
about young West Indians confronting the police in the Bull Ring
Shopping Centre and other localities. Such events helped to create a
climate in which the local police became centrally preoccupied with
the issue of young unemployed blacks.

This concern was in turn fuelled by the study carried out in 1977 by
John Brown into the question of relations between young blacks and
the police in Handsworth. Published in November 1977 under the title
Shades of Grey, the essence of the study was an analysis of the issues
of crime and violence in the area, particularly as they related to a
group defined by Brown as consisting of 200 or so 'Dreadlocks' who
'form a criminalised sub-culture' and whose actions helped to create
and reproduce tensions between the black community and the police
(Brown, 1977: 7–8). For Brown the activities of this group of
'criminalised' youngsters needed to be counteracted by a combination of improved police contact with the local communities and wider
social policy measures. One result of the study was the strategy of

'community policing' developed by Superintendent David Webb from 1977–81, which aimed to create through direct police intervention more peaceful contact between the local black communities and the police. But perhaps its broader impact was to help popularise the notion that the 'Dreadlock' minority of black youth was the source of the problem. In their detailed sociological study of the Handsworth area John Rex and Sally Tomlinson commented that *Shades of Grey* fitted in with the popular image in the media that British society was being threatened by a 'menacing group of strangers', and that they found no evidence in their study for the existence of a group of 200 'Dreadlocks' terrorising the area and committing crimes (Rex and Tomlinson, 1979: 231–2). Such reasoned critiques of Brown did not prevent his sensational account of Handsworth from gaining wide coverage in the press and thus helping to popularise dominant police stereotypes of the situation.

Brown's sensational account of the Handsworth situation notwithstanding, the late 1970s saw a further escalation of concern about police–black youth relations – particularly in the context of growing black youth unemployment. Tensions were reaching new levels and the occurrence of conflict and violent confrontation became more commonplace as time went by.

A local resident of Handsworth described the groups of young blacks and other residents marching on Thornhill Road police station as 'more pleased than if they'd won the pools' (*The Observer*, 21 August 1977). Such a depth and intensity of opposition to the police was only partly overcome by the community policing approach adopted by the local police in Handsworth from the mid 1970s onwards. The background to the violent unrest of the 1980s lies precisely in this history of tension and confrontation between young blacks and the police in many localities. The 1970s may not have seen violent protests at the same level as recently seen but the foundations for the breakdown of relations between young blacks and the police were laid during this period.

Race, crime and statistics

The early 1980s were an important period in the racialisation of debates about law and order, crime and policing in at least two ways. First, the politicisation of the black youth unemployment issue helped to focus attention on the interrelationship between unemployment and crime. Second, the riots during 1980–1 forced the issue of crime and violence on the streets onto the mainstream political agenda. The widespread coverage given to the issue of race in connection with the riots helped to open up a wider debate about issues such as mugging and black crime under the wider concern of the future of British society.

One of the most important public debates about race and crime took place in the early 1980s. It followed the decision of the Metropolitan Police in March 1982 to release a previously unpublished racial breakdown of those responsible for street robberies, the statistics having been collated for some time (Scotland Yard, Press Release, 10 March 1982; *The Guardian*, 11 March 1982). These statistics showed a marked rise in street robberies, but the crucial statistic picked up by the press and other media concerned the disproportionate involvement of young blacks in crimes such as mugging, purse snatching and robbery from stores. The press reaction varied from sober commentaries on the nature and limitations of the statistics to sensational headlines about black crime and *The Sun*'s 'The Yard blames black muggers'. But a common theme was the argument that the statistics, along with the riots of 1980–1, were further evidence of the consequences of allowing alien communities to settle in the very heart of Britain. *The Daily Telegraph* articulated this argument succinctly:

> Over the 200 years up to 1945, Britain became so settled in internal peace that many came to believe that respect for the person and property of fellow citizens was something which existed naturally in all but a few. A glance at less fortunate countries might have reminded us that such respect scarcely exists unless law is above the power of tribe, or money, or the gun. But we did not look; we let in people from the countries we did not look at, and only now do we begin to see the result. Many young West Indians in Britain, and, by a connected process, growing numbers of young whites, have no sense that the nation in which they live is part of them. So its citizens become to them mere objects of violent exploitation (11 March 1982).

Such an argument amounted to a direct link between race and crime. A similar tone was adopted by papers such as the *Daily Mail* and *The*

Sun, which went even further in their use of images of mugging – harking back to Powell's 1976 definition of mugging as essentially a black crime. A year later the intervention of Harvey Proctor, the right-wing Tory MP, helped to secure the release of similar figures by the Home Office and led to a similar wave of articles in the press. Since then the Metropolitan Police have been much more reticent about publishing such statistics (although they continue to be kept) because of their potentially volatile political impact.

Not surprisingly, however, the issue of the involvement of young blacks in criminal or quasi-criminal activities remains a key area of concern for the police and other institutions, both locally and nationally. Because of this climate of official concern the issues of crime and violence remain central to the full understanding of how contemporary ideologies about young blacks as a social category were formed and how they are being transformed.

What is clear is that the successive shifts in political language about the black youth question since the early 1970s have involved the issues of policing and black crime as a central theme. Whether in terms of specific concerns about street crime, or with more general concerns about the development of specific subcultures, such as Rastafarianism, among young blacks, the interplay between images of race and crime have remained important symbols in political language. Since the late 1970s, and particularly after the 1980–1 riots, political debates about the black crime issue have also been heavily weighted by the phenomenon of urban unrest and civil disorder. But even within this context the issues of race, crime and the ghetto remain the bedrock for the shifts in official ideologies and public debate about black youth.

The ideological image of the involvement of young blacks in mugging and other forms of street crime has provided the basis for the development of strategies of control aimed at keeping young blacks off the streets and keeping the police in control of particular localities which have been identified both in popular and official discourses as crime-prone or potential trouble spots. It has also helped to bring to the forefront a preoccupation with the social and economic roots of alienation and criminal activity among young blacks. This was reflected in debates about the impact of unemployment on young blacks. But it was also reflected in the increasing preoccupation of the police and other agencies with particular localities where relations between the police and sections of the black community were becoming tense and politicised.

In this context it is worth noting that the police as an institution have been actively seeking to meet what they see as the challenge of policing multi-racial inner city localities by developing new strategies and tactics. They have sought, for example, to recruit more police officers from minority communities. Over the past decade a number of initiatives have attempted to overcome the reluctance of minorities to join the police, albeit with only limited success. More fundamentally, perhaps, the police have also attempted to develop longer term strategies for managing unrest and violence in inner city areas.

Summary and conclusion

In this chapter we have looked at the changing politics of race and policing over the past three decades. We have seen that the main themes in public debates about race and policing have tended to emphasise the interconnections between the social and economic position of minorities and the growth of conflict between the police and sections of minority communities. During the 1970s and 1980s a noticeable politicisation of this issue took place, leading in many areas to questions about policing occupying a prominent place on the political agenda. At the same time it became clear that the question of policing was inextricably tied up with the wider issue of urban unrest and public order. It is to this phenomenon that we now turn.

7 Protest, Racism and Urban Unrest in the 1980s

Introduction

In previous chapters we have seen that black and ethnic minority groups have by no means been passive political actors; rather they have been an active political force over such issues as immigration policy, race relations policies, social policies and policing. In Chapter 6 we looked at some aspects of the experience of policing in the 1970s and early 1980s, and explored the ideological and policy responses by the police and other agencies to racial issues. In this chapter we will advance the analysis a step further by looking at the experience of urban unrest in the 1980s, and the political repercussions of these events in the context of contemporary political trends. This will allow us to explore the question of how far these developments help to explain the new forms of racialised politics that have emerged in Britain in recent years.

Disorder and urban unrest

As was made clear in Chapter 6, examples of urban unrest and disorder have become a regular phenomenon in Britain. The riots of 1980–1 and 1985, in particular, attracted widespread attention from the media, the police, central and local government, voluntary agencies and black political and community groups on a scale never witnessed before in the politics of race in Britain.

During 1980 and 1981 three main examples of urban unrest were recorded. First, in April 1980 violent confrontations took place in the St. Paul's district of Bristol between groups of predominantly black residents and the police. Second, during April 1981 violent confrontations between the police and crowds of mostly black youths took place in the Brixton area of London. Finally, in July 1981 widespread outbreaks of urban unrest were reported in the Southall area of London, in the Toxteth area of Liverpool, and in Brixton and other localities in London. During both 1980 and 1981 other smaller scale disturbances also took place and attracted some attention in the media and within government (Benyon, 1984).

The Brixton events of 10–13 April 1981 led the government to set up the Scarman Inquiry, which, although much more limited than the various American inquiries in the 1960s, sought to explain what happened and also what should be done by government and other agencies in the future (Scarman, 1981; Benyon, 1984). The more widespread events during July 1981 led to a flurry of responses at both central and local government levels, and real and symbolic interventions which sought to prevent the further spread of disorder and violence. It is not surprising, for example, that after years of inaction many local authorities actively sought to develop equal opportunity strategies, that promises were made to reform police training to take account of multi-racialism, that initiatives to tackle the roots of racial disadvantage and discrimination were promised (Joshua and Wallace, 1983).

All of these responses are examples of the symbolic reassurance which was noted by American analysts (Lipsky and Olson, 1977), but they took different issues as the core variables. At least four basic explanatory frameworks were used, which emphasised in turn race, violence and disorder, the breakdown of law and order, social deprivation and youth unemployment and political marginality as the core issues.

Further large-scale riots occurred from September to October 1985. Serious outbreaks of violence took place in the Handsworth area of Birmingham, in the Tottenham and Brixton areas of London and in Liverpool. Other smaller scale disturbances occurred in 1986 and 1987 (Benyon and Solomos, 1987). The scale and locations of the 1985 riots seem to have surprised even some of the most astute commentators. Handsworth, for example, was widely perceived as a success story in terms of police–community relations, and therefore the outbreak of violence in this area was seen as an aberration. Similarly the spread of violence in London to areas such as the Broadwater Farm Estate in Tottenham was seen as a break from previous experience, which had centred on areas such as Brixton. In this sense the interpretation of the 1985 riots proved to be as difficult as that of the 1980–1 riots.

Explanations of urban unrest

The racialisation of the 1980-81 events was evident from the very first confrontation in Bristol on 2 April 1980, although in a somewhat convoluted manner. Under the headline 'Riot Mob Stone Police' the *Daily Mail* talked of 'mobs of black youths' roaming the streets (3 April 1980). This theme was repeated in the coverage of *The Sun*, *Daily Star* and *Daily Express*. *The Financial Times*, however, covered the same events under the headline: 'Bristol: a multiracial riot against the police' (5 April 1980). *The Guardian* was even more ambiguous, with the headline: 'The Bristol confrontation: racial but not racist' (5 April 1980).

The tension between the racial and non-racial elements in the media coverage of the Bristol events reflected, according to Joshua and Wallace (1983), a wider divergence in political responses to violent protest: between modes of explanations which saw race and law and order as the essential variables and those which saw the riots as the outcome of inner city decay and unemployment. This tension was partly the result of official resistance to the idea that Britain was experiencing race riots on the American model, and partly the wish to defuse the situation by separating out the actions of groups of youth from wider social, economic and political grievances. The very fact that the events occurred in Bristol, a city with a popular image of good race relations, was taken as evidence that they were not race riots, a local paper reporting that both William Whitelaw and Tony Benn were agreed that the events could not be described as such (*Evening Post*, 3 April 1980).

Reactions to Bristol are worth remembering, precisely because they highlight the changing symbolism attached to race as an explanatory factor in urban violence during the 1980s. Bristol represented a dilemma even for those who had warned of the possibility of urban violence, since such predictions were premised on areas such as Brixton, Handsworth, Moss Side and Toxteth rather than St. Paul's. Its very unexpectedness made it all the more difficult to locate the role of race or racism as causal factors. But the linkage between black youth and street violence was already established in popular media images.

This can be seen partly by the reactions to small-scale street confrontations that took place between the Bristol riots in 1980 and the next major outbreak, in Brixton on 10–13 April 1981. During this intervening period a number of smaller confrontations took place with the police. The most important was on 3 March 1980 during a demonstration held to protest the death of 13 young West Indians in a fire in Deptford, South London. The *Daily Express* covered the events under the headline 'Rampage of a Mob' (3 March 1980), while the *Daily Mail* saw them as, 'When the Black Tide Met the Thin Blue Line' (3 March 1980). Racialisation of the confrontation between the mostly-black marchers and the police was achieved around the themes of the 'mob' and 'young blacks'. As the *Daily Mirror* saw it:

A peaceful protest by 10,000 of London's West Indians was ruined by the hooliganism of 200 young blacks (4 March 1981).

The ambiguity of the coverage of the events in Bristol was replaced by the emphasis on the involvement of small groups of young blacks in street confrontations with the police, and the role of black militants and outside agitators in fostering violence for their own objectives.

Whatever the symbolic importance of Bristol and the Deptford march, however, there is no doubt that the period between April and July 1981 constituted the crucial phase in the racialisation of discourses about violent protest. Events in Brixton (April 10–13) and nationwide (July 3–28) led to a number of accounts of the events viewed through the prism of race. The most stark usage of racial symbols to explain the violence was articulated by Enoch Powell and a small but vociferous group of Conservative MPs and journalists. Powell had already intervened in a somewhat muted form during the Bristol events, but he made a series of interventions during 1981 when he articulated his view of why the riots could not be understood without reference to race and immigration. In a confrontation with William Whitelaw in Parliament he concluded by saying that in view of the 'prospective future increase in the relevant population' future outbreaks were inevitable, and that 'Britain has seen nothing yet' (*Hansard*, 1981, vol.3, col. 25). By July 1981 he had warmed up to this theme and argued his case in a number of articles in the popular press, as well as in his parliamentary speeches. During a vigorous speech in the House he disagreed with Roy Hattersley that the three main causes of the July riots were poverty, unemployment and deprivation. Pouring scorn on this analysis he offered his own causal factor and constructed the linkage with race without actually uttering the words:

> Are we seriously saying that so long as there is poverty, unemployment and deprivation our cities will be torn to pieces, that the police in them will be the objects of attack and that we shall destroy our own environment? Of course not. Everyone knows that, although those conditions do exist, there is a factor, the factor which the people concerned perfectly well know, understand and apprehend, and that unless it can be dealt with – unless the fateful inevitability, the inexorable doubling and trebling of that element of a population can be avoided – their worst fears will be fulfilled (*Hansard*, 1981, vol. 8, col. 1313).

He repeated his argument in a series of graphic warnings in the popular press over this period. In addition a number of right-wing Conservative MPs, newspaper columnists and commentators took up Powellite themes and embellished them with different symbols, as did the extreme neo-fascist groupings.

If Powellite imagery was the most stark usage of race as the main explanation for the riots, it was by no means the only one, whether it be in the official reports about the riots, in press and television coverage or in the general public policy debate. In all of these categories such as race, racial discrimination or black youth played a central role either implicitly or explicitly. During both the Brixton riot of April 1981 and the nationwide riots of July 1981 the press was full of images, both pictorial and written, that emphasised that race was somehow a central variable or even the main one. The strength of these images was particularly clear during July 1981 when headlines proclaimed the hatred that blacks had for the police, their alienation or detachment from the mainstream values of British society and the growth of racial tension in certain important localities. Among the early reports on the riots the *Daily Mail*'s headline proclaimed simply: 'Black War on the Police' (6 July 1981). This was perhaps the most extreme, but *The Sun* was only marginally less direct when it talked of 'The Cities that Live in Fear' while the *Daily Mirror* proclaimed the words of Merseyside's Chief Constable, Kenneth Oxford, when it argued: 'This was not a race war. It was blacks versus the police.'

A number of lead articles in both the popular and the serious press from 6 July to 25 July devoted much attention to the race issue, which they saw as important in various degrees. In addition Enoch Powell's statements and those of other politicians in favour of repatriation were widely reported, though usually with a disclaimer which distanced the paper from such extreme views. Ronald Butt, writing in the *Daily Mail*, argued that the culprits in the riots were for the most part black and that this meant that one could not blame white society for the kinds of attitudes that led young blacks to stage disturbances. Rather the blame lay with the attitudes of young blacks and with those agitators who directed such attitudes to their own ends (10 July 1981).

The ambivalence about whether the events in Bristol had been a race riot had been replaced by July 1981 by the imagery that since a sizeable number of riot participants were black the riots were racial or at least the outcome of bad relations between the police and young blacks. But racism as such was only rarely talked about, since the riots were not seen as linked to real grievances but only to the perceptions that young blacks had of their position in society, and to the wider processes which were undermining the role of law.

Law and disorder

Another important line of argument used in relation to the unrest was the issue of law and order, and the difficulty of policing multiracial inner city areas. This was by no means an accident, since throughout the 1970s a powerful body of media, political, policy and academic opinion had been constructed around the theme of how Britain was drifting into a violent society, and how the basis of consent was being shifted by the pressures of forces undermining the moral fabric of British society (Hall *et al.*, 1978). An article by Peregrine Worsthorne during this period underlined this fear:

> The spectre haunting most ordinary people is neither that of a totalitarian state nor Big Brother but of other ordinary people being allowed to run wild. What they are worried about is crime, violence, disorder in the schools, promiscuity, idleness, pornogra-

phy, football hooliganism, vandalism and urban terrorism (Worsthorne, 1978: 151).

The riots, however, were instrumental in popularising Worsthorne's image of 'ordinary people being allowed to run wild' beyond the readership of neo-conservative tracts and readers of the *Daily Telegraph*. By forcing the debate on law and order onto the streets they helped give actuality to the warnings which had been expounded by a number of commentators for over a decade that lawlessness and corrosive violence were undermining traditional British values and institutions.

A glimpse of the impact of the 1980–1 riots at this level can be seen through two important debates in Parliament. The first took place in the midst of the July riots and had as its theme: 'Civil Disturbances'. The importance of the debate is indicated by the fact that more than 60 MPs had indicated their wish to participate in it. The tone of the debate was set by William Whitelaw's introductory statement which spoke of the need to (a) 'remove the scourge of criminal violence from our streets' and (b) the urgency of developing 'policies designed to promote the mutual tolerance and understanding upon which the whole future of a free democratic society depends' (*Hansard*, vol. 8, 1981, col. 1405). The 'scourge of criminal violence' was, Whitelaw argued, a danger to the whole framework of consent and legality upon which the political institutions of British society were based. In reply Roy Hattersley supported the call for the immediate suppression of street violence, but warned that the roots of such riots could not be dealt with until all people felt they had a stake in our society (ibid.: cols 1407–9).

The second debate took place on 26 November 1981 and had as its theme: 'Law and Order'. The importance of the riots in pushing the law and order issue, and specifically policing, onto the main political agenda was emphasised by the Liberal Leader, David Steel, who argued that urgent action to prevent a drift into lawlessness was necessary from both a moral and political perspective (*Hansard*, vol. 13, 1981, cols 1009–11). A subsequent debate on the same issue in March 1982 was also full of references to the experience of 1981, the impact of street violence, crime, decaying urban conditions, the breakdown of consent between the police and many local communities, and the spectre of more violence to come if changes at the level of policing tactics and social policy were not swiftly introduced (*Hansard*, vol. 20, 1982, cols 1107–81).

The psychological and symbolic impact of the riots was also grasped by Lord Scarman, whose report on Brixton contained the following graphic description:

> During the week-end of 10–12 April (Friday, Saturday and Sunday) the British people watched with horror and incredulity an instant audio-visual presentation on their television sets of scenes of violence and disorder in their capital city, the like of which had not previously been seen in this century in Britain. In the centre of Brixton, a few hundred young people most, but not all of them, black attacked the police on the streets with stones, bricks, iron bars and petrol bombs, demonstrating to millions of their fellow citizens the fragile basis of the Queen's peace. These young people, by their criminal behaviour – for such, whatever their grievances or frustrations, it was – brought about a temporary collapse of law and order in the centre of an inner suburb of London (Scarman, 1981: para. 1.2).

It is perhaps all too easy to forget this sense of shock and the fear that more violence was to come, and this pervaded much of the discussion of the riots during and after 1981. But even a brief glance at both the popular and quality press during April and July 1981 reveals the deep sense of shock at the street violence which was popularly perceived as not having occurred on the same scale during this century. On the 13 April *The Times* reported that looters and mobs of young people had virtually taken over the Brixton area from the police. *The Guardian* saw it somewhat differently, but it still talked of 'The Battle of Brixton'. The *Daily Mail* talked of an 'army of rioting black youths' taking to the street, the *Daily Star* talked of 'Flames of Hate'. The *Daily Mirror* took a longer term view when it warned that the Brixton events were 'The Shape of Things to Come' and that the next riots could come in Birmingham, Manchester or many other inner city localities. Under a picture of groups of youth facing and throwing stones and missiles at the police it ran the following headline:

> THE BATTLE RAGES: Youths, white and black, hurl their barrage of missiles at point blank range as police attempt to take cover behind their shields.

Similar, and more detailed reports were to be found in most of the papers on 14 and 15 April, and intermittently throughout April and into May.

The messages which such reporting contained were complex and quite often contradictory. But the centrality of the law and order theme, the fear that disorderly street violence was becoming an established fact of the English way of life, and the linkages constructed with black youth as the main group involved highlight the symbolic evocation of the reestablishment of order as the main concern of official political language during this period. Under the headline 'Order Before Research' a *Daily Telegraph* editorial asserted:

Mob violence must be stopped. Existing laws should be used to the full to punish the offenders and guarantee safety in our cities. If the Public Order Act . . . cannot cope with the threat of disorder now, then new riot legislation must be enacted (6 July 1981).

The need to support the police was accepted by both the Labour and Conservative speakers in the parliamentary debate on the riots, and was established as a benchmark for the official response to the riots long before the Scarman Report was published in November 1981. Any substantive disagreement centred around the issue of what role social deprivation and unemployment had in bringing young people to protest violently on the streets.

A particularly interesting sub-theme within the law and order arguments was the emergence of the outside agitator and the middle men who were seen by some sections of the press as directing the violence. Under the headline 'Search for the Masked Men' the *Daily Mail* reported on 7 July:

Masked figures on motor cycles were seen issuing instructions to groups of rioters on the second night of violence in the predominantly black district [of Toxteth]. They appeared to be giving tactical orders to sections of the 500 strong mob of mainly white youths. As the battle developed, groups armed with petrol bombs and stones were moved quickly from street to street.

During July 1981 a whole sub-mythology grew up around this imagery of outside forces directing the actions of mobs on the street, and of the purposes they had in mind. As we shall see later this image was taken up and reworked in 1985 to become one of the main symbols used to analyse the causes of the riots in Handsworth, Brixton and Tottenham.

Racial disadvantage and urban unrest

Intermingled with the discourses about race and law and order but somewhat autonomous were constant references to unemployment, particularly among the young, and various forms of social disadvantage and poverty. The attack by Enoch Powell on the arguments articulated by Roy Hattersley was but one example of the clash between explanations of the riots on the basis of social deprivation. Throughout 1980 and 1981 debates about the riots in the media, Parliament and in various official reports hinged around the interrelationship between racial, law and order and social factors. The importance of this debate can be explained, partly, by the political capital which could be made by the opposition by linking the social and economic malaise of the country at large with violent street disturbances. Hence throughout this period numerous government ministers strenuously denied that unemployment and social deprivation were the most important roots of urban unrest.

The tone of this debate and the ambiguities contained in social explanations of the riots highlight the complex dilemmas faced by the political establishment during 1980–1. These dilemmas became even greater when the Scarman Report was published in November 1981, to be followed by a vigorous public debate about how the report could be implemented, what other policy initiatives were necessary and what immediate measures could prevent a recurrence in 1982 of the July 1981 events.

Although the Scarman Report is often taken to be the central text which argues for a link between social conditions and disorder, the terms of the debate were by no means set by Scarman. During both April and July 1981 vigorous exchanges took place both in the press and in Parliament about the role that deteriorating social conditions and unemployment may have played in bringing about the riots. During the 16 July parliamentary debate on civil disturbances Roy Hattersley's formulation of this linkage provided a useful summary of the social conditions argument. After some preliminary remarks about the Labour Party's support for the police, he went on to outline his opposition to the view of the riots as essentially anti-police outbursts:

> I repeat that I do not believe that the principal cause of last week's riots was the conduct of the police. It was the conditions of deprivation and despair in the decaying areas of our old cities – areas in which the Brixton and Toxteth riots took place, and areas from which the skinhead invaders of Southall come (*Hansard*, vol. 8, 1981, col. 1408).

He went on to outline the four common features shared by such areas, namely:

- Inadequate housing and inadequate government spending on improvements.
- A lack of social, cultural and welfare amenities.
- Inadequate provision of remedial education for deprived families.
- High levels of unemployment, particularly youth unemployment.

Much of the subsequent controversy about this analysis, apart from Powell's retort which is discussed above, centred on the question of youth unemployment. Hattersley had suggested that the riots were a direct product of high levels of youth unemployment, and a furious debate ensued in both Parliament and the media about this assertion. A similar debate took place in the aftermath of the publication of the Scarman Report, linking up many of the report's arguments with the Hattersley version of the social conditions argument.

What is interesting about the debate surrounding this symbol, however, are the different emphases which were put on the four common features identified by Hattersley in his parliamentary speech. While challenging any causal link between unemployment and violent protest, both William Whitelaw and Margaret Thatcher accepted that social conditions in many inner city areas were bad. What they disputed, however, was the jump from such conditions to violent confrontations on the streets between youth and the police. During the Brixton riots the Prime Minister replied angrily to Labour suggestions that unemployment was a primary cause of the riots:

> If you consider that unemployment was the only cause – or the main cause – of the riots I would disagree with you. Nothing that

has happened to unemployment would justify these riots (as quoted in *Financial Times*, 15 April 1981).

A number of exchanges along the same lines took place during July 1981 about unemployment and urban poverty. The existence of unemployment as such was not denied, though its impact was disputed, but the formula which established a link between high levels of young unemployed and urban disorder remained a hotly debated issue.

Alienation and powerlessness

The final symbolic cue used to make sense of the 1980–1 protests is more difficult to categorise, but its basic meaning can be captured by the term political marginality. While a number of discussions of the roots of urban unrest in the US have noted the salience of political marginality in determining participation in violent protests (Skolnick, 1969; Fogelson, 1971; Edelman, 1971), this issue has received relatively little attention in Britain. Nevertheless, during the 1980–1 events and their aftermath the political context was discussed from a number of perspectives.

The Scarman Report, for example, located part of the explanation for the riots in the feelings of alienation and powerlessness experienced by young blacks living in depressed inner city areas. A successful policy for tackling the roots of urban disorder was seen as one which sought to involve all the community in dealing with the problems of each area so that they could come to feel they had a stake in its future (Scarman, 1981: para. 6.42).

A good number of examples of the political marginality argument can also be found in the media coverage during 1980–1. After the Bristol riot, for example, *The Observer* reported the events by quoting a 'lanky Rastafarian with dangling dreadlocks' who argued:

Discrimination accumulates; chickens come home to roost. They wanted to strike fear in people's hearts with law and order. You have no say in your life. People may give you some grant, some urban aid, but they are not really interested in getting to the root of the situation (6 April 1980).

While such a viewpoint was rarely heard, throughout this period the question of politics and power did enter into some aspects of the public debate about the causes of urban violence. Precisely because it raised questions about power, however, the issue of political marginality was difficult to handle and touched upon the thorny problem of how far the riots were in fact a form of political action.

The ambiguity and tension which the 1980–1 riots created meant that though the statements of 'lanky Rastafarians' could be repeated and to some extent taken on board, they were not accorded the detailed coverage in the mass media that the other symbols were given. Where such arguments did not fit in with the overarching themes of race, violence and disorder and social deprivation they were either sidelined or pushed into the sub-clauses of official reports. The Scarman Report, for example, contained the following policy proposal:

> I . . . recommend that local communities must be fully and effectively involved in planning, in the provision of local services, and in the management and financing of specific projects (Scarman, 1981: para. 8.44).

Such a move towards greater political integration was seen by Lord Scarman as essential if the gap between inner city residents and the forces of law and order was to be bridged and constructive cooperation developed.

But the concern with overcoming political marginality remained on the sidelines of the main public debate because it questioned the perception of the rioters as driven by irrational, uncivilised, and criminal instincts. According to Martin Kettle:

> The attempt to depict the riots as irrational was very important. It denied legitimacy to the rioters, their actions and their views. It made them events without cause, and events that therefore posed no direct threat to any existing assumption (Kettle, 1982: 404).

This did not, however, stop the question of political marginality and the need to reform existing policies from being raised at all, as can be seen subsequently by the numerous attempts after 1981 to introduce measures both locally and nationally which were meant to address some of the grievances of the rioters and to ensure that further disturbances did not occur. It is to this issue that we now turn.

Power, legitimacy and political disorder

Perhaps the most important lesson of the 1980–1 riots was the way they emphasised the role of political protest as a channel for challenging racial injustice after decades of ameliorative reforms. But in the aftermath of the riots many of the issues that were raised and the reforms that were promised did not become a central item on the political agenda of the Thatcher administration. Part of the reason for this may have been the hope that the events of 1980–1 were an aberration outside the normal pattern of British politics and that urban disorders on a similar scale were not likely to recur.

Between 1982 and 1985 the differential nature of the government's response to the riots became clear and a matter of comment both in the media and in academic research. Writing in 1985 John Clare, the BBC's community affairs correspondent, noted that although the government had carried out many changes in relation to the police after 1981 it had done remarkably little in relation to political, social and economic issues (Clare, 1985). Indeed during this period many of the conditioning factors which had commanded attention during 1981 had steadily worsened. This is particularly the case when one looks at issues such as unemployment, housing and welfare provision. Government policies, far from remedying the employment situation, for example, had helped to produce levels of unemployment in inner city areas which were up to two or three times higher than during the 1980–1 disorders (Cross and Smith, 1987). Perhaps even more disastrously the government had steadfastly refused to strengthen either the legislation on race relations or to take administrative measures to tackle racial inequality. After the 1981 riots the government seemed to believe that it had the situation under control, and that future violent disorders were unlikely.

What is clear is that the dominant political language used during the 1985 events sought to establish the senselessness of violent protest by arguing that the lessons of 1980–1 had been learned and that solutions were being applied to the main problems. Responding to the Handsworth events Douglas Hurd was moved to argue with some force that such events were senseless and reflected more on those who participated in them than on the society in which they took place:

> The sound which law abiding people in Handsworth heard on Monday night, the echoes of which I picked up on Tuesday, was not a cry for help but a cry for loot (*Financial Times*, 13 September 1985).

The Chief Constable for the West Midlands, Geoffrey Dear, took this argument further by pointing out that the day before the riots a successful carnival had taken place, with the support of local community leaders. He drew the conclusion from this that the riot 'came like a bolt out of the blue' (*The Guardian*, 21 November 1985). Such language focused attention on the individuals or groups who were 'breaking the law', 'committing criminal acts', and threatening the interests of the law-abiding 'majority'.

It also helped to rework some of the main themes that were evident in the aftermath of 1980–1 around the central role of law and order in relation to (a) race and social disadvantage, (b) urban decline and unemployment, (c) crime, drugs and hooliganism and (d) internal enemies and political disorder.

Let us take the example of the political debate about race and urban unrest in the aftermath of the 1985 riots. There are many continuities between 1980–1 and 1985 in relation to the race issue. But responses in 1985 can be said to be different at least in terms of degree, and probably in relation to the extent to which the riots were seen as a race phenomenon by a wider body of opinion. The ambiguities and sub-clauses to be found in much of the press coverage during 1980–1 had at least acted as a countervailing tendency against the more extreme forms of discourse which blamed the riots completely on blacks. During the 1985 riots and their immediate aftermath, however, the imagery of race was used by sections of the press without the sense of ambiguity which could still be found in 1980–1. The silence over race was breached in 1980–1, but in a more limited way than in 1985.

An example of this greater openness about racial issues is the way new right commentators used the urban unrest in 1985 to question the possibility that a multi-racial society could develop without conflict. Peregrine Worsthorne, for example, argued that the ferocity of confrontations in Handsworth, Brixton and Tottenham posed a major question mark over the possibility of assimilating the 'coloured population' into mainstream 'British values' (*Sunday Telegraph*, 29 September 1985). To be sure there was still strong opposition to Enoch Powell's call for repatriation, from all shades of political opinion, but the racialisation of public debate about the riots went even further than in 1980–1. Consider for example the following headlines the day after the outbreak of violence in Handsworth, 11 September:

Bloodlust (*Daily Mail*)
Hate of Black Bomber (*The Sun*)
War on the Streets (*The Mirror*)
Torch of Hate (*The Star*)
England, 1985 (*Daily Express*)

All five headlines were next to a picture of a black petrol bomber, who was variously described as 'stalking the streets of Handsworth' or as a 'prowling West Indian'. These images fitted the official view that this was not a social phenomenon but crime, which was also reported by the press on the same day. They established a linkage between race, crime and disorder much more firmly than the riots of 1980–1 had done.

In this context it was the externality of West Indians and Asians which was highlighted rather than the racist institutions and processes which worked against blacks at all levels of society. The usage of race during the 1985 riots took on new meanings, which had little if anything to do with the impact of racism as such, since the emphasis was on the cultural characteristics of the minority communities themselves. After Handsworth part of the press response was to blame the riot on rivalry between West Indians and Asians, and even after the arguments were criticised by local residents and community leaders they were used to explain what happened. In addition, the questions of whether the cultures and values of the black communities, their family structures and their political attitudes bred violence were constantly raised.

The actual facts of who was arrested during the riots, whether black or white, were hardly debated since it was assumed that they were mostly black and mostly unemployed and involved with crime. The imagery of the black bomber used in Handsworth was extended to the notion that there were groups of alienated and criminalised young blacks who saw the riots as a chance to engage in an orgy of looting. The Dear Report on Handsworth captures this image and links it to the social condition of young blacks:

> The majority of rioters who took part in these unhappy events were young, black and of Afro-Caribbean origin. Let there be no doubt, these young criminals are not in any way representative of the vast majority of the Afro-Caribbean community whose life has con- tributed to the life and culture of the West Midlands over many years and whose hopes and aspirations are at one with those of every other law abiding citizen. We share a common sorrow. It is the duty of us all to ensure that an entire cultural group is not tainted by the actions of a criminal minority (Dear, 1985: 69).

This black criminal minority was constructed not only into the leading force behind the riots, but sometimes as the only force. Indeed through September and October 1985, and during the following months, the imagery of race continued to dominate debate both about the causes and the policy outcomes of the riots.

As pointed out above the social causes argument was another major plank of public debate about the 1980–1 riots, particularly in relation to the highly politicised issue of unemployment. During 1985 this issue was raised once again, though by then the extent of mass unemployment and urban deindustrialisation and decay was more stark than it had been in 1981. Images of urban decay, tinderbox cities, and ghetto streets linked up with the images of race inequality and black ghettoes to produce an analysis based on more complex but contradictory sets of arguments.

An interesting mixture of the various images was provided by a story in the *Daily Telegraph* under the headline: 'Broadwater Farm: Like the Divis Flats with Reggae' (8 October 1985). *The Mirror* described the estate as 'Living Hell', and quoted one resident as saying that 'You've no idea how awful daily life is' (8 October 1985). Such images were reworkings of arguments already used about Toxteth and Brixton in 1981, but they were used more widely than in 1980–1. Even the *Daily Mail*, which deployed the clearest use of race and outside agitator type arguments, ran a major story on Broadwater Farm under the headline: 'Burnt-out hulks litter this concrete jungle . . . despair hangs heavy' (8 October 1985). A number of stories using such imagery were run by both the quality and popular press during this period, but similar arguments are to be found in parliamentary debates (*Hansard*, vol. 84, 1985, cols 30–46, 368–88), and even in official reports produced by the police on the riots in Birmingham and London.

The following editorial from *The Mirror*, printed in the aftermath of the Brixton riot illustrates the point:

The fire down below
The fires in Brixton have been damped down but the spark that ignited them is still glowing in every inner-city area with a large black population. That spark will not be extinguished easily or painlessly.

There is no excuse for what happened on Saturday and there can be no mercy for those who committed crimes . . .

But bad conditions make bad people of some who would otherwise be good. If they had pleasant housing, secure jobs and favourable prospects, they would be far less likely to behave as they did on Saturday (1 October 1985).

The imagery of a fire down below and the policy implication that as well as tackling the criminal acts the government should be doing something about housing, employment and leisure facilities challenged the notion that the riots were a mere cry for loot, but only to a limited extent. It did so largely by including the causes for the crimes under a broader social explanation of the roots of disorder.

The cities of inner despair were conceived as the breeding ground for disorderly protest, and however hard the government tried to break the causal link between the two it was forced to take on board the need to restore order not only through the police but through promises of help for the inner cities. Much as in 1980–1 the social causes argument cannot be seen separately from the broader debate about the future of the British economy and society more generally. The government's record on unemployment was a heavily politicised issue, and just as in 1981 it vehemently denied any responsibility for the riots through its pursuit of free-market policies. But the government did find a way of accepting a link between the riots and social problems without bringing its main policies into the debate, namely by linking the growth of violent disorder to crime and drugs.

Policing after the riots

The emphasis on crime and the criminal acts of the rioters in the official responses to the 1985 riots took a general and a specific form. The general form relied on the argument that the riots were not a way of protesting against the unbearable social conditions of inner city areas or the actions of the police, but a criminal act or a cry for loot. This argument was put most succinctly by Geoffrey Dear, Chief Constable of the West Midlands (Dear, 1985) and by Douglas Hurd, the Home Secretary, in relation to Handsworth. But it recurred as a theme in official and press responses to the other riots. The specific form was built upon the notion that the outbreak of violence in Handsworth and Brixton in particular was brought about by drug barons who saw the police attempting to curb their activities and control their territory. Numerous examples of this line of argument can be found in Dear's report on Handsworth and in a number of major press stories published during the riots.

The attack on criminal acts and the emphasis on order resonated through a long debate in Parliament on 23 October 1985 on urban Disturbances. Rejecting the Labour Party's call for an independent inquiry into the causes of the riots the government succeeded in pushing through the following resolution:

> That this House recognises the crucial importance of the main-
> tenance of public order; applauds the courage and dedication of the
> police and responsible community leaders in restoring order; and
> welcomes Her Majesty's government's commitment to early
> effective action in the light of the recent urban disturbances
> (*Hansard*, vol. 84, 1985, col. 388).

A measure of how the law and order argument was used can also be found in the numerous calls made by Douglas Hurd for people to rally round the police in order to defend the rule of law, and the acceptance by virtually all the media that, in the short term at least, the restoration of police authority on the 'streets of fear' was the first priority.

Taking the specific argument about the role of drugs and drug barons in stimulating the riots, this seems to have served two purposes. First, it distanced the riots from the social, economic, political and other grievances which had been linked to them by locating the cause outside of the social problems of inner city dwellers and in the simple greed of the drug barons. Second, just as Dear's image of a few hundred 'young black criminals' was used to explain what happened in Handsworth, the problem of drugs was used to explain what happened at a national level. The issue of drugs provided an everyday image, already a national issue through saturation media coverage and public debate, around which the police, the Home Office and other institutions could desocialise the riots.

What is clear, therefore, is that the public pronouncements branding the riots as criminal acts and a cry for loot were only one element of a wider ideological construction of the events around the theme of a drift towards crime. While the branding of the riots as criminal seemed to depoliticise them, it is quite clear that a more complex analysis of why crime and disorder were a growing phenomenon exercised an influence on police and other official ideologies.

The theme of outside agitators had been widely used to explain the 1980–1 riots, but 1985 saw a massive explosion of this imagery and its use to explain the causes of the attacks on the police. The masked men of 1980–1 were to some extent unmasked. Take for example the treatment by the press of Bernie Grant and other black and white local Labour Party leaders. They were labelled by Douglas Hurd as the 'high priests of race hate', and then followed lurid press stories which attempted to show how 'GLC leftists', 'black activists' or plain reds were behind a campaign to undermine the police, to stimulate urban violence and to bring about a collapse of law and order. Such stories served a double function. First, they unmasked the forces supposedly behind the riots and gave credibility to claims that even if they were not preplanned they had been sparked off by agitation from leftists and other folk devils. Second, they helped to decontextualise the riots from the issue of racism and the social position of inner city black communities by laying the blame for racial hatred squarely at the door of the extreme left and black activists. Indeed according to Ronald Butt, a regular columnist for *The Times* and other papers on racial issues during 1980–1 and 1985, race had become a new weapon in the class war.

If blaming assorted types of reds for the outbreak of street violence had taken on new forms in 1985, the traditional outside agitator theme of masked men and foreign agents did not exactly disappear. A classic of its own kind is the following story from the *Daily Express* about the death of PC Blakelock on Broadwater Farm:

Moscow-trained hit squad gave orders as mob hacked PC Blakelock to death
The thugs who murdered policeman Keith Blakelock in the Tottenham riots acted on orders of crazed left-wing extremists. Street-fighting experts trained in Moscow and Libya were behind Britain's worst violence.

The chilling plot emerged last night as detectives hunted a hand-picked death squad believed to have been sent into North London hell-bent on bloodshed.

They include men and women from Commonwealth countries like Jamaica, Barbados and Nigeria, who have been trained in Russia and Libya in street revolutionary tactics (8 October 1985).

A number of similar stories resonated through the pages of the popular press, even when there was no evidence supplied or when the links seemed to be a matter of assertion. Looking for the 'men behind the riots' turned out to be less a matter of the individual 'leftists' who were named in such stories but of the construction of symbolic cues about the threat posed to Britain by 'outside agents', 'men and women from Commonwealth countries'. In fact what is interesting about the *Daily Express* story, apart from the classic headline, is the way it highlights the supposed use of 'immigrants' by Russia and Libya to undermine order and stability.

The symbolic political value of such metaphors has been noted in studies of riot response in the US, where the 'outside agitators' argument was used to deflect attention away from social, economic and policing issues (Edelman, 1971; Lipsky and Olson, 1977). The experience of 1980–1 and 1985 in Britain suggests that such an analysis needs to be contextualised against a broader historical perspective, since 'outside agitators' type of arguments do not seem to have any relation to the 'facts' of the riots as such. They seem to form part of a wider use of symbolic political language to help make sense of the crises facing British society. Ambiguous political situations such as riots help engender anxieties about the role of external threats to order, but they do not create such beliefs. But when they are contextualised against the background of wider political debates about race and immigration in post-1945 Britain it becomes easier to see the interconnections between images of outside agitators and the popular stereotypes of blacks as 'alien'.

The notion that the growth of street violence was the product of a combination of social problems leading to the emergence of a 'criminal element' and 'hooliganism' was one of the main themes in accounts of the 1980–1 riots, as pointed out above. But in the responses to the 1985 riots we see not only a popular use of such ideas but a more sophisticated use by sections of the police. Some reference to this development has been made in relation to Dear's report on Handsworth. A more developed version was offered in the aftermath of the 1985 riots by Sir Kenneth Newman, Commissioner of the Metropolitan Police. During of 1982–5 he had already made a series of influential speeches on the issue of disorder and the growth of violence in British society. In a paper delivered in 1983 he had warned that in many inner city areas the police were under threat and unable to maintain order:

> In many multi-ethnic areas police encounter not merely apathy and unhelpfulness when making enquiries or engaging in order maintenance, but outright hostility and obstruction (Newman, 1983: 28).

He warned that such a situation could result in a cycle of increasing crime, law-breaking, police inability to maintain order and the reinforcement of urban decay. He argued that increasingly policing was not an isolated service but part of a wider set of agencies which helped to maintain social stability and order and prevent a drift towards crime and lawlessness. He saw such agencies as particularly important in the areas of education, health and social services, housing and environment, and employment.

In the aftermath of the 1985 riots Newman extended his analysis by arguing that crime and the fear of crime helped to reinforce attitudes towards the police and society which allowed violent protests to break out and challenge the legitimacy of the established order (Newman, 1986a, 1986b). Crime, according to Newman, provided not so much a causal explanation for riots, but one element in a broader crisis of social policy and control. He saw this as particularly important in areas of a 'multi-ethnic' nature where cultural and political hostility towards the police was growing.

Scarman and beyond

As argued above the 1980–1 riots resulted in a wide variety of responsive measures, emanating from both central and local government, as well as other agencies. The very multiplicity of ideological constructions of the riots is an indication of the complexity of the responses which resulted in policies and programmes of action. There are, however, three analytically distinct and important political and policy responses which need to be analysed: (a) the Scarman Report; (b) policing and law and order; (c) economic and social policies.

In the aftermath of the April 1981 riots in Brixton the Home Secretary, William Whitelaw, used his powers under the 1964 Police Act to appoint Lord Scarman to inquire into the events, produce a report and make recommendations. This brief was subsequently widened to cover the occurrence of other disturbances during July 1981. Lord Scarman's inquiry was not on the same scale as the famous Kerner Report on the US riots, but since the publication of his report in November 1981 his views and prescriptions have played an important role in fashioning political debate about the riots. It is therefore important to look into the basic analysis put forward by the Scarman Report in order to understand how the political agenda of riot response has developed since 1980.

The starting point of Lord Scarman's explanation of the riots is important here. He began his analysis by distinguishing between the background factors which had created the potential for urban disorder in areas such as Brixton and the precipitating action or event which sparked off the riots. Scarman identified two views that were commonly held as to the causation of the disorders. The first explained them in terms of oppressive policing, and in particular the harassment of young blacks. The second explained them as a protest against society by deprived people who saw violent attacks upon the forces of law and order as a way of calling attention to their grievances. For Scarman both views were a simplification of a complex reality, or at least 'not the whole truth'. He linked the social and policing aspects of the complex reality of areas like Brixton in an analytic model which emphasised the following issues:

(i) the problems which are faced in policing and maintaining order in deprived, inner-city, multi-racial localities;

(ii) the social, economic, and related problems which are faced by all residents of such areas; and

(iii) the social and economic disadvantages which are suffered particularly by black residents, especially young blacks (Scarman, 1981, paras 2.1 to 2.38).

He saw the existence of all these features in certain deprived areas as 'creating a predisposition towards violent protest' which could be sparked off by incidents such as confrontations between local residents and the police or by rumours about the actions of the police or other authority figures.

From this account Lord Scarman drew the conclusion that once the roots of a 'predisposition towards violent protest' had taken hold it was difficult to reverse the situation. Talking about the position of young blacks, he noted that because they felt neither socially nor economically secure many of them had drifted into situations where more or less regular confrontations with the police were the norm of their daily experience. Noting that despite the evidence of academic and government reports, which had pointed to widespread discrimination against young blacks, very little had been done to remedy the situation, Scarman concluded that (a) many young blacks believed that violence was an effective means of protest against their conditions and (b) that far from the riots being a meaningless event, they were 'essentially an outburst of anger and resentment by young black people against the police' (ibid., paras 3.110, 2.38). What is important to note here is that aside from Lord Scarman's condemnation of the criminal acts committed during the riots, the report was a strong argument in favour of a historical and social explanation of the riots.

Another line of argument embodied in the Scarman Report related to the social and family structures of the black communities in the inner cities, particularly the West Indian family. Explaining the drift towards violence and crime it painted the following picture of the young black in Brixton:

Without close parental support, with no job to go to, and with few recreational facilities available, the young black person makes his life on the streets and in the seedy commercially run clubs of Brixton. There he meets criminals, who appear to have no difficulty in obtaining the benefits of a materialist society (ibid., para. 2.23).

Though the report went on to point out that many young black people do not of course resort to crime, it can nevertheless be said that it used the image of the rootless black youngster as a visible symbol of the despair and injustice suffered in areas such as Brixton. This despair had to be remedied through the actions of the government and local government departments, which were seen as the agencies that could help the minority communities overcome their special problems.

Given the close link which the Scarman Report established between questions of policing and the wider social context, the programme of action which it outlined contained proposals not only about the reform of the police and the introduction of new methods of policing and riot control, but about employment policy, social policy and policies on racial discrimination. In a telling phrase Lord Scarman argued:

> The social conditions in Brixton do not provide an excuse for disorder. But the disorders cannot be fully understood unless they are seen in the context of complex political, social and economic factors which together create a predisposition towards violent protest (ibid., para. 8.7).

Although some of these issues went beyond the main remit of his inquiry he drew the conclusion from this basic finding that only a national government-led initiative to deal with problems of policing, unemployment, poor housing and racial disadvantage could get to the roots of the unrest.

Parliamentary and media responses to the report varied widely, although it was widely seen as making an important contribution to the debate about how to respond to the riots and prevent the outbreak of violence in the future. But what became clear after the immediate debate on the report in late 1981 and early 1982 was that the government was not going to implement all the recommendations uniformly. Some aspects of its proposals for reforming the police and rethinking police tactics were implemented during 1982 and 1983 (Reiner, 1985), but evidence of the urgent action which it called for in other areas remained scarce (Benyon, 1984; Benyon and Solomos, 1987).

This returns us to the point we made earlier about the other major forces which contributed to the development of political responses to the riots: the media, Parliament, political parties and popular debate.

The Scarman Report formed a part – and a vital one – of this process of political debate, but its role cannot be understood in isolation. This can be seen if we look more closely at the issues of policing and economic and social problems.

Although the Scarman Report considered issues of policing in some detail and influenced the course of subsequent government responses in this field, it should be clear from Chapter 6 that the construction of a law and order response drew on a wider set of pressures and influences. Indeed in the aftermath of the Scarman Report's publication police opinion was divided on the question of whether its proposals for reforming the police and the adoption of new methods of policing could be implemented, or whether such changes could insure against further violence and unrest. Sim (1982) has argued that the police were particularly worried by Scarman's recommendations that they should (a) tackle racial prejudice and harassment, (b) improve their methods of policing inner city multiracial areas and (c) develop new methods of managing urban disorder. He sees the police, sections of the media and right-wing parliamentarians as launching a counteroffensive to counteract criticisms of the police handling of the riots or their handling of the black community in general.

Certainly even before the publication of the Scarman Report the police and sections of the media were engaged in constructing a rather different explanation of the riots and of the participants in such events. During July 1981 a number of accounts of the events focused on the issue of the family background of riot participants and the decline of 'firm parental control' over children. Kenneth Oxford, the Chief Constable for Merseyside, made a number of statements which argued that the main responsibility for the riots lay with parents who either could not control their children or who did not care. The *Daily Telegraph* reported Mr Oxford as saying:

> What in the name of goodness are these young people doing on the streets indulging in this behaviour and at that time of night? Is there no discipline that can be brought to bear on these young people? Are the parents not interested in the futures of these young people? (8 July 1981).

According to this model the cause of the riots lay not in the conflict between young people and the police but in the failure of families to control the actions of their children. Such arguments were articulated with regularity throughout the period of the riots. Both the Prime Minister and the Home Secretary supported such arguments. *The Times* reported the Prime Minister as saying that if the parents could not control the actions of their children what could the government do to stop them from engaging in hooliganism and a 'spree of naked greed' (10 July 1981). At the same time the Home Secretary was reported as saying that the government was looking at plans to involve parents in 'the consequences of offences committed by their children' (*The Times*, 10 July 1981).

Such arguments were not necessarily linked to race, but as we saw earlier Lord Scarman himself partly explained the drift of black youngsters into crime and violence by reference to the weak family units of the West Indian communities. And during 1981 much media coverage was given to the supposed pathology of the West Indian family and the isolation of young blacks from both their families and society as a whole. Moreover it has been shown in earlier chapters how the history of political response to black immigration is deeply infused with the notion that blacks were intrinsically a problem, either in social or cultural terms. Thus even when such arguments were not racialised per se, popular common sense helped to link the notion of weak family structure to the West Indian communities, and it was a short step from this to explaining the riots as an outcome of pathological family structures.

Arguments around the question of the family were linked to other issues: for example the crisis of youth, the growth of violence in society generally, the phenomenon of youth hooliganism, the drift of young people into crime. Whether such images were based on factual evidence or not they succeeded in becoming part of the public debate about the 1980–1 riots and became even more important during 1985. By becoming part of public debate they helped to construct a model of the riots which saw them as the outcome of causes outside the control of either the government or the police. They thus helped to deflect attention away from the broader social context of Lord Scarman's report and towards specific social problems which undermined law and order.

In terms of economic and social policies the impact of the 1980-1 riots was equally ambiguous and contradictory. Part of this ambiguity, as has been shown above, resulted from the government's strenuous efforts to deny any link between its policies and the outbreak of violence and disorder. This denial was particularly important, since at the time the Thatcher administration was going through a bad period in terms of popular opinion on issues such as unemployment, social services and housing (Leys, 1983; Thompson, 1986). While Lord Scarman was careful not to enter the political dispute between the government and the Labour Party on issues such as unemployment and housing, his call for more direct action to deal with these problems, along with racial disadvantage, posed a challenge to the political legitimacy of the policies the government had followed from 1979 onwards. It also posed a delicate problem for the Home Secretary himself, since Lord Scarman had been appointed by him to carry out his inquiry. Having spent the whole summer denying any link between its policies and the riots, the government had to tread warily in responding to the economic and social policy proposals of the Scarman Report when it was published in November 1981.

The parliamentary debate on the report shows the Home Secretary adopting a two-pronged strategy in his response. First, he accepted many of the recommendations of the report, particularly in relation to the role of the police. Additionally he accepted the need to tackle racial disadvantage and other social issues. Second, he emphasised the government's view that, whatever broader measures were taken to deal with racial and social inequalities, the immediate priority was to restore and maintain order on the streets. When the Home Secretary talked of the need for the government to give a lead in tackling racial disadvantage he therefore saw this as an issue for the longer term. On the other hand he was much more specific about the reform of the police and the development of new tactics and equipment for the management of urban disorder (*Hansard*, vol. 14, 1981, cols 1001–8).

The changing politics of policing

The policy responses after the 1985 riots, and subsequent events, show some of the same characteristics as those during 1980–1, but as was argued above the emphasis on the criminality of the riot participants favoured explanations that linked disorder to the pathological characteristics of inner city residents which pushed them towards lawlessness and crime. This in turn produced a sharper contrast than in 1980–1 between (a) responses which emphasised the need to strengthen and buttress the role of the police and (b) responses which called for greater emphasis on the rejuvenation of the social and economic fabric of the inner cities. As Douglas Hurd argued after the 1985 Handsworth disturbances, this is not a case history for sociologists to pore over, but a case for the police (*The Guardian*, 23 September 1985).

The above quote from the Home Secretary, which can be backed up by numerous others from government ministers and MPs, reflects the most important shift in political language between 1981 and 1985, namely the emphasis given to the interpretation of the riots as a criminal enterprise more suited to investigation by the police than by social analysts or judicial experts such as Lord Scarman. The question of policing and law and order had been central in 1981 as well, but it had been balanced to some extent by an emphasis (for example in the Scarman Report and the interventions of opposition parties) on the wider social policy context.

In 1985, however, the government specifically rejected calls for another Scarman type inquiry, arguing that since the riots were a criminal enterprise it was useless to search for social explanations or to have yet another report advising it about what to do. Implicitly the government was saying that it knew what the problems were, and how they could be tackled.

While some senior policemen, like Newman, wanted to stress the link between the police and other areas of social policy, the official government response attempted to decontextualise the riots and see them as the actions of a small minority who were either criminalised or influenced by extreme political ideas. The dominant approach of the government attempted to emphasise two main arguments:

1. That the riots were 'a lust for blood', an 'orgy of thieving', 'a cry for loot and not a cry for help',
2. That the riots reflected not a failure to carry out the 'urgent programme of action' recommended by Lord Scarman in 1981, but were the outcome of a spiralling wave of crime and disorder in inner city areas.

The logic of this approach, articulated by Douglas Hurd most clearly, was that the riots were both 'unjustifiable' and a 'criminal activity'. In a widely reported speech to police chiefs at the time of the disorders Hurd made this point clear:

> Handsworth needs more jobs and better housing. But riots only destroy. They create nothing except a climate in which necessary development is even more difficult. Poor housing and other social ills provide no kind of reason for riot, arson and killing. One interviewer asked me whether the riot was not a cry for help by the rioters. The sound which law-abiding people heard at Handsworth was not a cry for help but a cry for loot. That is why the first priority, once public order is secure, must be a thorough and relentless investigation into the crimes which were committed (*Daily Telegraph*, 14 September 1985).

Such arguments resonated through the media and in the various parliamentary debates during September and October. They became part of the symbolic political language through which the riots were understood by policy makers and by popular opinion.

The ascription to the rioters of 'wickedness' and 'pure naked greed' did not go unchallenged, as the analysis in the previous section has shown. Indeed Lord Scarman and numerous other commentators have sought to implicitly or explicitly challenge such simplifications. American experience, however, shows that the official espousal of explanations which see riots as irrational outbursts of criminal activity cannot be easily countered by oppositional forces, however well founded and empirically sound their arguments are (Edelman, 1971; Lipsky and Olson, 1977). This certainly seems to be one of the dangers in the aftermath of the 1985 riots, particularly if one looks at the nature of the response to the social and economic issues which underlay the riots.

The preoccupation with law and order responses did not preclude initiatives on other issues, most notably inner city and employment policies. The parliamentary debates during September–December 1985 were full of promises from the government and the opposition that they were both interested in transforming the social conditions of inner city areas (*Hansard*, vol. 84, 1985, cols 348–88; *Hansard*, vol. 88, 1985, cols 929–1004). The media showed similar concerns, and a number of feature articles analysed the problems of the 'inner cities', the 'ghettoes', and the lives of people living in such areas. A feature article in *The Mirror* on the Broadwater Farm Estate described it as a

'Living Hell'. and went on to summarise what it saw as the feelings of the local people:

> If you don't live in desolate apartments where no one seems to care – and even the police have declared a no-go area, you have no idea how awful your daily life can be (8 October 1985).

When combined with no jobs, inadequate social facilities, and no real help from either central or local government, *The Mirror* went on, such areas can become 'another world', a world where disillusion and violence are everyday facts of life.

During the late 1980s and early 1990s the government announced a number of initiatives on the inner city and employment, and it presented these as part of an effort to rejuvenate depressed areas on a sound basis. Examples of such actions include the introduction of more government finance to encourage black business enterprise, promises to regenerate inner city localities, the setting up of 'task forces' to generate jobs in 'problem areas', and attempts to integrate black youngsters into the training schemes run by the Manpower Services Commission. Additionally, having done little if anything to implement the Scarman Report's recommendations on 'positive action' the government belatedly promised to look at what new initiatives it could take to tackle racial discrimination in employment and other areas.

The evidence that has emerged since then, however, points to a major discrepancy between the government's promises of action and the allocation of resources to implement them. This discrepancy again became evident in the aftermath of the inner city initiatives launched by the government after the June 1987 general election. It is perhaps too early to reach a conclusion on this point, but a repeat of the period of inaction between 1982 and 1985 cannot be ruled out within the current political context. Indeed a number of researchers and commentators have argued that this is the most likely course of development (see the papers in Benyon and Solomos, 1987). A number of local authorities have attempted to take more positive action to deal with the issues raised by the 1985 riots, but such local initiatives are often severely limited by the actions of national government, the police and broader economic and political pressures. We shall return to this issue in Chapter 10, which will look specifically at the possibilities for reform and the limits faced both nationally and locally.

Summary and conclusion

During the late 1980s there was much discussion about whether the lessons of the urban unrest of 1980–1 and 1985 had been learned, whether the political response to the riots had been adequate and whether forms of collective violence had become a permanent feature of British political life. The array of inner city initiatives, expressions of government concern, and promises of more effective action to tackle unemployment are in many ways responses to this overriding concern about how to manage and depoliticise the impact of the riots.

The actual impact of these initiatives on the lives of inner city residents has been minimal. This is not to say that the political objectives of these forms of state intervention have not been achieved. Precisely because it is the symbolic political language about the riots which most people experience, promises of reform seem to reassure popular opinion that something is being done and thus help ensure the 'political viability of unsuccessful policies' (Edelman, 1977). But the limits of symbolic action, which does little to change the underlying problems, are clear enough today when we see constant complaints from black groups and other inner city residents that promises without actual change are not enough.

This focus on the interconnections between the social position of young blacks and urban unrest did not produce uniform policy conclusions. The proposals made by Lord Scarman in his report on the Brixton disturbances, for example, differed markedly from the policy conclusions of the law and order lobby. There were also marked differences between the approach of the Labour Party, which tended to emphasise social deprivation as the central issue, and the Conservative Party, which saw the events as yet another example of the growth of violence and disorder in British society.

The implications of these different responses to the 1980–1 disturbances for policy remained to be worked out, but from 1981 onwards the emphasis of the Thatcher administration was already on (a) the need to strengthen the police and (b) to train them more fully in the management of riot situations. The assumption seemed to be that the main objective of the government should be to contain social protest by strengthening the forces of law and order.

This is an inherent contradiction since it is clearly impossible to separate the analysis of the riots from the wider social and economic changes in contemporary Britain. Nor is it possible to ignore the deep political and ideological shifts which have taken place, particularly the development of nationalist and neo-racist ideologies at both the academic and the popular level (Troyna and Williams, 1986; Gilroy, 1987). Such transformations inevitably overdetermine the possibilities of implementing reforms of existing inequalities, however limited these reforms may be. But it seems clear that this pattern, if reproduced over the next period, will result in a situation where the symbolic value of violent protest will become an even more important form of action for oppressed and marginalised social groupings. The reforms necessary to tackle the core issues may well be beyond the limits of the current political realities. It is to this question of the limits and possibilities of political action that we now turn, in order to provide a rounded analysis of the political dynamics of racism in contemporary Britain.

8 Racism, Nationalism and Political Action

Introduction

Previous chapters have provided both a chronological and thematic analysis of racialised politics from 1945 to the present. The concerns of this and the following two chapters are somewhat different, though they are closely linked to the themes already covered at a more general level. The main objective of these chapters is to analyse in more detail something we have only touched upon in previous chapters: the role of racial ideologies, political action and social movements in the racialisation of contemporary British politics.

This chapter will look at how the racialisation of British political culture has been achieved through the social construction of ideological notions of the nation, culture and politics. This is a relatively neglected issue, despite the importance of racialised discourse in the political language of the new right and the usages of racial symbols in the construction of national identity in contemporary Britain.

By analysing the changing meanings attached to race and nation, particularly in the political discourses of the old and the new right, we shall be able to explore the interaction between racist politics and broader ideologies about the 'British way of life' and 'national consciousness' (Seidel, 1986; van Dijk, 1988). Additionally, this exploration should allow us to see how the symbolic political language which attempts to define who is British and who is not represents a powerful and volatile political force in contemporary Britain.

Chapter 9 will then take the analysis a step further by looking in more detail than has been possible so far at the development of forms of black and minority political consciousness and the changing discourse about race, culture and social change in contemporary British society. Both these issues have been raised in previous chapters, but we have been unable to explore the dynamics in any depth. Yet it is becoming clear all the time that the question of political mobilisation is at the centre of current debates about processes of racialisation in Britain society.

Given the wealth of empirical material which can be included in these chapters I have opted to be selective rather than exhaustive. For example, the analysis of the National Front and other extreme right-wing groups is limited to some of the broader features. A number of case studies of such groups exist, and I have no wish to duplicate the analysis which they offer (Billig, 1978; Fielding, 1981; Taylor, 1982). A similar point can be made about black political organisations and pressure groups. They also have a long and dynamic history of struggles and achievements. On both these issues it would have been possible to write separate books. My concern here, however, is to provide an outline of the complex ways in which notions of race and national identity have been articulated to give support to political movements and pressure groups.

Changing forms of racial ideology

The impact of post-1945 debates about black immigration on the definition of national identity and Britishness was discussed in some detail in Chapters 3 and 4, but there are a number of dimensions of this issue which remain to be analysed. In particular there are the questions of (a) the changing forms of racial ideology between the 1970s and the 1990s, (b) the transformation of ideologies of race and nation and (c) the emergence of what is sometimes called a new racism. I have hinted at these processes in previous chapters, but in this section I want to make a more detailed analysis of their development.

In Chapter 4 we looked at the rise of Powellism as a process of political mobilisation which helped to redefine the terms of political discourse about racial relations in British society during the late 1960s and early 1970s. The responses of the Labour government from 1968–70 and the Conservative government from 1970–4 in their different ways showed how powerful a political symbol this mobilisation was. Both administrations responded to the appeal of Powell's ideas about immigration and race by attempting to depoliticise these issues (Freeman, 1979; Layton-Henry, 1984). The two most important manifestations of this process were the acceptance by both the

Labour Party and the Conservative Party of (a) the need for tight restrictions on immigration and (b) the necessity to allay the fears of those attracted to Powell's ideas.

In this sense the period embracing the late 1960s and early 1970s has been quite rightly characterised as one in which Powellite ideas helped to racialise British political life. Quite apart from the impact of Powell's intervention at the political level, however, it is important to acknowledge a less evident aspect of his role, namely his influence on the political language used to discuss race and immigration issues. His emphasis on the social and cultural transformations brought about by immigration helped to create or recreate in popular political debate understandings of Englishness and Britishness which relied explicitly or implicitly on notions of shared history, customs and kinship which excluded black minorities from the polity (Powell, 1969, 1972).

From the late 1960s through to the 1990s Powell's interventions have continually returned to two themes. First, the growth of the black population, and the prospect that by the end of the century a large proportion of Britain's population was likely to be made up of black immigrants and their descendants. From the 1960s onwards this concern with the size of the black population has become part of the wider political common sense about immigration. Second, Powell's speeches have emphasised that the scale of black migration represented a threat to the national character of such a magnitude that the whole social and cultural fabric of British society was likely to be undermined by the presence of immigrants from a different cultural, racial or religious background.

It is this second theme that has increasingly occupied a central role in Powell's politics during the 1970s and beyond. A good example of this emphasis in Powellite discourse can be found in his interventions during the urban unrest of 1981 and 1985, when he continually emphasised the threat to the nation posed by the danger of a civil war on the streets of Britain's inner cities and the growth of multi-racialism.

More recently, he has reiterated some of the themes from his 1968 'Rivers of Blood' speech in a series of articles which coincided with the twentieth anniversary of this speech. As we have already emphasised, for Powell the source of the main threat to the British nation is the volatile mixture of different nationalities and cultures that black immigration has created in many inner city areas, rather than any external enemies. It is to this issue that he returned repeatedly in 1988. For example, in a speech given in Birmingham he chose to speak on the theme of 'Englishness' and the current threats to its survival. He identified a number of factors which he saw as representing a threat to national identity, and among these he emphasised the danger posed to the distinctiveness of English culture by the presence 'of those who not only visibly do not share with them a common identity but are to be encouraged to maintain and intensify their differences' (*The Independent*, 23 April 1988). In Powell's terms this was a danger not so much because of the number of immigrants and their descendants, though this was an issue, but because the nation itself had lost its identity to such an extent that it had failed to respond to the dangers it faced from the presence within its major cities of minorities whom he perceived as outside of the primordial ties of nation and culture.

By the 1980s therefore the language that Powell used to describe the politics of race in contemporary Britain had as much to do with a definition of Englishness or Britishness as it had with character-istics of the minority communities themselves. He makes no claim to know all the sources which 'since neolithic times, or earlier, have contributed to the gene pool of the English people' (ibid.), but he warns of 'The spectre of a Britain that has lost its claim to be a nation':

> The spectacle which I cannot help seeing . . . is that of a Britain which has lost, quite suddenly, in the space of less than a generation, all consciousness and conviction of being a nation: the web which binds it to its past has been torn asunder, and what has made the spectacle the more impressive has been the indiffer-ence, not to say levity, with which the change has been greeted (*The Guardian*, 9 November 1981).

From this perspective the loss of Britain's national identity is caused not just by immigration, but by the failure of 'the nation' to recognise the importance of this process for the unity of the national culture. This kind of argument links up with earlier themes in Powell's interventions on this issue, although the presentation of his argument is less dependent on immigration as a political symbol and more reliant on a definition of the cultural basis of 'Englishness' (Seidel, 1986; Gilroy, 1987).

Such arguments are by no means limited to Powell. During the early 1980s and 1990s Powellite arguments about national identity and culture have indeed been given more respectability by the growing influence of the arguments of the new right, whose proponents have adopted race as one of the main components of their political discourse.

Conceptions of race and nation

As in other areas of political life, since the 1970s the new right has begun to exercise is influence in public debates about racial questions. Through channels such as the Centre for Policy Studies, the Social Affairs Unit and the *Salisbury Review*, a number of new-right commentators have attempted to define what they see as a critique of established dogmas and policies in areas such as multiracial education, race and housing and anti-racism generally (Flew, 1984; Palmer, 1986). These writings are a clear example of how ideologies about race are not static, but constantly changing.

The political language of the new right still resonates with old Powellite themes, such as immigration and stereotypes of black muggers, aliens and black criminals. But since the early 1980s, as with Powell's political language, we have seen two main shifts in the concerns of the new right. First, there has been a move away from the language of nativism and anti-immigration. By the late 1970s the concern with the social position of young blacks was signalling a new preoccupation with the dangers of the political and social alienation of sections of the black communities for the polity as a whole (Keith, 1987; Solomos, 1988). The image of inner city areas becoming 'black enclaves' where 'British' law and order could not be easily enforced is one of the recurrent themes in new-right writings in this field. The very presence of black communities is presented as a potential threat to the 'way of life' and culture of white citizens.

Second, new-right racial discourses increasingly present black people as an 'enemy within' that is undermining the moral and social fabric of society. In both popular and élite discourses about immigration and race, black communities as a whole, or particular groups such as young blacks, are presented as involved in activities which are a threat to social order and political stability.

Such ideological constructions do not necessarily have to rely on notions of racial superiority in the narrow sense. In practice the most resonant themes in contemporary racial discourses are not concerned with absolute notions of racial superiority, but with the 'threats' which black communities are seen to represent to the cultural, political and religious homogeneity of white British society.

Commonly-held images of black people include assumptions about differences between the culture, attitudes and values of black people compared with the white majority. Additionally the attempts by black groups to assert their rights and lay claim to social justice have often been presented in the media as a sign of the failure of the minority communities to adapt to British society, and not as a sign that racial injustice is deeply embedded.

This type of argument has been summarised by van Dijk (1988) as amounting to the claim that the demands of black minorities are not legitimate, that they are in fact the product of attempts to claim special privileges and thus a threat to the majority. Because such claims are presented as coming from groups which are outside the traditions and culture of British political life they are more easily portrayed as a challenge to the values of the majority communities, and by a twist of logic as unjust.

As we saw in Chapter 7 the emergence of urban unrest during the 1980s, and the widely publicised involvement of young blacks in these events, also provided an important cue in the use of racial symbols by sections of the popular media and the extreme right. The media coverage of the 1985 riots in particular did much to reinforce the popular image of young blacks as involved in antisocial acts such as crime, and to allow the extreme right to present them as a threat to social and political stability.

The notion that the seeds of 'racial conflict' were sown by the failure of successive governments to 'tackle' immigration has been a major theme in the interventions by Enoch Powell since the 1960s. The outbreak of urban unrest, however, allowed Powell to expand his notion of the threats posed by immigration to include within it the notion that the whole nation and society was under threat from actual rather than impending 'civil war', and that the origins of this situation could be traced back to the imposition of 'alien cultures' on British society. This theme has proved to be particularly attractive to the new right in the present political climate, as will be shown in more detail in Chapter 10.

New-right ideologies and national identity

What has become increasingly clear in recent years is that racial discourses are rarely concerned only with the role of minority communities and cultures. They are also typically an attempt to define the characteristics of the dominant national culture and the ways in which these differ from those of racial and ethnic minorities. It is precisely on this issue that the ideologists of the new right have begun to concentrate, though it has to be said that this is by no means a new phenomenon.

Over the centuries, for example, the meanings attached to 'Englishness' and 'Britishness' have changed constantly. Or as one account puts it: 'Englishness has had to be made and re-made in and through history' (Colls and Dodd, 1986: i). The symbols used in this process have included ideas about shared language, customs, religion, colour, family and numerous other assumed attributes of the 'national culture'.

Within the context of more contemporary debates about race and immigration it is noticeable that a recurrent issue is the definition of the historical and cultural attributes of the 'British way of life'. While the position of black minority communities in the inner cities may be the immediate point of reference in discussions of crime and disorder, the overarching concern is about the 'threat' posed to the majority culture by the development of multiracial communities.

One example of this process is the attention given to young Afro-Caribbeans. During the 1980s this group became in many ways the centre of much political debate, particularly in the aftermath of urban unrest (Solomos, 1988). But although the immediate source of concern was the outbreak of violent unrest on the streets of major cities, the underlying concern of new right commentators was the argument that the permanent settlement of black communities, a phenomenon which young blacks symbolically represented, was a threat to the unity of British society.

John Casey, writing in 1982 in the *Salisbury Review*, expressed such views succinctly when he argued that black immigration had broken down the social order established during the Victorian period and was therefore a threat to the way of life of the majority population. From this he drew the conclusion that the source of the problem was a failure to understand the role of national identity in the development of British society:

There is no way of understanding British and English history that does not take seriously the sentiments of patriotism that go with a continuity of institutions, shared experience, language, customs, kinship. There is no way of understanding English patriotism that averts its eyes from the fact that it has as its centre a feeling for persons of one's own kind (Casey, 1982: 25).

This 'feeling for persons of one's own kind' thus becomes a way for Casey to argue that any opposition to the settlement of black migrants in Britain is not necessarily based on racial antipathy but is a 'natural' response to outsiders.

The famous swamping statement made by Margaret Thatcher on television in February 1978 is another example of how this image of the threat of black immigration can be utilised to mobilise political support without resorting directly to racist language. Referring to trends in immigration, Thatcher argued that the present rate of immigration would, by the end of the century, mean that there would be four million people from the new commonwealth or Pakistan in Britain. She drew the following conclusion from this:

That is an awful lot, and I think it means that people are really rather afraid that this country might be swamped by people of a different culture. The British character has done so much for democracy, for law, and done so much throughout the world that if there is any fear that it might be swamped, then people are going to be rather hostile to those coming in.

In the same interview she sought to explain the support achieved by the National Front during the 1970s as the result of the failure to deal with immigration through the mainstream political institutions. She went on:

We are a British nation with British characteristics. Every nation can take some minorities, and in many ways they add to the richness and variety of this country. But the moment a minority threatens to become a big one, people get frightened (*The Guardian*, 31 January 1978).

The use of notions such as 'British nation' and 'British character' helps in this context to establish Thatcher's concern for protecting the interests of the nation against threats from within and from without. And in the context of the political climate of the late 1970s there is evidence that this helped the Conservative Party to draw support from National Front sympathisers, who saw the party as a more likely channel for translating their views into policy (Layton-Henry, 1986).

Taken together, these processes have helped to redefine the terms of political discourse about race in British politics. What is interesting, however, is that unlike the simmering controversy aroused by Powell's speeches during the late 1960s and 1970s, new-right arguments about race and nation have achieved a certain respectability in both popular and élite political discourses. This does not mean that the more extreme arguments of the new right have not aroused anger and opposition. But within the present political climate the ideas of the new right on culture, nation and identity represent a potent political force whose political impact has yet to be fully understood.

Neo-fascist politics

One of the most important features of the politics of racism was the emergence, and decline, during the early 1970s of the National Front – and other minor neo-fascist groups – as a more or less credible political force (Walker, 1977; Billig and Bell, 1980; Husbands, 1983). Indeed at that time there was serious concern that the National Front could become an established political force in the way the French National Front has during the 1980s and 1990s.

The history and political impact of the National Front have been given widespread attention, and there have been numerous studies of its rise and decline, of the social context of support for neo-fascist and racist political groups, of the role of racialised ideologies and of the prospects for the future mobilisation of racist beliefs and ideologies by political parties and movements. These studies date mostly from the 1970s, which represents the high point of the impact of the National Front on both local and national political life.

The National Front was founded in 1967 as a unified organisation of groups supporting neo-fascist and anti-immigration viewpoints (Walker, 1977). One of the primary motivations behind the formation of the group seems to have been the relative neglect of immigration and race-related issues by the mainstream political parties. This was seen as providing an opening for a party openly committed to the defence of racial purity and to a clear anti-immigration stance to capture support from both main political parties.

As a union of the right wing British National Party and the League of Empire Loyalists, the National Front inherited the ideological baggage of anti-semitism and resistance to Britain's postwar decolonisation, two prominent themes among far right-wing political groups in the 1960s. In its political rhetoric it made clear its links with the politics of anti-semitism, and there is evidence that both its leadership and membership were committed to a nationalist ideology based on a notion of racial purity (Thurlow, 1975; Edgar, 1977).

Research on the social basis of support for the National Front and racist political groups has brought out two important features. First, Phizacklea's and Miles's study of working class racism argued that it was important to look at the social and economic context in order to understand the attraction of sections of the white working class to the politics of the National Front. Drawing upon research in London they argued that one of the most important factors in the growth of support for racist political groups was the wider context of economic and social restructuring in many inner city working class areas (Phizacklea and Miles, 1980).

Husbands' study of support for the National Front in particular localities, such as the East End area of London, argued that it is important to look particularly at the influence of such issues as the presence of black communities, changes in the national and local politics of race and the restructuring of local political economies in order to understand the level and solidity of National Front support in some areas and its relative weakness in others (Husbands, 1983).

These studies emphasise the need to locate the support for racism within a wider social, economic and geographical context. A similar theme was been taken up by Cashmore (1987) in his detailed analysis of the social basis of racism in Birmingham and its surrounding area during the 1980s. But it is important not to lose sight of the role of politics and ideology in the mobilisation of this support.

It is interesting to remember, for example, that during the 1970s both the Conservative Party and the Labour Party lost voters to the National Front. Throughout the 1970s the National Front's membership and level of electoral support ebbed and flowed with the tide of political debate and public controversy over racial questions. Its membership peaked at 14000–20000 between 1972 and 1974, at the height of the moral panic about the arrival of Ugandan Asians. In 1973 it achieved a vote of 16.2 per cent in the West Bromwich by-election. It also achieved respectable results in the local elections of 1976 and the local elections in London in 1977 (Taylor, 1982).

This level of support and political mobilisation was not maintained, however, and fell dramatically in the aftermath of Thatcher's swamping statement in 1978 and the attempt by the Conservative Party to draw the support of National Front sympathisers. From 1977 to 1979 the activities of the National Front also became the focus for anti-racist political mobilisation orchestrated by the Anti-Nazi League and Rock Against Racism. This counter-mobilisation helped to counter its claim to be a defender of the national interest and helped to increase awareness of the political dangers which its growth as a major political force was likely to lead to.

From its foundation, however, it was the issue of black immigration which occupied a central role in its political rhetoric and propaganda. Despite periodic attempts by the National Front's leadership to broaden the movement's appeal and political platform, immigration and race remained the single most salient issue among Front members and sympathisers during the 1970s and it was the ability of the party to utilise this issue at both a local and a national level that allowed it to mobilise electoral support and attract members.

In neo-fascist political discourses about race popular images resonate with references to racial purity, cultural superiority or difference and the defence of 'the nation' from the threat posed by immigration and racial mixing. The alien, the stranger or the subhuman are repeatedly struck themes.

Since 1979 there has been a decline in the electoral performance of the National Front and other overtly racist political groups. The National Front in Britain has not had the same political impact as the National Front in France. This has been interpreted from a number of perspectives as (a) representing a marginalisation of the racist political message that the National Front was propounding (b) as the outcome of the incorporation of the National Front's ideas within mainstream political institutions and (c) the result of factional strife and conflict within the racist groups themselves. Certainly since 1979 the National Front and other extreme right-wing organisations have splintered in a number of directions and have failed to make any significant intervention in electoral politics.

of a multiracial society is not necessarily an 'irrational or superstitious reaction':

> Opposition to the creation of a multi-racial society may well spring primarily from a deep concern about the future of one's country, one arising from a belief that its transformation over a short period from a relatively homogeneous population to one of a particular racial mix may, on balance, have adverse effects on its institutions and character or, at any rate, may be more likely to do harm than good (p. 18).

For Mishan, and other new-right commentators on racial issues, opposition to immigration and support for the repatriation of black communities already settled in this country is thus a 'natural' response to the new 'racial mix' in British society, and not a sign of racism.

Some of the policy implications of new-right political discourses are not fundamentally different from those of Powellite discourse. John Casey, for example, writing in the *Salisbury Review* in 1982, argued that the only feasible 'solution' to the 'problems' caused by the presence of black communities was the voluntary repatriation 'of a proportion of the immigrant and immigrant-descended population' or the retrospective withdrawal of the rights of black immigrants to citizenship and the creation of a status analogous to the position of 'guest-workers' in Europe (Casey, 1982: 27).

Even those of the new right who do not go along with such a scenario accept that the 'social problems' which they see as caused by black immigrants require constructive measures to encourage repatriation or to ensure the integration of those who want to remain in Britain. What is interesting, however, is that increasingly such arguments are presented not as extreme solutions but as a rational political response to what the new right presents as an intractable problem. Within the logic of the politics of the new right any attempt to create a multicultural society can only lead to social conflict and present a threat to the values and culture of the majority.

Anti anti-racism

Today some of the most strident voices in the mass media a academic discourse are raised not against racism but against on

Whatever the reasons for the decline in electoral support for the National Front and other neo-fascist political groups, their influence in other arenas of British political life has persisted and they continue to mobilise effectively in a number of localities. Their role, however, cannot be seen in isolation from other forms of political mobilisation around the symbols of race and nation. This can be illustrated in relation to the question of racial attacks.

The politics of racial attacks

Racially motivated attacks have a long history, but it was during the late 1970s and 1980s that increasing public attention was given to the phenomenon of racially motivated attacks on black people.

The context within which such attacks take place is complex, and far right-wing groups are not always involved, but the impact that they have had on the everyday lives of many black people in Britain is clear. One report lists the following as relatively typical cases of this phenomenon:

> As a boy sleeps, a pig's head, its eyes, ears, nostrils and mouth stuffed with lighted cigarettes, is hurled through the window of his bedroom. A family do not leave their home after 7 in the evening; they stay in one large room, having barricaded their ground floor. A family are held prisoner in their own flat by a security cage bolted to their front door by white neighbours. A youth is slashed with a knife by an older white boy as he walks along a school corridor between classes. A family home is burned out and a pregnant woman and her three children killed. A ticket collector is stabbed in the eye with a metal stake and killed simply because he refused to take racial abuse from some white passengers (Gordon, 1986: v).

A number of surveys by the Home Office, the Commission for Racial Equality and local authorities have confirmed the widespread nature of these types of attack, as well as everyday forms of racial harassment (Home Office, 1981; GLC, 1984; CRE, 1987a, 1987b).

The involvement of far-right racialist groups in some of these cases has been clearly shown. What seems to have happened is that as the National Front found itself electorally isolated after 1979 sections of its membership, along with supporters of other far-right groups, turned to more direct forms of attack on black communities.

But it also seems clear that the overall political climate has contributed to the growth of this phenomenon. Given the prevalence of racialised political discourses, and the emphasis of the new right on the need to reassert the importance of patriotism and nationalism in British political culture, it is perhaps not surprising that it was during the early 1980s and 1990s that racial attacks became such a major issue.

This may explain the low key nature of the response to racial attacks both by the government and the police for most of the past decade. This contrasts sharply with the oft-expressed views of the police and government on the criminal activities of young blacks, and the amplification of images of black crime in the popular media on an almost daily basis. By contrast the policy response to racial attacks and related phenomena has been at best muted and at worst non-existent.

Racialised politics and the enemy within

Perhaps the most important theme in contemporary political discourse about race in British society, even after successive attempts to develop anti-discrimination policies, is the image of blacks as a whole, or particular groups of them, as a threat to the unity and order of British society. Cohen (1988) notes that one way in which this tendency is expressed in contemporary political discourse is in attempts to attribute the persistence of racial inequality not to racism but to the presence of black minorities and the problems that result from this presence.

Such images are by no means unique to the post-1945 period, or to Britain. Edelman (1971), writing about the US, has shown how in situations of conflict and protest one of the ways in which dominant groups or political institutions defend themselves is to rationalise threats as the product of outsiders and enemies who are seen as being outside the social and moral values of the society as a whole. Referring to the political debates about the race riots of the 1960s he argued that one of the ways in which the dominant élite of American society

attempted to reduce the political impact of the events was to portray them as the work of enemies of American society and its values.

In contemporary British political life, however, we have seen a somewhat different variant of this process in the context of racial relations. In the language of the new right, black people are increasingly portrayed not as an enemy without but as an enemy within: as a threat to the cultural and political values of the nation. They are increasingly presented in the media and other channels of communication as a threat to the way of life of the majority white community and as a group which is difficult to integrate into the mainstream of British society.

Two of the ways in which this process has influenced recent political debates about race are to be found in new-right discourses about the naturalness of racial antipathy and the increasingly vociferous attacks on anti-racism which are to be heard in the popular media and in public political debate.

Naturalisation of racism

Barker (1981) notes that one important aspect of contemporary rac[ist] ideologies in Britain is the tendency to obscure or deny the mean[ing] and implications of the deployment of race categories. This fits with the wider tendency (a) to deny the importance of racism [in] British society and (b) to deny that hostility to the presence of bl[ack] communities in Britain is a form of racism. According to this lin[e of] argument it is only natural that, given the choice, people should pr[efer] to live with their own kind and not become a multiracial society. S[uch] a wish is not seen as a manifestation of racialist attitudes, but [a] natural response to the presence of people of a different cultural [and] racial background.

Thus when in 1978 Margaret Thatcher expressed the view tha[t the] moment a minority threatens to become a big one, peopl[e get] frightened', she was giving voice to an argument that has [now] become part of the accepted common sense of new right writin[g on] racial questions. A more recent expression of this kind of arg[ument] can be found in the arguments developed in the *Salisbury R[eview.]* Mishan (1988), for example, argues that opposition to the eme[rgence]

the favourite targets of the new right, namely anti-racism. Sections of the media are almost daily concerned with aspects of the work of either local authorities or of agencies such as the Commission for Racial Equality. Additionally it has become an important focus of concern for the various right-wing think tanks, who see anti-racism as an intrusion on individual freedom and a threat to the interests of the white majority.

According to van Dijk (1988) the strategy of such attacks on anti-racism is to defend the assumed virtues of British tolerance and decency against attacks from enemies within :

> Within a more embracing framework of defending white British culture and its values, the targets of such press campaigns were obvious: assumed positive discrimination, ethnic projects, cultural pluralism, multicultural education, and in general each initiative based on the recognition that Britain is no longer white (p. 184).

Over the past few years these are precisely the targets which sections of the popular media and new-right pressure groups have singled out for particular attention. There has been a whole series of controversies over the actions of local authorities which have sought to take a positive stance on racial equality and on anti-racism. Increasingly what the new right calls the ideology of anti-racism has become the subject of virulent attack, and indeed the whole notion of racism has been dismissed in some circles as an invention of the loony left and the race relations industry.

Russell Lewis's *Anti-Racism: A Mania Exposed* represents one of the most strident attacks on the work of what he sees as anti-racist fanatics. It was published amid much publicity, with a preface by Enoch Powell, and has been taken up by the new right as a fundamental critique of anti-racist politics. Starting out from a denial of the importance of racism in contemporary Britain Lewis argues that the source of current problems was the failure of successive governments to control immigration, and the creation of the race relations industry by successive Labour and Conservative administrations. Indeed for Lewis the main harm to race relations results not from racism but from the lunatic outrages done in the name of anti-racism and the failure of the black minorities to respect the way of life and customs of the white majority.

Arguments such as these are still a minority position. But they represent an important phase in the politics of racism in post-1945 Britain. In attacking the activities of the anti-racists they have helped to shift public attention away from the processes of racial discrimination and racism and focus it instead on the activities of the black communities themselves and the anti-racists who are seen as having a vested interest in claiming that Britain is a racist society.

One consequence of these attacks on anti-racism is that they have helped to legitimise the relative inaction of the three Conservative administrations since 1979 to tackle racial inequality and allow open discussion of issues which have tended to be talked about at the margins of political life since the 1970s. In a commentary on Lewis's book, William Deedes, a former Conservative minister, argued that it proved that Britain needed to have less guilt over race and more open discussion about the impact of minority communities on the majority values (*Daily Telegraph*, 30 June 1988).

But interestingly the debate on this issue has also led to attempts by those on the left and in the Labour Party to rethink the politics of racial equality. The controversy over the events at Burnage High School in Manchester has led to a debate among sections of the left about the role and future of anti-racist initiatives (*New Statesman*, 9 May 1988; *New Socialist*, 27 July 1988). In the medium term therefore it is likely that there will be a fundamental rethinking of these questions from both the left and the right.

Nationalism and the interests of the majority

It is perhaps no accident that the prevalent theme in political debate over the past few years has been the issue of anti-racism. Such a preoccupation fits in with the mobilisation of national symbols and the attack on enemies within which Thatcherism as a political philosophy did much to foster. As Thatcher's swamping statement of 1978 made clear, a recurrent theme in her political discourse in 1980s and early 1990s was her commitment to defending the interests of the white British majority against the claims of minority communities. The emphasis in her political rhetoric on the shared history, customs and values of Britishness was one way in which she attempted to draw together a social basis for her political project.

This was emphasised to some extent in the aftermath of the Falklands war, and the mobilisation of nationalism against the 'Argies'.

But within the context of domestic British politics it is emphasised continuously by debates about the role of multiculturalism in British society. Thatcher's expressed sympathy for the fears of the majority and about the impact of immigration and race on 'their' localities, 'their' schools and 'their' cultural heritage was not an isolated rhetorical statement. It was part of a wider debate about the politics of national identity, to which we shall return in Chapter 10.

Summary and conclusion

Much of the substance of this chapter has been concerned with unravelling and exploring the role of ideology and political language in contemporary processes of racialisation. But the various forms of racist mobilisation, at both theoretical and practical levels, analysed in this chapter also provide a basis for understanding how policy issues as diverse as urban change, law and order, unemployment and youth policy are racialised and constantly transformed.

The transformations in racist ideologies that we have witnessed in the 1980s point to the need for a deeper understanding of the logic of racist ideologies and mobilisations, particularly by those interested in challenging the roots of racism as well as its everyday manifestations. The prevalence of racialised ideologies about Englishness and national identity shows perhaps how far we have to go before we can achieve a situation of racial justice and equality, but it also highlights the importance of understanding the complex forms of racial thought in contemporary British society.

9 Race, Politics and Mobilisation

Introduction

In previous chapters we have seen that the politicisation of race and race-related issues since 1945 has been a complex process involving interventions by successive governments, political parties, pressure groups, politicians and other political actors. The sequence of events that we have witnessed since 1945 have been the product of political mobilisation of one sort or another, rather than the inevitable consequence of processes beyond political control.

It is also clear, however, that black and ethnic minority groups have played an active role in the political debates about questions of race and immigration. Both at national and local levels black political groups, or anti-racist alliances between black and white groups, have attempted to mobilise either in order to counteract the activities of racist groups or to promote measures aimed at bringing about racial justice and equality (Pearson, 1981; Sivanandan, 1982; Anwar, 1986; Carter, 1986; Saggar, 1992). Such mobilisations have proved to be as controversial as the activities of extreme right-wing groups, and in some localities the actions of black political activists have attracted widespread media attention. Recent examples of such controversies are the debates about the politics of anti-racism and the long drawn out debate during the 1980s on black sections within the Labour Party.

Indeed, as we have seen, one of the ironies of the present situation is that in the media and in popular political discourse it is the anti-racists who are often seen to be doing more harm to good race relations than extreme right-wing racist groupings. Peregrine Worsthorne reflected this type of argument when he argued force-fully that the Notting Hill Carnival was not threatened by white racists or the police, but by black racists who were keen to use the occasion for their political ends (*Sunday Telegraph*, 28 August 1988). Within the logic of this argument the greatest threat to the development of racial harmony lies in the politicisation of racial issues by black activists and politicians and by race relations professionals.

This approach helps to marginalise the issue of white racism, and at the same time to invoke the threat of black racism. It thus fits in with the view, articulated most recently in the language of the new right, of black communities being a threat to the political and social unity of British society.

In this chapter we will examine in greater detail the nature and impact of black political mobilisation, and responses to it. The focus will be on delineating the basic forms of black mobilisation, the interplay between race and class, the role of anti-racist political alliances, minority political participation and the impact of racial factors on local political processes. In the final part of the chapter we shall reflect on the prospects for black political mobilisation, particularly in the context of the social changes that are taking place within the various black communities.

Before moving on to the central concerns of this chapter, however, it is necessary to introduce some general arguments about political participation and processes of political mobilisation.

Political participation and exclusion

Political participation and action are an essential element in the development of political systems and institutions. Historically the development of political systems in different societies has involved the integration of disparate groups into the polity and the development of channels of political participation and inclusion.

In liberal democratic societies such as Britain the most obvious means for enabling, as well as constraining, participation are elections, parties, trade unions and pressure groups. Such processes and institutions tend to reinforce identification with the rules, procedures and values of the polity, they enable the articulation of demands, they facilitate consent and they strengthen acceptance of the legitimacy of the political system (Edelman, 1977; Alford and Friedland, 1985).

What is clear, however, is that not all groups enjoy the same opportunity to participate politically through channels defined as legitimate (Piven and Cloward, 1977; Bowles and Gintis, 1987). According to Katznelson and Weir, groups in society may be (a)

incorporated fully and equally and may possess the capacity to affect
the contours of policy change, (b) incorporated fully and equally but
have relatively little influence on the political system, (c) incorporated
in a partial and structurally subordinate way, but possess the capacity
to influence policy outcomes at some moments, or (d) be structurally
subordinate and without resources to affect what the state does
(Katznelson and Weir, 1985: 204).

Thus once individuals or groups gain access to channels of political
participation they do not necessarily gain equal access to agenda
setting and decision making. Some groups and individuals have far
greater power to place issues on the agenda. Indeed it has been argued
that certain types of problems and many groups of people are
systematically excluded from participation: there is a mobilisation
of bias whereby some issues are organised into politics while others
are organised out.

Prevailing social and political values, as well as institutional
practices, can also limit the political agenda. A good example of
this is the way in which, with the shift in political values to the right
since 1979, calls for political intervention to promote greater racial
equality and positive action have been politically marginalised.
Because such calls do not fit in with the development of an enterprise
culture, the four Conservative administrations since 1979 have
systematically refused to make any major initiatives to strengthen
race relations legislation or to allocate more resources to those bodies
charged with promoting greater racial equality.

The context of black political participation

As argued above, racist political mobilisations, whether in the form of
Powellism or the actions of extreme right-wing groups, have tended to
attract most of the attention since the 1960s. Yet it is clear that during
the same period black and anti-racist political mobilisations have
played an important role in shaping the politics of race in contemporary Britain.

What explanation can be given to the relative neglect of this
important facet of the politics of race and racism in contemporary
Britain? It seems to stem partly from the noticeable failure of political
scientists to study the growth and development of this form of
political action. Until the mid 1970s the common assumption seemed

to be that there was little, if any, political mobilisation by the ethnic minority communities at the political level. This assumption seemed to be supported by national studies of electoral behaviour and local political studies such as Newton's study of Birmingham, which found no significant evidence of political mobilisation (Newton, 1976).

Another factor which worked against the serious study of black politics was the sensitivity of research on political issues. Research on either the national or local politics of race proved to be a highly controversial issue and there was a marked reluctance by social scientists to carry out research in the face of opposition from local black community groups and activists (Jenkins, 1971; Rex and Tomlinson, 1979; Mullard, 1985).

The combination of these two processes helped to produce a situation where the political participation of Afro-Caribbean and Asian communities was little understood or analysed, with the exception of a few studies during the late 1960s and early 1970s which looked at the experience of specific cities or of ethnic minority organisations.

From the mid 1970s onwards, however, the issue of black political participation attracted the attention of a number of researchers and political commentators. Although this interest was not as yet clearly focused it helped to clarify some aspects of emergent forms of black political organisation, of electoral participation and of the response of political parties and institutions to black political action (Fitzgerald, 1984; Anwar, 1986).

One of the main concerns of a number of studies has been the question of the future development of black politics, particularly as the black communities become more established and incorporated into political processes. These studies have suggested three possible patterns for the future political incorporation of minority black communities within the British political system.

First, it has been argued that with the passing of time it is possible that black immigrants and their descendants will become incorporated fully, if unequally, within the political institutions of British political life, including political parties, pressure groups and trades unions. Second, it has been argued that immigrant communities could be incorporated into the political system through their own ethnically or regionally based organisations. Such organisations would seek to advance the interests of particular ethnic groups by political means. Third, it has been argued that in response to institutionalised racism

and the politicisation of racial issues in British society black
communities, whatever their ethnic origins, could develop a common
political identity as an excluded 'black' minority.

There is little agreement as yet about the most likely course of
political incorporation which the various black minorities are likely to
follow, or to the degree of choice they have in this process. But it
seems to be generally agreed by both Marxists and pluralists that
black political participation is likely to follow one of the above three
patterns.

For example, a study by Phizacklea and Miles (1980), which was
based on fieldwork in London during the late 1970s and utilised a
Marxist framework, concluded that what seemed to be happening in
Britain involved a combination of class-based and ethnically-based
political mobilisation. Because of their class composition minority
black communities showed a strong interest in traditional forms of
working-class participation in the British political system, expressed
through their support for the Labour Party and involvement in trades
unions. But because of the pervasiveness of racial exclusionism at all
levels of British society, according to Phizacklea and Miles, minority
communities were also forced to organise autonomously on ethnic or
racial lines to defend their interests. In broad terms this is also the
argument developed by Layton-Henry (1984), though his account
lays more stress on the incorporation of minority politics within
political parties and electoral processes.

It has to be said, however, that as yet there are few research-based
studies of the patterns of political incorporation or autonomous
political mobilisation among the various minority communities. It is
very difficult therefore to draw firm conclusions about the future of
black politics in British society without such detailed accounts, but in
the rest of this chapter we shall attempt to outline some of the main
aspects of black political involvement since the 1940s and look briefly
at prospects for the future. In the course of this account we shall
return to the themes that have been outlined in this section.

Origins of black political mobilisation

During the 1940s and 1950s the position of the newly arrived black
communities can be seen in terms of the pattern of political exclusion
and marginalisation from the political system. Black organisations or

groups at that time had little or no resources to affect what the state did. This does not mean that there was an absence of political involvement or organisation within the newly arrived minority communities. Throughout this period there is evidence of a lively interest in both the mainstream of British politics and in community-based associations and groupings (Sivanandan, 1982; Ramdin, 1987; Gilroy, 1987).

In the 1960s, however, a number of black groups and individuals began to challenge this exclusion and invoke fundamental issues of citizenship and equality. Afro-Caribbean and Asian immigrants launched a series of local and national organisations that sought in various ways to challenge the exclusion of blacks from equal participation in British society. Such organisations included the already established Indian Workers' Association, the West Indian Standing Conference and other ethnically based groups (Pearson, 1981; Jacobs, 1986; Carter, 1986).

The organisation that received widespread public attention during the 1960s, however, was the Campaign Against Racial Discrimination (CARD). This organisation was formed in 1964–5 by a coalition of black political groups, white liberals and campaigners against racism. It had as its main objectives the struggle to eliminate racial discrimination in British society, opposition to racially discriminatory legislation and the coordination of the work of local and national organisations fighting racial discrimination (Heineman, 1972: 20–35). Although it collapsed after a brief and highly controversial power struggle within the organisation during 1967, it did play a role in public debates about the development of policies to tackle racial discrimination and it also served as a catalyst for a wide-ranging debate about the need for autonomous black political organisation to tackle the roots of racial inequality at all levels of British society.

Forms of black political organisation

From the early 1970s there has been a noticeable growth in the levels of political involvement and mobilisation among the Afro-Caribbean and Asian communities. A growing literature of sensitive studies of the black experience in Britain has shown that in practice there is a complex and rich diversity of political and cultural expression at the local level within many black communities. This diversity can be seen at the levels of electoral politics, community mobilisation, political party involvement and more recently in parliamentary politics.

Electoral politics

During the 1970s the political participation of the various black communities attracted the attention of both political parties and researchers. A study carried out by the Community Relations Commission on the importance of the black vote in certain constituencies during the general elections of 1974 helped to arouse media and public interest in this issue.

In the period leading up to the 1979 general election Thatcher's 'swamping' statement helped to politicise the race issue further, particularly in relation to the question of party allegiances. Despite the attempt by the Conservative Party to draw support among the white electorate away from the National Front, this did not prevent the party from attempting to draw the support of sections of the black communities in some constituencies. This was particularly the case with respect to Asian voters.

During the late 1970s and early 1980s all the major political parties showed some interest in attempting to draw support from the black communities, particularly in important inner city constituencies where the black vote could make a difference to the outcome. In practice both Asian and Afro-Caribbean voters have tended to express a preference for the Labour Party in both national and local elections over the years. This trend goes back to the 1950s, though we have clear evidence only for the period since the 1970s. In the general elections of 1974 and 1979 there was strong evidence of support for the Labour Party among both Asian and Afro-Caribbean voters. This was the case for both working class and professional black voters, though there was some variation according to class position. This trend was repeated, but with some changes, in the 1983, 1987 and 1992 general elections.

In broad outline the evidence from such sources shows a depth of support for the Labour Party among both major minority communities, though increasingly less so among Asian voters. But what is also clear is that as compared to the majority white electorate, in England at least, the black electorate is overwhelmingly likely to support the Labour Party.

There are, however, other issues that need to be taken into account. Some evidence exists of a lower turnout at elections among some sections of the Afro-Caribbean communities, particularly the young. Such groups are more likely to be disillusioned with the ability of politicians to bring about changes in major issues that concern them. Additionally it may be important to look at the issue of generational differences in voting behaviour. The trend of sections of the Asian electorate towards the Conservative Party may not be uniform, and there is a need to look into the class and generational patterns behind this transformation (Crewe, 1983; Layton-Henry and Studlar, 1985; Anwar, 1986).

Interestingly, although during both the 1983 and 1987 general elections there was much speculation about a major move towards the Conservative Party by middle class Asians and Afro-Caribbeans the scale of the change does not support such generalisations. Layton-Henry (1988) argues that the trend towards class based voting may be more limited than some studies have suggested:

In the future, one would expect that class voting will increase among members of the black electorate but there are a number of reasons why this is likely to be rather slow. These include Mrs Thatcher's determination to bring New Commonwealth immigration to an end, her lack of sympathy for anti-discrimination measures and her willingness to allow the Labour Party to be identified with what she regards as unpopular minorities (p. 22).

Whether the shift towards more class-based voting behaviour among the Afro-Caribbean and Asian communities is likely to become more pronounced is the subject of much academic debate and it has aroused the interest of the major political parties. But before we can begin to analyse this issue in more detail there is a need to look more deeply into the question of the sociology of the black electorate and its different component parts.

Community politics

During the past four decades a variety of community-based organisations and groups have been formed within the various minority communities. Indeed one of the features of both Afro-Caribbean and Asian self-organisation has been the array of communal, religious, political and issue-oriented groups that have arisen over the years. Such organisations have frequently been of a local or community-based character, and have involved a variety of different forms of autonomous organisation in a number of different contexts, rather than unified ethnic movements.

Few detailed studies of the history and political ideologies of such groups have been carried out. During the 1960s and 1970s some studies of Asian political and cultural organisations were undertaken, particularly in relation to their political involvement and ideological commitments. A more limited number of studies of Afro-Caribbean organisations and groups were also carried out during this time. Such studies were, however, limited both in scope and in geographical context.

Part of the reason for the neglect of this dimension of black political action may have been the assumption that such organisations and groups were not very influential at the political level. Goulbourne (1987), however, argues forcefully that without looking at the role played by such groups it is impossible to understand the growing political impact of minority politics on the major political parties and mainstream institutions. He sees this influence as particularly important in placing such issues as the education of black children, police relations with black people, black unemployment and racial attacks on the political agenda at both local and central government levels.

Other studies of black community organisations have helped to show how active self-organisation is an everyday feature of the political life of various black communities. Cheetham (1988) notes that the most important feature of ethnic associations in Britain seems to be their extraordinary vitality, energy and commitment. She concludes from her study of a sample of ethnic associations that two issues were held to be important by most of the groups she studied. First, the question of culture, language and ethnic identity, including the politics of the country of origin of the associations' members. Second, the issue of how to bring about greater equality and integration into British society without losing minority traditions and values (p. 150–1).

The importance of the role played by community-based and ethnic associations in the political life of the various ethnic minority organisations is only now being fully appreciated. This is likely to lead to more detailed studies of the processes of political mobilisation and community organisation, both in relation to issue-centred politics and electoral and party politics. One example of this trend is the attention which has been given to the growth of political mobilisation among ethnically and religiously based community groups in recent years. The two most important examples in this context are the Muslim and Sikh communities, which have developed high levels of political organisation and community-based mobilisation on issues related to British politics and the politics of their countries of origin.

The Labour Party and black sections

As we have already seen, from the very earliest stages of postwar black immigration one of the themes in the discussion of the political allegiances of black immigrants was their tendency to give their support in elections to the Labour Party. Yet it is clear that the Labour Party itself made little serious attempt until the late 1970s to incorporate its black supporters fully into its own organisations or to tackle the institutionalised racism in its own organisational structures.

During the late 1970s, however, both black and white Labour Party members begun to press for more action on issues concerned with racial inequality and racism. In 1975 the Labour Party Race Action Group was established as a pressure group within the party, and along with other individuals it helped to increase awareness of the politics of racism within the party. From the late 1970s internal debates and policy changes helped to bring racial inequality, along with other previously neglected issues, onto the political agenda of the party at both national and local levels.

These pressures were given greater force during the early 1980s in the aftermath of the political attention given to the outbreaks of urban unrest. In many local Labour Party constituencies, as well as at a national level, race-related issues became the focus of intense policy debate. The early 1980s were a period of innovation as a number of left-wing Labour local authorities took the initiative in developing race equality policies, in promoting anti-racist initiatives and in tackling institutionalised racism within their own institutions.

It was in the context of these changes that black Labour Party politicians and activists begun to demand both greater attention to racial issues and more black representation in local and national political institutions. Such demands for increased black representation were seen as a way of (a) including black politicians in the institutions of political power, (b) helping to put black issues on the political agenda and (c) giving a voice to the demands of those excluded from equal political participation.

Increasingly the focus for these demands became the issue of the formation of black sections within the Labour Party, which were seen as a way of increasing the influence of black Labour Party members on policy making and encouraging more black people to become involved in political activity. Resolutions calling for the recognition of black sections were debated at the annual conferences of 1983 and 1984, and at subsequent conferences. The leadership of the party came out against the idea of black sections, largely on the grounds that it could be seen as divisive and as a form of apartheid. There seems also to have been an underlying fear among the leadership that the black sections movement could become a political liability if it was led by radical left-wing black groups.

Marc Wordsworth, a leading figure in the black sections campaign, expressed the thinking behind the campaign when he warned that:

> If the Party did not begin actively to take the issue of black representation seriously, it must face the possibility of increased abstentions, a tide of black independents and perhaps a tendency, particularly amongst black youth, to redress their grievances through extra-parliamentary action (*The Times*, 16 April, 1984).

Within the terms of this argument the recognition of black sections within the Labour Party would help to institutionalise black representation and allow black members a channel through which to press for changes in the political programme of the party both locally and nationally.

According to Diane Abbott, a leading figure in the black sections movement who was elected to Parliament in 1987, a number of factors helped to make the black sections issue a central theme. First, the long-standing institutionalised racism in the Labour Party and the increasingly glaring contradiction between the Labour Party reliance on the black vote and the fact that the structures of the Labour Party were almost all white. Second, the way in which in the late 1970s the left wing of the Labour Party had used constitutional means, like mandatory selection, as a way of organising against the status quo. Finally, there was 'the emergence in the Labour Party of a different generation of black activists, who took for granted that they should organise themselves as black people' (*Marxism Today*, September 1985: 31).

Despite the failure of the black sections movement to achieve formal recognition from the party it has continued to exercise some influence on political debates within the Labour Party (Jeffers, 1991). A number of active groups exist in various localities. These groups continue to campaign for formal recognition and to meet regularly at both local and national level. During 1988 they produced a detailed *Black Agenda* which seeks to put forward proposals on such issues as inner city policy, education, policing and housing (Labour Party Black Section, 1988). The agenda has proved to be controversial and it is unlikely at this stage to influence the policies being pursued by the Labour Party, particularly given the identification of the document with a number of controversial issues. But in the longer term the likelihood is that, as black representation becomes more established, black pressure for increased political incorporation into political institutions will be difficult for the Labour Party to resist (Back and Solomos, 1992a, 1992b). It is also clear that the question of black participation in the Labour Party has now moved beyond the question of black sections as such. Many black and ethnic minority politicians who were not active in the black sections movement are also demanding increased representation in party institutions and in elected posts. It is clear that despite opposition their demands are already beginning to have some impact.

Representation in Parliament

The final aspect of black political involvement that needs to be mentioned in this context is the issue of representation in Parliament. In 1987 four black Labour Party MPs were elected: Bernie Grant for Tottenham, Diane Abbott for Hackney North and Stoke Newington, Paul Boateng for Brent South and Keith Vaz for Leicester East. Their election meant that black people were represented in Parliament for the first time in sixty years, and because of this it was popularly represented as a major change in British political life.

In the 1992 general election the number of minority Labour MPs increased to five and we saw the election of the first Conservative minority MP (*Runnymede Trust Bulletin*, May 1992). During the 1992 general election all the political parties claimed that race was no longer an issue in British political life. All of the black Labour MPs elected in 1987 were returned to Parliament, many of them with significantly increased majorities. Bernie Grant in the north London constituency of Tottenham managed the second largest swing to Labour: 9.4 per cent. Equally Keith Vaz in Leicester East increased his majority, winning a 10.4 per cent swing to Labour. Despite the defeat of Ashok Kumar, who was elected as Labour Member of Parliament for Langaugh in a 1991 by-election, two new black MPs were also elected to Westminster, Piara Khabra held the Labour seat of Ealing Southall and Nirj Deva became the first black Conservative Member of Parliament in Brentford and Isleworth.

In all, twenty-three black candidates stood: ten for Labour, eight for the Conservatives and four for the Liberal Democrats. The success of black candidates in the election was offered as evidence that Britain was becoming a multi-racial democracy. This was contrasted with the experience of other European societies where immigration was becoming a highly politicised issue.

Part of the reason for the interest in the election of the black MPs since 1987 can be found in the controversy surrounding their selection, which was popularly presented as the outcome of pressure from the black sections movement and sections of the left-wing of the Labour Party. Certainly one of the most controversial aspects of the rise of black political power at both local and national levels has been the election of black politicians, particularly those seen as representing left-wing or black-power views. Many black politicians have been represented in the media and in popular political discourse as representatives of black power or of the extreme left.

When in the period leading up to the 1987 general election the Labour Party selected a number of black candidates in winnable seats there were clear signs of unease about the possible impact of black representation in Parliament. *The Sun* warned that the election of black MPs would not help the majority of the black population since they were 'all holders of loony left ideas which have shocked the nation' (14 February 1987). At a broader level the selection of black candidates became embroiled in the wider controversies about the influence of the 'loony left' on Labour Party politics and on the activities of left-wing local authorities such as Lambeth and Brent. The controversy over the selection and deselection of Sharon Atkin as the candidate for Nottingham East in the lead-up to the election was a clear example of how these issues coalesced in popular political debate.

In the aftermath of the 1987 and 1992 General Elections much attention was focused on the parliamentary performance of the black MPs and their impact on debates in Parliament and in committee. It is certainly too early to make a reasoned judgement on the role of black MPs or whether they will be able to use their position to influence debates in and out of Parliament on race and related issues, as well as on wider policy questions. But already there are signs that their presence in parliament has given rise to quite unique pressures and has rendered their position very difficult both as constituency MPs and as black politicians. Black MPs face pressure on the one hand to become integrated into the rules of parliamentary politics, while on the other hand they are often treated as spokespersons on a variety of race and ethnic issues. A similar situation faces the increasing number of black politicians who have been elected as local councillors, and who are often represented as speaking for whole communities regardless of ethnic, cultural or religious differences (Solomos and Back, 1991).

Anti-racist politics and political alliances

One of the recurrent themes in debates about the development of black political action is the question of political alliances between black and anti-racist political groups. The search for such alliances is based on two main assumptions. First, it is argued that the relatively small size of the minority population means that black demands would have a greater chance for success if they received the support of sections of the majority white population. The second assumption is that racism in British society is as much a problem for the white majority as it is for the black minorities, and that racialist political groups can best be dealt with on the basis of an alliance between black and white anti-racist groups.

One example of a national attempt to develop an alliance of anti-racist political groups was the Anti-Nazi League (ANL), which was founded in 1977. The league was particularly active from 1977 to 1979 and it concentrated its interventions on political action to counter the propaganda of the National Front and other extreme right-wing groups. It drew its support from members of the Labour Party, the Socialist Workers Party and from other left-wing organisations that had become concerned about the growing popularity of racist political groups. One of these organisations was Rock Against Racism, which had been active since 1976 in mobilisations aimed at turning young people against the National Front and other racist organisations, and which helped to draw many supporters to the ANL (Widgery, 1986; Gilroy, 1987).

The ANL used a variety of initiatives to organise against the National Front and emphasised in particular two modes of action. First, direct extra-parliamentary initiatives such as rallies and demonstrations which helped to publicise its arguments on racism and on the political dangers which the extreme right represented. The ANL in particular chose to emphasise the links between the ideologies of the National Front and the Nazi Party in order to mobilise opposition to it, and to dwell on the links between the National Front and underground fascist groups. This helped to mobilise opposition to the Front in the period leading up to the 1979 election.

Second, during 1978 and 1979 it organised a series of successful musical events in association with Rock Against Racism, which were aimed at attracting to the anti-racist cause the young people who were seen as particularly vulnerable to National Front propaganda.

The speed of the rise of the ANL was matched by the rapidity of its decline as a political force from 1979 onwards. Although it continued to exist for some time afterwards its high point was over and it had little impact on public political debate.

This does not mean that attempts to organise anti-racist political alliances have not persisted. Ben-Tovim *et al.* (1986) have argued, on the basis of research in Liverpool and Wolverhampton, that locally based anti-racist alliances have played an important role in promoting black political demands and mobilising opinion against racist organisations. From this they conclude that at the local level at least the role of anti-racist political alliances remains an important aspect of the politics of racism in contemporary Britain.

The politics of race and class

The interplay between race and class in the formation of black political action has been one of the most resonant themes in studies of this question. As we saw in Chapter 1 the theoretical debate about how race and class interact is far from being resolved, and indeed it is still one of the causes of heated debate among social scientists.

Underlying these theoretical controversies, however, are more practical questions about the relationship between autonomous black political mobilisation and class-based politics.

This theme is central, for example, in the controversy surrounding the electoral behaviour of the black communities and the formation of black sections within the Labour Party. Similar questions have been raised about the development of black politics in the US, particularly in the debate between Marxists and black nationalists (Marable, 1981).

In Chapter 1 we looked at some of the ways in which a number of scholars have attempted to overcome the dichotomy between race and class relations. At that stage no attempt was made to provide full answers to the problems. After the above discussion, however, we are in a better position to look more deeply into this issue.

In broad outline there are two questions we have to confront in rethinking the terms of political debate about race and class. First, there is the question of what is meant by class. The role of political mobilisation in determining the formation of class consciousness, national consciousness and other identities has been the focus of a lively debate over the years. One of the sharpest formulations of this problem is to be found in a study of the politics of schooling in the US by Ira Katznelson and Margaret Weir, who argue that:

> It is important to think of the formation of a class as a conditional process. Whether people who share objective traits in the material organisation of society will form a class in action cannot be predicted from the profiles of the social structure, nor can the rhetorical and practical bases of their action be deduced from such profiles (1985: 62).

Within the terms of this perspective what is important in the development of political mobilisation is not the objective position of political actors in the social structure but their actual experiences and responses to the social, economic and political processes of the societies in which they live.

Second, and following on from the above, there is a need to understand the connection between race as a political category and wider social processes and conflicts.

In contemporary Britain the main problem with trying to see black politics from a purely class perspective is that it is impossible to see contemporary forms of black political mobilisation as separate from the everyday experiences of discrimination and exclusion which have operated over four decades. The distinctive experiences of Afro-Caribbeans, Asians and other minority groups need therefore to be understood, and this necessarily takes us beyond a dogmatic conception of class formation. At the same time it is important to remember that their distinctive historical experiences are joined by a common thread: either a full or partial denial of citizenship or the rights that accompany it.

Politics, social movements and reform

The central question which underlies all accounts of black political mobilisation is: What impact can black communities have on the political agenda? Another related question is: What are the prospects that an effective challenge to racism can be mounted within the current political environment?

These questions have certainly become a common reference point in debates about such specific policy issues as education and policing, which have been areas of active concern among the various black communities for some time.

What is also clear, however, is that there is by no means a uniform answer to these question. Responses range from deep scepticism as to the possibility of blacks exercising a major influence on the mainstream political agenda, to a degree of optimism about the ability of black politicians to transform political institutions.

Perhaps the most noticeable political development in recent years, however, has been the attempt by black politicians to gain access to positions of political patronage and power at both national and local political levels. The assumption behind this strategy is that it is only through their integration into the mainstream channels of political power and patronage that black communities can move beyond political exclusion and powerlessness to a situation where they are incorporated equally into the political system and have the resources to bring about policy changes in their interest.

Such an optimistic view of the possibilities for black advancement through the political system is not shared by all commentators. The relative failure of the mainstream political institutions to tackle the root causes of racial inequality and racism in British society has led some commentators to look beyond the channels of formal politics for a way out of the present problems.

Gilroy (1987), for example, concludes his account of urban social change and the role of black community struggles by arguing that:

In the representation of the recent riots, it is possible to glimpse a struggle, a sequence of antagonisms which has moved beyond the grasp of orthodox class analysis. Unable to control the social relations in which they find themselves, people have shrunk the world to the size of their communities and begun to act politically on that basis (p. 245).

While it is difficult from this rather general and cryptic statement to fathom a clear political strategy, Gilroy seems to be suggesting (a) that the view which sees black communities becoming increasingly incorporated into existing class-based political institutions is inadequate, and that (b) excluded groups are likely to develop forms of political involvement at the micro rather than the macro level.

This line of argument stands in direct contrast to the attempts by other black radicals to prioritise the need to see more direct black involvement in national and local political institutions. This tension is also reflected in the on-going debate about the formation of black sections within the Labour Party and the wider debate about increasing black representation in the mainstream political institutions.

At the present time, even the election of four black MPs and the election of a sizable number of black councillors in many local authorities is unlikely to have much effect on the allocation of resources and political influence. This seems to be implicitly recognised by the so-called Black Agenda issued by the black sections movement during 1988 (Howe and Upshal, 1988).

Black demands for full citizenship will not easily be achieved in the present political climate. Urban unrest such as that which occurred sporadically throughout the 1980s may be better managed in the future, but the underlying conflicts which produced it are not going to disappear. Ordinary patterns of dispute resolution have so far proved to be incapable of managing conflict with this content, meaning and intensity, and the prospects for the future are not hopeful.

Yet it is important to note that this situation is not likely to result in any wholesale withdrawal from all types of political activity. This is perhaps the best hope in the long-term struggle of the black communities for equality and full citizenship. Reflecting on the history of attempts to form a national body to fight for black interests at the political level, Hall (1985b) has argued that one reason for the failure of such attempts is the distance between such organisations and the 'actual day-to-day experience of repression and exploitation which the black community has gone through'.

Summary and conclusion

This chapter has looked at the role of black and anti-racist political mobilisation in the context of the racialisation of British political life since 1945. It has shown that, far from being helpless victims, black communities have actively attempted to challenge racialism and injustice. Indeed the experience of the past few years would seem to indicate that the political participation and involvement of both the Asian and Afro-Caribbean communities is likely to increase.

Anti-racist political mobilisations have also played an important role at various stages since the 1950s and have attracted widespread sympathy and support from outside the black communities. Local and national attempts to create alliances against racism have been inherently contradictory and have proved to be unstable, but the experience of groups such as the Anti-Nazi League and Rock Against Racism, along with various locally based initiatives, seems to indicate that the potential for political mobilisation against racism is there.

The prospects for the 1990s are already becoming a focus of debate. Concern seems to be particularly focused on young blacks and other disaffected groups within the black communities. Rose (1985) has warned, for example, that the main question in the 1990s is likely to be whether public policy succeeds in bringing about greater social integration or a situation where 'a small, politically alienated and active group will identify themselves as blacks rather than Britons' (p. 59). From a rather different perspective, Gilroy has put forward the argument that the immediate prospect of change from the present situation is to be found among 'those groups who find the premises of their collective existence threatened' (Gilroy, 1987: 246).

Perhaps the most important lesson we can learn from the experience of the 1980s is that it is far too simplistic to search for one model of either black or anti-racist political mobilisation. Rather it is important to recognise the volatile, and to some extent unpredictable, nature of political struggles over race and whether such struggles have a racist or an anti-racist political objective. Once this is done it becomes clear that the active involvement of black and ethnic minority communities is an integral element of any realistic strategy for challenging the existing political agenda about race in British society.

10 Race, Culture and Social Change

Introduction

According to one recent commentator modern nation states seem to offer minorities the status of (a) complete assimilation or (b) despised difference or exclusion (Asad, 1990b). While this argument may seem somewhat overstated it is also reflective of an on-going struggle in contemporary societies, including Britain, over the definition of who belongs and who does not.

The previous chapter highlighted the complex forms of political mobilisation that have emerged over the past decade among black and ethnic minority communities. In this chapter the focus shifts to another feature of the changing face of contemporary race relations, namely political debates about the meaning of British national identity in an increasingly multicultural society. We shall deal with some of the key aspects of recent debates about the changing dynamics of culture, religion and identity in contemporary Britain. In particular the focus will be on the implications of these developments for an understanding of the changing role of national identity in the context of growing multiculturalism in British society.

This issue has provoked an increasingly vociferous public debate in recent years, and the question of just who possesses the dominant national identity is preoccupying politicians, journalists and commentators alike (Nairn, 1981 and 1988; Crick, 1991). This process of public debate has been given added impetus in recent years by heated public debates about the Rushdie affair, the role of Islamic fundamentalism in British society and concern about the future of the British national identity within a broader European framework (Appignanesi and Maitland, 1989; Asad, 1990a; CRE, 1990; Ruthven, 1990; Ahmed, 1992; Samad, 1992). At a broader level debates about such diverse issues as the Gulf War, immigration from Hong Kong and the arrival of refugees and asylum seekers are conducted largely around the question of their impact on national identity.

Additionally, there has been a vigorous public debate in recent years about the changing balance between civil society and the state in contemporary British society and the need to redefine citizenship rights to take account of the claims by minority communities to specific religious and cultural identities (Parekh, 1991; Asad, 1990b). This has been reflected in debates about what it really means to call Britain a 'multiracial' or a 'multicultural' society, and in a questioning of the possibility of achieving such an objective through the policies and initiatives that have been pursued by successive governments.

Such debates have linked up with a growing preoccupation in academic studies of this field with questions of culture and identity (Rutherford, 1990; Grossberg *et al.*, 1992). Within the context of debates about the changing dynamics of racial relations in Britain one reflection of this concern has been the growing literature on the relationship between racial and gender identities (Grewal *et al.*, 1989; Brah, 1992; Anthias and Yuval-Davis, 1992; James, 1992; James and Harris, 1993). It is also interesting to note that many radical writers in this field have increasingly begun to point to the need to analyse the dynamics of racial and ethnic identities in Britain and other European societies (Hall, 1991a; Gilroy, 1991; Rattansi, 1992). Additionally, a number of writers have begun to question whether the use of a general category like 'black' to describe all racial minorities in British society has the effect of simplifying the complex ethnic, cultural and religious identities that characterise minority communities.

Imagined communities

One way to begin to think about the range of issues to be covered in this chapter is to raise the following question: What is the acid test for who is and who is not English or British? Simple as it sounds it has in practice been a difficult question to answer in the context of the important social changes that have taken place in British society over the past few decades. There is no longer, if there ever was, any certainty about the meaning of 'Englishness' and 'Britishness' in the current political environment. Such uncertainty is certainly not new in the context of British history (Samuel, 1989b; Colley, 1992), but what we are seeing at the present time is a profound debate about the definition of the 'nation' and its boundaries in the context of internal

processes of social change and external patterns of political transformation.

It is interesting to note in this regard that the question of
nationhood and identity has become contested in public debate.
During the early 1990s, for example, we have seen a succession of
controversies which have focused specifically on this issue. The on-
going debate about the Rushdie affair, Nicholas Ridley's comments
about 'the Germans', Norman Tebbit's 'cricket test' and public
debate about the Gulf War are perhaps the most well known
examples of this process. But what is interesting is that these widely
publicised cases are only the tip of the iceberg. Recent research has
pointed to the way in which in many multi-ethnic communities
everyday processes involve a dialogue about such issues as race,
culture and ethnicity (Gilroy, 1991; Back, 1991). Alluding to the
cultural expressions to be found in popular youth cultures and in
other contemporary cultural forms a number of writers have argued
that we are witnessing the emergence and flowering of 'new
ethnicities' which challenge the boundaries of national identity by
asserting the possibility of being both black and English (Mercer,
1990; Hall, 1991a). Recent feminist writings have also begun to
explore the changing dynamics of culture, race and identity in shaping
the position of both white and black women in British society
(Parmar, 1990; Brah, 1992; Ware, 1992).

In this environment the difficulty of providing a clearcut definition
of the distinctivenesss of Englishness has itself become a matter of
political controversy. The furore caused by Nicholas Ridley's remarks
in July 1990 about the threat to Britain posed by the 'German nation'
highlighted the increasing importance of ideas about national identity
and difference in contemporary political discourse (*The Spectator*, 14
July 1990). In a sense Ridley was expressing a much broader sense of
mistrust within the Thatcher administration and the Conservative
Party more generally of the implications of (a) the development of
political and economic unity through the European Community and
(b) of the unification of Germany. A clear example of this wider
preoccupation was provided by Norman Tebbit's attempt in April
1990 to use the 'cricket test' as a bench mark for measuring the loyalty
of migrants to Britain. According to Tebbit many migrants were
disloyal to Britain because they failed to support the English cricket
team in games involving their countries of origin (*Daily Express*, 21
April 1990). Despite the ferocity of some of the opposition to his

remarks Tebbit chose to stick to his comments and has expressed similar views subsequently.

In her famous Bruges speech in September 1988, for example, Margaret Thatcher had warned of the dangers of diluting Britain's national identity under the rubric of a wider European identity. She argued that although Britain's future was as part of Europe it was important to protect the uniqueness of different national cultures. Additionally she pointed to the danger of Europe falling under 'the dominance of a single power' (Thatcher, 1988: 2).

It is also interesting to note that a few months before the controversy about Ridley's remarks Thatcher herself organised a meeting of experts to discuss the implications of German reunification for Britain and other societies. The record of this discussion was subsequently published and led to controversy about the language used to describe the German nation and the possible dangers that may result from reunification (*The Independent on Sunday*, 15 July 1990).

Such controversies also highlighted the fact that ideas about race and nationhood are as much to do with the 'others' within Europe as with those outside. Ridley's comments and the wide-ranging debate surrounding them can be seen as symbolic of an uncertainty of the future of Britishness and Englishness in a period of global changes in economic and political power relations. This uncertainty is by no means new and has a long history going back to the transformation of Britain's imperial role and the decline of its economic power over the past century (Rich, 1986; Goulbourne, 1991).

But it seems clear that in the present political environment debates about the future of the nation are likely to be expressed in new ways in relation to the position of racial and ethnic minorities within British society. It is to this issue that we now turn.

Multiculturalism, identity and the nation

One of the trends that has become clear since the early 1980s is that there is a clear attempt to reinvent a British national identity in line with antecedent images of the 'island race'. Media images and political language have continually used such images to reconstruct popular images of national identity in line with myths of origin and cultural uniqueness.

A number of events have highlighted the ways in which nationhood connects with the politics of race and racism in British society. The death of the nation state is being proclaimed within public discourse simultaneously with the recirculation of a national imagery that is increasingly chauvinistic, defensive and racially exclusive. New and not so new expressions of national identity have dominated the public imagination as it grapples with changes occurring within the world geopolitical order.

Rushdie and Islam

Following the publication of *The Satanic Verses* the most notable attacks on Rushdie were published in India, where he was accused of being anti-Islamic and writing blasphemous statements about the Prophet. The first notable public response in Britain was a staged book burning in Bradford in January 1989. This was followed by other protests in Bradford and other major cities in Britain. Other demonstrations against Rushdie took place in Pakistan and other Islamic countries, leading to Ayatollah Khomeini's *fatwa* in February 1989. Such events helped to politicise the debate about *The Satanic Verses*, and ensured that it influenced popular and élite debates about the future of minority communities in British society.

The Rushdie affair reinforced public interest about the role of fundamentalism among sections of the Muslim communities in various localities and gave a new life to debates about the issue of cultural differences and processes of integration and assimilation. The full impact of the Rushdie affair on both the local and national politics of race is not as yet clear, but even at this stage it is obvious that it has influenced debates about such issues as multiculturalism and anti-racism in Britain (Asad, 1990b; Ruthven, 1990; Samad, 1992).

This has happened at two levels. First, at the national level, there are already signs that the Rushdie affair has given a new impetus to debates about issues such as immigration, integration and public order. Second, it has had a direct impact on local politics, both in terms of formal and informal political processes, with various local Muslim political activists adopting a high profile in areas such as Bradford, Leicester, Birmingham and elsewhere (Akhtar, 1989; Appignanesi and Maitland, 1989). In the aftermath of the affair local political debates about race and ethnicity have increasingly had to take on board a range of issues about religious identity which were not a priority in the policies of radical local authorities during the 1980s. Recent research in Birmingham has highlighted the complex ways in which the affair influenced broader debates about race and ethnicity within the local political context (Back and Solomos, 1992c).

Additionally, political mobilisations around the Rushdie affair also brought to the fore organisations such as the Bradford Council of Mosques which consciously sought to mobilise and exert political influence on the basis of representing particular religious communities, and rejected the idea of organising within the limits of traditional party politics. In the context of Bradford the role of the Council of Mosques became a symbol of attempts to use the Rushdie affair as a means of mobilising Muslims as a specific political constituency.

It is also clear that the events surrounding the affair have led to some reappraisals of the role of gender in the politics of race and ethnicity (Sahgal and Yuval-Davis, 1992). A number of black feminist organisations, along with other groups, have sought to question the image that there was simply one unified Muslim response to the Rushdie affair, regardless of gender and politics. In particular groups such as Women Against Fundamentalism sought to support Rushdie while at the same time attempting to challenge stereotypes about 'Asian' and 'Muslim' women.

The hostile media coverage of the events surrounding the political mobilisations around the Rushdie affair has served to reinforce the view that minorities who do not share the dominant political values of British society pose a threat to social stability and cohesion (Asad, 1990b). Some commentators have argued that as a result of the affair more attention should be given to the divergent political paths seemingly adopted by sections of the Afro-Caribbean and Asian communities. The affair has also given added impetus to debates about the multiple cultural and political identities that have been included in the broad categorisation of black and ethnic minority communities (Modood, 1992).

In his response to the events arising from the affair John Patten, Minister of State at the Home Office, argued that:

The last few months have been difficult ones for British Muslims. The issue of race relations has been thrown into sharp relief and all of us have had to think deeply about our objectives and priorities; about what it means to be British, and particularly what it means to be a British Muslim (*The Times*, 5 July 1989).

From this premise Patten then went on to argue that it was important to link the rights of Muslims to their responsibilities to British society:

[If Muslims] are to make the most of their lives and opportunities as British citizens, then they must have a clear understanding of the British democratic processes, of its laws, the system of government and the history that lies behind them, and indeed of their own rights and responsibilities.

Pronouncements along the same lines were a common theme in much of the media and political debate about the affair during 1989 and 1990. They highlighted the racialisation of political debates brought about by the affair and the tensions between ideas about race and ideas about national belonging. They also demonstrated the interplay of nation, culture and xenophobia which linked up with a concern that cultural difference presented a threat to Britishness.

Aspects of the media response focused specifically on the implications for race relations in the future. The *Daily Telegraph*, for example, alleged in an editorial headed 'Races Apart' that the events surrounding the publication of *The Satanic Verses* highlighted the 'difficulty of integrating Moslem communities into British life'. It went on:

In the wake of *The Satanic Verses*, there must be increased pessimism about how far different communities in our nation can ever be integrated, or want to be (*Daily Telegraph*, 17 May 1989).

Arguments such as this show the complex way in which the Rushdie affair has helped to push back onto the agenda questions about the integration of minority communities and they have helped the case of those who question the viability of an ethnically plural society. They have also given an added impetus to the argument that the development of ethnic pluralism is interfering with the social and political cohesion of British society.

Partly in response to media attacks on 'fundamentalism', supporters of the political stance taken by some radical Muslim groups defended

perhaps not surprising that these have not been heard. The reimposition of order on the streets is seen within the current dominant political discourse as an objective which can be achieved without the economic and political reforms called for by the liberal project, at least in the medium term. In the long term the strong free-market economy which the present government espouses is seen as the best insurance against social disorder, rather than short-term reform measures.

Caught between the repeated calls for reform voiced by liberals since 1980 and the logic of the free market and the strong state, the inner city areas which have witnessed violent protest seem to have little chance of any fundamental change in the medium term (Gamble, 1988). Given such a situation, and there is little evidence of change, the occurrence of violent protest is not merely a possibility – it is a likelihood. Promises of a better future in some future free-market paradise will do little to transform the economic and social fabric of inner city areas, overcome political powerlessness or challenge the differential policing patterns which brand certain racial and ethnic groups as criminal. In such a situation the preservation of authority and order will be secured as much by force as by consent.

Rethinking the politics of racism

Few analytically clear attempts have been made to theorise the interrelationship between racism and the state in Britain or in other advanced capitalist societies. There are, by contrast, numerous accounts of the relationship between class structure and the state, and even some accounts of gender relations and the state. This omission has serious consequences for the adequacy of theoretical models of the state in capitalist society. For instance, how adequate are accounts of welfare and social policy, employment policy and housing policy which ignore the position of black and ethnic minorities? Yet there are numerous studies of these issues which ignore the question of racial inequality and the role it plays in structuring social conditions in advanced industrial societies.

At the beginning of this book I argued that there was a need for greater theoretical clarity about the interplay between racism, politics and society. But as I have shown throughout the basic problem confronting any account of the complex relations between race, class and the state is to be found in the very nature of racism in contemporary capitalist societies. From the brief survey in Chapter 1 of the competing approaches to this question in sociological, neo-Marxist and political discourses it should be clear that there are at least two problems which have so far defied resolution. First, the question of the interplay between racial and ethnic categorisations and economic and class determination. Second, the role of the state and the political institutions of capitalist societies in the reproduction of racism, including the complex role of state intervention in many countries to control immigration, to manage race relations and, more broadly, to integrate racial and ethnic groupings into the wider society.

Aspects of these issues have been addressed in this book, but it must be said that I have not sought to develop a polished theoretical framework. In the rest of this chapter, however, I want to outline some of the fundamental questions that arise from the substantive case studies of racialised politics in contemporary Britain.

Michael Omi and Howard Winant, in their analysis of the politics of race in the US, have suggested that it is wrong to conceive of the state as an external factor in the shaping of racial relations. Rather, they argue that:

> The state is inherently racial. Far from intervening in racial conflicts, the state is itself increasingly the pre-eminent site of racial conflict. . . . Every state institution is a racial institution, but not every institution operates in the same way. In fact, the various state institutions do not serve one co-ordinated racial objective; they may work at cross-purposes. Therefore, race must be understood as occupying varying degrees of centrality in different state institutions and at different historical moments (Omi and Winant, 1986: 76–7).

Such arguments have been made in a number of other theoretical contributions to the analysis of the politics of racism. But whatever the merit of theoretical propositions such as these the difficulty has been that they have not been used systematically to inform historical and empirical analysis of particular racial situations. There have been some ad hoc attempts to do this, but they have been both partial and based on limited research on the dynamics of racism across historical and spatial boundaries. While not diminishing the importance of these studies, the relative absence of empirical analysis has left a major gap in existing writings on this subject. Without analysing the interaction between racist structures and other social structures in capitalist societies it becomes difficult to explain how certain types of racialised ideologies and inequalities develop and help to shape the fundamental institutions of a society.

Part of the problem has been the lack of a fruitful dialogue on theoretical and methodological issues among those involved in research on various aspects of the politics of racism in Britain. Another problem is the absence of detailed studies of the genesis, development and transformation of racial institutions.

An example of this failure to integrate theory with research can be found in the work of Stuart Hall. In his account of the interplay between racism and other social relations in capitalist societies, he argues:

> At the economic level, it is clear that race must be given its distinctive and 'relatively autonomous' effectivity, as a distinctive feature. This does not mean that the economic is sufficient to found an explanation of how these relations concretely function. One needs to know how different racial and ethnic groups were inserted historically, and the relations which have tended to erode and transform, or to preserve these distinctions though time – not simply as residues and traces of previous modes, but as active structuring principles of the present society. Racial categories alone will not provide or explain these (Hall, 1980: 339).

Hall's approach implicitly criticises those approaches which assume that there is a harmonious articulation between racism and the capitalist mode of production. His emphasis on the ways in which racial and ethnic groups are incorporated historically into different societies, and how their position changes over time, suggests that the relationship between racism and wider social relations should be seen as historically and spatially variable and contradictory.

But such broad generalisations need to be tested out and analysed in accounts of processes of racialisation in particular historical situations. In order to develop a dynamic framework which can help us understand the historical and contemporary intersection between racism and politics in specific societies there is a need for an analytic framework that focuses attention on the processes that lead to the politicisation of racial and ethnic issues. Yet there is no attempt in Hall's work to go beyond general theoretical propositions by analysing the development of racism in particular societies. This failure to integrate theory with detailed historical and political analysis is to be found in much of the radical literature on racism.

This separation between theoretical analysis and political analysis needs to be overcome if we are to understand the history and present forms of racialised politics in British society. There is a need to move away from a notion of racialisation which is uniform across different historical formations or even particular societies.

The paradox of attempts to construct a uniform conception of racism is that they seem to lose the ability to explain the dynamics of change and conflict. In so doing they fail to analyse the processes which lead to the racialisation of social relations in particular societies.

This has been my main concern in this book. In particular I have focused on two broad questions. First, how do political structures and institutions in Britain function in relation to race and in what ways do they produce and reproduce or help overcome racism? Second, how does racism shape the ways in which class, gender and other social relations are actually experienced and how do they structure political action? The limits of one volume have allowed me to cover only the essential aspects of these issues, but in doing so I have tried to open up areas for further debate and analysis.

Racism and nationalism in Europe

The current resurgence of racist and extreme nationalist movements in a number of European societies is perhaps the most widely commented upon aspect of public and media debate about the new Europe. The role of the Front National in France, the Vlaams Blok in Belgium and a number of political movements in the now unified Germany have helped to draw attention to the increased support for such groupings. Such movements have drawn much of their support on the basis of their opposition to immigration and their open manipulation of nationalist symbols.

What is interesting, however, is that extreme right-wing political parties have not made a major impact in Britain, despite the fact that immigration and race remain heavily politicised issues. According to

Husbands (1992) such movements have not yet become a major force in British society because of (a) the limited appeal of extreme right, such as the National Front and the British National Party, outside of a few specific localities and (b) the ability of the Conservative Party to maintain the support of voters who may otherwise be attracted to the extreme right. Other researchers have commented on the way in which the electoral system in Britain has made it difficult for small parties to become major political forces at the national level.

Robert Miles (1989) has recently observed it is important to move beyond descriptive accounts of racism to an explanation of the forms that racism actually takes on in contemporary societies. He argues that perhaps what is novel about contemporary forms of racism is not the proliferation of racist social movements but an intensification of ideological and political struggle around the expression of a racism that often claims not to be a racism. It is certainly clear that racism is taking on new forms in the present political environment and there is widespread confusion about the boundaries of national identity, and the role of cultural, religious and linguistic differences. The experience of the former Yugoslavia is a case in point. In the aftermath of the break up of Yugoslavia we have seen not only the development of forms of 'ethnic cleansing' but the articulation of new types of cultural racism based on the construction of fixed religious and cultural boundaries.

This raises the question of what is meant by racism in the context of contemporary British society. This question has been hotly debated in recent years, with some writers arguing that we can no longer use the term racism while others talk of the emergence of more subtle forms of new racism which eschew notions of racial supremacy in favour of the celebration of patriotism and fixed cultural boundaries. Whatever the merits of this argument it is also clear that recent events in a number of European countries have highlighted the persistence of neo-fascist political ideas which are virulently anti-semitic and anti-foreigner. This seems to indicate that it is best to see racism not as a monolithic set of ideas but as an ideology that takes particular forms within given social and political relations.

What is interesting is that, despite the absence of a mass racist political movement, political discussion about immigration and race relations in Britain still has much in common with the more recent debates in the rest of Europe. British immigration policy is increasingly concerned with the twin issues of immigration from Hong Kong and the arrival of asylum seekers and refugees. Despite claims by the government that it is interested in developing a non-racial response to these issues political debates about them remain heavily racialised. What is also interesting is that despite strong pressure for the reform of existing immigration controls the Labour Party has found it difficult to adopt a clear policy on this issue, fearing that it would pay an electoral penalty if it did.

What other recent studies show, however, is that there is no easy model that we can use to explain the power and role of new types of racism in contemporary Europe and elsewhere (Miles, 1989; Goldberg, 1990). We need to be aware that simplistic notions of racism, or notions derived from one specific socio-historical context, cannot be used to explain the growing role of racist ideologies and movements in the new Europe. Part of the problem is that the role of the Front National in France and similar movements in Belgium, Germany, Austria and elsewhere needs to be contextualised against the background of developments in particular national political settings and trends in European societies more generally. Researchers have generally not been good at combining these two levels of analysis and ensuring that they explain as well as describe the development of new forms of racism.

But perhaps the most glaring absence is the lack of serious debate about the best ways to tackle the growth of racism and the articulation of appropriate anti-racist initiatives. This is certainly a difficult aspect of policy in this field, as we can see by the confused and conflicting accounts of anti-racism that are found in current political debates in Britain. In the present political context it is impossible to ignore the urgent need for measures to tackle the growth of racism, and the need to develop initiatives to challenge the influence of the visions articulated by racist movements and parties.

What kind of future?

The subject matter of this book represents one of the most controversial and volatile questions in contemporary British politics. Indeed, it is clear from the analysis of trends in the period covered in this book that race is a divisive issue at all levels of British society and is likely to remain so in the future. This makes it all the more important that the history of these decades is analysed fully and any lessons for the future are learned quickly.

The failure so far to tackle the roots of racism and racial inequality means that it is difficult to be optimistic about the likely future of racial relations. The need for urgent political action on this issue is clear, but there is no commonly accepted political basis for such action. Indeed, in the 1980s and early 1990s the most notable features of governmental policy have been the further institutionalisation of immigration controls and a complete failure to promote positive measures to overcome racial inequality and injustice. The political climate generated by the Conservative administrations since 1979 is such that it is difficult to imagine a fundamental change in political priorities and policy change in this area in the medium term (Gamble, 1988). Certainly there are no signs that the present administration will radically change the policy stance of the previous two.

At the same time the Labour Party and the other opposition parties do not seem able to offer a coherent radical alternative to the policies pursued by successive governments since 1950. Indeed the growing influence of the new right and the public attention given to the loony left and the anti-racist lobby has resulted in attempts by the Labour Party to distance itself from the actions of many Labour-controlled local authorities and to reduce the identification of the party with minority causes.

Within the context of the present political climate, therefore, the prospects of a radical reorientation of policies remain slim. The outbreaks of urban unrest during the 1980s resulted in a short-lived flurry of activity, but this did little to tackle the broader context of racial inequality and urban neglect. The election of four black MPs in 1987, and a further two in 1992, may have a bearing on the nature of the parliamentary politics of race. But on current evidence their influence is likely to remain marginal and limited. In the longer term increasing black political involvement and political representation, and alliances with other political forces, may help to fundamentally transform the terms of political debate about racial inequality in British society.

It is all the more important in this situation for those interested in tackling the roots of racism and racial inequality in British society to look more deeply into the questions discussed in this book. The lessons of the four decades between 1950 and 1990 need to be learned and internalised if we are to move towards a more just and egalitarian society, one in which racism does not structure the life chances of Britain's black citizens. If this book has raised a few issues for further thought and debate on this question it will have achieved its task.

Guide to Further Reading

The object of this guide is to point to specific works of relevance to the subjects covered in each chapter. It is not intended as an exhaustive literature review, although the references in the Bibliography provide an overview of the literature in the areas covered by this book. The object rather is to suggest works which give an up-to-date view of a specific topic and which allow you to come to terms with divergent perspectives. You may also find it useful to have a look at issues of the journals *Ethnic and Racial Studies*, *Equal Opportunities Review*, *Immigrants and Minorities*, *New Community*, *Patterns of Prejudice*, *Race and Class*, and *Sage Race Relations Abstracts*. The Runnymede Trust publishes a monthly bulletin called *The Runnymede Bulletin*, which provides detailed coverage of current issues in this field.

Chapter 1

The literature on this area is vast. A useful overview of divergent theoretical perspectives is contained in J. Rex and D. Mason (eds) (1986). Other important texts are M. Banton (1987), P. Gilroy (1987), R. Miles (1989), J. Rex (1983). For more recent debates see D. T. Goldberg (ed.) (1990).

A useful review of recent American debates can be found in M. Omi and H. Winant (1986). Other useful American studies are M. Marable (1985) and W. J. Wilson (1980 and 1988).

Chapter 2

On the history of race and immigration in British society the best starting point is C. Holmes (1988). Two important collections of original papers are to be found in C. Holmes (ed.) (1978) and K. Lunn (ed.) (1980). On the history of Irish immigration and attitudes towards the Irish see R. Swift and S. Gilley (eds) (1985) and L. P. Curtis (1968). On the politics of Jewish immigration see B. Gainer (1972) and L. P. Gartner (1973). P. Fryer (1984) takes a historical view of the black presence in British society, and two other sources on this subject are R. Ramdin (1987) and P. Rich (1986).

Chapter 3

There are no up-to-date studies of the politics of immigration since 1945. Two studies worth looking at are G. Freeman (1979) and Z. Layton-Henry (1984) though they are limited in their coverage. Other studies widely referred to are: P. Foot (1965), R. Miles and A. Phizacklea (1984) and A. Sivanandan (1982). The socio-legal context is covered fully in I. A. Macdonald (1983).

Chapter 4

This field is relatively neglected, though it has recently begun to attract more interest. An interesting overview of the early history of legislation on this issue can be found in A. Lester and G. Bindman (1972), while the papers in S. Abbott (ed.) (1971) look at various aspects of race relations policies during the 1960s. On the legal context since the passage of the 1976 Race Relations Act see the divergent perspectives of L. Lustgarten (1980), C. McCrudden (1982) and C. McCrudden *et al.* (1991). On the political and social context see: N. Glazer and K. Young (eds) (1983), R. Hepple (1983) and R. Jenkins and J. Solomos (eds) (1989).

Chapter 5

A number of recent books have looked at various aspects of the local politics of race, the most important being W. Ball and J. Solomos (eds) (1990) and G. Ben-Tovim *et al.* (1986). More specific case studies can be found in F. Reeves (1989) and S. Saggar (1991). A pioneering work in this area was J. Rex and R. Moore (1967). For more recent trends and a comparative perspective see M. Cross and M. Keith (eds) (1993).

Chapter 6

Because of recurrent controversies about relations between black communities and the police there is a large literature on this subject. Good starting points for recent developments are R. Reiner (1985) and D. Smith and J. Gray (1987). Other important studies are: S. Hall *et al.* (1978) and D. Humphry (1972). On the history of police relations with young blacks see J. Solomos (1988). On the politics of urban unrest see: Scarman (1981) J. Benyon (ed.) (1984) J. Benyon and J. Solomos (eds) (1987) and M. Keith (1993).

Chapter 7

The experience of urban unrest and social change during the 1980s has led to a growing interest in the politics of protest and violent unrest. For an up-to-date review of some of the main issues see the papers in J. Benyon and J. Solomos (eds) (1987). For other perspectives see: M. Kettle and L. Hodges (1982) and H. Joshua and T. Wallace (1983). A discussion of some of the major problems in some popular discussions of urban unrest can be found in M. Keith (1993).

Chapter 8

Much of the literature on this general area is fairly limited in scope. It remains a relatively neglected topic. A good starting point for the theoretical aspect of this question is R. Miles (1989). Useful attempts to look at the changing political language about race and nation are to be found in G. Seidel (1986) and P. Gordon and F. Klug (1986). On the politics of the extreme right see the papers in R. Miles and A. Phizacklea (eds) (1979) and the study by C. Husbands (1983). For a selection of new-right perspectives on these issues see F. Palmer (ed.) (1986). You may also find it useful to look at copies of the journal *Searchlight*, which covers the activities of neo-fascist and extreme right wing groups.

Chapter 9

Due to the relative neglect of this question there is no detailed up-to-date study of all the dimensions of the question. An early attempt to argue that this dimension had been neglected in traditional studies of the subject was CCCS Race and Politics Group (1982). Useful studies of aspects of Afro-Caribbean and Asian political mobilisation can be found in: D. Pearson (1981); M. Fitzgerald (1987) and T. Carter (1986). Recent developments are examined in J. Solomos and L. Back (1991) and L. Back and J. Solomos (1992a and 1992b). Another useful collection is W. James and C. Harris (eds) (1993).

Chapter 10

The best overview of the issues covered in this chapter can be found in the papers in J. Donald and A. Rattansi (eds) (1992). See also F. Anthias and N. Yuval-Davis (1992) L. Appignanesi and S. Maitland (eds) (1989) T. Asad (1990a and 1990b) and W. James (1992). For a more theoretical and comparative perspective see the papers in D. T. Goldberg (ed.) (1990). On the role of the media see T. A. van Dijk (1991).

Chapter 11

The best starting point for the issues discussed in this chapter are the overviews provided by P. Gilroy (1990b) and J. Solomos (1991). For useful American comparisons take a look at M. Marable (1985) and W. J. Wilson (1988).

Bibliography

Abbott, S. (ed.) (1971) *The Prevention of Racial Discrimination in Britain* (London: Oxford University Press).

AFFOR (1978) *Talking Blues* (Birmingham: AFFOR).

Ahmed, A. S. (1992) *Postmodernism and Islam* (London: Routledge).

Akhtar, S. (1989) *Be Careful With Muhammad! The Salman Rushdie Affair* (London: Bellew Publishing).

Alderman, G. (1983) *The Jewish Community in British Politics* (Oxford: Clarendon Press).

Alderson, J. and Stead, P. (1973) *The Police We Deserve* (London: Wolf).

Alford, R. and Friedland, R. (1985) *Powers of Theory: Capitalism, the State and Democracy* (Cambridge: Cambridge University Press).

Amin, K. and Richardson, R. (1992) *Politics for All: Equality, Culture and the General Election 1992* (London: Runnymede Trust).

Anthias, F. (1990) 'Race and class revisited – conceptualizing race and racism', *Sociological Review*, 38, 1: 19–42.

—— (1992) 'Connecting "race" and ethnic phenomena' *Sociology* 26, 3: 421–38.

Anthias, F. and Yuval-Davis, N. (1992) *Racialized Boundaries: race, nation, gender, colour and class and the anti-racist struggle* (London: Routledge).

Anwar, M. (1986) *Race and Politics* (London: Tavistock).

Appignanesi, L. and Maitland, S. (ed.) (1989) *The Rushdie File* (London: Fourth Estate).

Applebey, G. and Ellis, E. (1984) 'Formal Investigations: the Commission for Racial Equality and the Equal Opportunities Commission as law enforcement agencies' *Public Law* Spring: 58–81.

Asad, T. (1990a) 'Multiculturalism and British Identity in the Wake of the Rushdie Affair', *Politics and Society*, 18, 4: 455–80.

—— (1990b) 'Ethnography, Literature, and Politics: Some Readings and Uses of Salman Rushdie's *The Satanic Verses*', *Cultural Anthropology*, 5, 3: 239–69.

Back, L. (1991) 'Youth, Racism and Ethnicity in South London', PhD thesis, Goldsmiths' College, University of London.

—— (forthcoming) 'Race, Identity and Nation within an Adolescent Community in South London' *New Community*.

Back, L. and Solomos, J. (1992a) 'Who Represents Us? Racialised Politics and Candidate Selection', *Research Papers No 3* (Department of Politics and Sociology, Birkbeck College).

—— (1992b) 'Doing Research, Writing Politics: the dilemmas of political intervention in research on racism', unpublished paper.

—— (1992c) 'Black politics and social change in Birmingham, UK: an analysis of recent trends', *Ethnic and Racial Studies*, 15, 3: 327–51.

Baldwin-Edwards, M. (1991) 'Immigration after 1992', *Policy and Politics*, 19, 3: 199–211.

Balibar, E. (1991) 'Es Gibt Keinen Staat in Europa: Racism and Politics in Europe Today', *New Left Review*, 186: 5–19.

Balibar E. and Wallerstein, I. (1991) *Race, Nation, Class* (London: Verso).

Ball, W. and Solomos, J. (eds) (1990) *Race and Local Politics* (London: Macmillan).

Ballis Lal, B. (1990) *The Romance of Culture in an Urban Civilisation* (London: Routledge).

Banton, M. (1955) *The Coloured Quarter: Negro Immigrants in an English City* (London: Jonathan Cape).

—— (1959) *White and Coloured* (London: Jonathan Cape).

—— (1967) *Race Relations* (London: Tavistock).

—— (1983) *Racial and Ethnic Competition* (Cambridge University Press).

—— (1985) *Promoting Racial Harmony* (Cambridge: Cambridge University Press).

—— (1987) *Racial Theories* (Cambridge University Press).

—— (1989) 'Minority Rights and Individual Rights', paper presented to CRE–PSI Seminar on Freedom of Speech, 28 September 1989.

—— (1991) 'The Race Relations Problematic' *British Journal of Sociology*, 42, 1: 115–30.

—— (1992) 'The Nature and Causes of Racism and Racial Discrimination' *International Sociology* 7, 1: 69–84.

Barkan, E. (1992) *The retreat of scientific racism* (Cambridge University Press).

Barker, M. (1981) *The New Racism* (London: Junction Books).

Baubock, R. (1991) *Immigration and the Boundaries of Citizenship* (Centre for Research in Ethnic Relations, University of Warwick, Monographs in Ethnic relations, No 4).

Beetham, D. (1970) *Transport and Turbans* (London: Oxford University Press).

Benedict, R. (1943) *Race and Racism* (London: Routledge).

Ben-Tovim, G. and Gabriel, J. (1979) 'The politics of race in Britain: a review of the major trends and of the recent literature', *Sage Race Relations Abstracts*, 4, 4: 1–56.

Ben-Tovim, G., Gabriel, J., Law, I. and Stredder, K. (1986) *The Local Politics of Race* (London: Macmillan).

Benyon, J. (1986), 'A Tale of Failure: Race and Policing', *Policy Papers in Ethnic Relations No. 3* (University of Warwick, Centre for Research in Ethnic Relations).

Benyon, J. (ed.) (1984) *Scarman and After* (Oxford: Pergamon Press).

Benyon, J. and Solomos, J. (eds) (1987) *The Roots of Urban Unrest* (Oxford: Pergamon Press).

Berghahn, M. (1984) *German-Jewish Refugees in England* (London: Macmillan).

Berghe, P. L. van den (1967) *Race and Racism* (New York: Wiley).

Berkeley, H. (1977) *The Odyssey of Enoch* (London: Hamish Hamilton).

Bevan, V. (1986) *The Development of British Immigration Law* (London: Croom Helm).

Bhabha, H. K. (1990) 'Interrogating Identity: The Postcolonial Prerogative', in D. T. Goldberg (ed.) *Anatomy of Racism* (Minneapolis: University of Minnesota Press).

Bhabha, H. K. (ed.) (1990) *Nation and Narration* (London: Routledge).

Bhachu, P. (1991) 'Culture, Ethnicity and Class Amongst Punjabi Sikh Women in 1990s Britain', *New Community*, 17, 3: 401–412.

Billig, M. (1978) *Fascists: a social psychological view of the National Front* (London: Academic Press).

Billig, M. and Bell, A. (1980) 'Fascist Parties in Post-War Britain', *Sage Race Relations Abstracts*, 5, 1: 1–30.

Bindman, G. (1980) 'The law, equal opportunity and affirmative action', *New Community* VIII, 3: 248–60.

Bovenkerk, F., Miles, R. and Verbunt, G. (1990) 'Racism, migration and the state in Western Europe. A case for comparative analysis', *International Sociology* 5, 4: 475–490.

Bowles, S. and Gintis, H. (1987) *Democracy and Capitalism* (London: Routledge and Kegan Paul).

Bozzoli, B. (ed.) (1987) *Class, Community and Conflict* (Johannesburg: Ravan).

Brah, A. (1992) 'Difference, diversity and differentiation', in J. Donald and A. Rattansi (eds), *'Race', Culture & Difference* (London: Sage).

Brown, C. (1984) *Black and White Britain* (London: Heinemann).

—— (1992) '"Same difference": the persistence of racial disadvantage in the British employment market' in P. Braham, A. Rattansi and R. Skellington (eds) *Racism and Antiracism: Inequalities, Opportunities and Policies* (London: Sage).

Brown, C. and Gay, P. (1985) *Racial Discrimination: 17 Years After the Act* (London: Policy Studies Institute).

Brown, J. (1977) *Shades of Grey* (Cransfield: Cransfield Police Studies).

Browning, R. P., Marshall, D. P. and Tabb, D. H. (1984) *Protest is Not Enough* (Berkeley: University of California Press).

Brubaker, W. R. (1990) 'Immigration, Citizenship, and the Nation-State in France and Germany: A Comparative Historical Analysis', *International Sociology*, 5, 4: 461–74.

Burgess, J. R. (1985) 'News from nowhere: the press, the riots and the myth of the inner city', in J. R. Burgess and J. R. Gold (eds), *Geography, the Media and Popular Culture* (London: Croom Helm).

Burleigh, M. and Wippermann, W. (1991) *The Racial State: Germany 1933–1945* (Cambridge University Press.

Butler, Lord (1971) *The Art of the Possible* (Harmondsworth: Penguin).

Cain, M. (1973) *Society and the Policeman's Role* (London: Routledge and Kegan Paul).

Cambridge, A. X. and Feuchtwang, S. (eds) (1990) *Antiracist Strategies* (Aldershot: Avebury).

Carr, J. (1987) *New Roads to Equality: Contract Compliance for the UK?*, Fabian Tract 517 (London: Fabian Society).

Carter, B., Harris, C. and Joshi, S. (1987) 'The 1951–55 Conservative government and the racialisation of black immigration', *Policy Papers in*

Ethnic Relations No. 11 (University of Warwick, Centre for Research in Ethnic Relations).

Carter, T. (1986) *Shattering Illusions* (London: Lawrence and Wishart).

Casey, J. (1982) 'One nation: the politics of race', *The Salisbury Review*, Autumn: 23–8.

Cashmore, E. (1987) *The Logic of Racism* (London: Allen and Unwin).

Castles, S. (1993) 'Migrations and Minorities in Europe. Perspectives for the 1990s: Eleven Hypotheses', in J. Wrench and J. Solomos (eds) *Racism and Migration in Western Europe*, (Oxford: Berg Publishers).

Castles, S. with Booth, H. and Wallace, T. (1984) *Here for Good: Western Europe's new ethnic minorities* (London: Pluto Press).

Castles, S. and Kosack, G. (1985) *Immigrant Workers and Class Structure in Western Europe*, (London: Oxford University Press).

Castles, S. and Miller, M.J. (1993) *The Age of Migration* (London: Macmillan).

CCCS Race and Politics Group (1982) *The Empire Strikes Back: race and racism in 70s Britain* (London: Hutchinson).

Chambers, I. (1989) 'Narratives of Nationalism: Being British', *New Formations* 7: 88–103.

Cheetham, J. (1988) 'Ethnic Associations in Britain', in S. Jenkins (ed.), *Ethnic Associations and the Welfare State* (New York: Columbia University Press).

Clare, J. (1985) 'Time to dust off the Scarman report', *The Listener*, 3 October: 6–7.

Clarke, C. F. D. (1970) *Police/Community Relations: Report of a Conference at Ditchley Park*, May-June, Ditchley Foundation.

Coates, D. (1984) *The Context of British Politics* (London: Hutchinson).

Cohen, P. (1988) 'The Perversions of Inheritance: Studies in the Making of Multi-Racist Britain', in P. Cohen and H. Bains (eds), *Multi-Racist Britain* (London: Macmillan).

Cohen, R. (1991) 'East–West and European migration in a global context', *New Community*, 18, 1: 9–26.

Colley, L. (1992) *Britons: Forging the Nation 1707–1837* (New Haven and London: Yale University Press).

Collins, P. H. (1990) *Black Feminist Thought* (Boston: Unwin Hyman).

Colls, R. and Dodd, P. (eds) (1986) *Englishness: Politics and Culture 1880–1920* (London: Croom Helm).

Commission for Racial Equality (CRE) (1977–) *Annual Reports* (London: Commission for Racial Equality).

—— (1983) *The Race Relations Act 1976 – Time for a Change?* (London: Commission for Racial Equality).

—— (1985a) *Review of the Race Relations Act 1976: Proposals for Change* (London: Commission for Racial Equality).

—— (1985b) *Immigration Control Procedures: Report of a Formal Investigation* (London: Commission for Racial Equality).

—— (1985c) *Positive Action and Equal Opportunity in Employment* (London: Commission for Racial Equality).

—— (1987a) *Training: The implementation of equal opportunities at work*, London: Commission for Racial Equality).

—— (1987b) *Principles of practice for contract compliance*, London: Commission for Racial Equality).

—— (1990) *Free Speech: Report of a Seminar* (London: Commission for Racial Equality).

—— (1991) *Second Review of the Race Relations Act 1976* (London: Commission for Racial Equality).

Cox, O.C. (1948) *Caste, Class and Race* (New York: Monthly Review Press).

Crewe, I. (1983) 'Representation and the Ethnic Minorities in Britain', in N. Glazer and K. Young (eds) *Ethnic Pluralism and Public Policy* (London: Heinemann).

Crick, B. (ed.) (1991) *National identities* (Oxford: Blackwell).

Cross, M. and Keith, M. (eds) (1993) *Racism, the City and the State* (London: Routledge).

Cross, M. and Smith, D.I. (eds) (1987) *Black Youth Futures* (Leicester: National Youth Bureau).

Crossman, R. (1975) *Diaries of a Cabinet Minister*, Volume 1 (London: Hamish Hamilton).

Curtis, L.P. (1968) *Anglo-Saxons and Celts* (Connecticut: University of Bridgeport).

—— (1971) *Apes and Angels: The Irishman in Victorian Caricature* (Washington: Smithsonian Institution Press).

Curtis, L. (1984) *Nothing But the Same Old Story* (London: Information on Ireland).

Dangerfield, G. (1976) *The Damnable Question: A Study of Anglo-Irish Relations* (Boston: Little, Brown).

Daniel, W.W. (1968) *Racial Disadvantage in England* (Harmondsworth: Penguin).

Deakin, N. (1965) *Colour and the British Electorate* (London: Pall Mall Press).

—— (1968) 'The Politics of the Commonwealth Immigrants Bill', *Political Quarterly*, 39, 1: 24–45.

—— (1970) *Colour, Citizenship and British Society* (London: Panther).

—— (1972) 'The Immigration Issue in British Politics', Unpublished PhD thesis, University of Sussex.

Dean, D. (1987) 'Coping with Colonial Immigration, the Cold War and Colonial Policy', *Immigrants and Minorities*, 6, 3: 305–34.

Dear, G. (1985) *Handsworth/Lozells, September 1985: Report of the Chief Constable, West Midlands Police* (Birmingham: West Midlands Police).

Dearlove, J. (1973) *The Politics of Policy in Local Government* (Cambridge University Press).

—— (1982) 'The Political Science of British Politics', *Parliamentary Affairs*, 35: 436–454.

Dearlove, J. and Saunders, P. (1984) *Introduction to British Politics* (Cambridge: Polity).

Deedes, W. (1968) *Race Without Rancour* (London: Conservative Political Centre).

Demuth, C. (1978) *'Sus': A Report on the Vagrancy Act* (London: Runnymede Trust).

DO 35/5219 (1957) 'Commonwealth Immigration: Social and Economic Problems' (London: Public Record Office).

Donald, J. and Rattansi, A. (eds) (1992) *'Race' Culture & Difference* (London: Sage).

Drake, St Clair (1954) 'Value systems, Social Structures and Race Relations in the British Isles', unpublished PhD Thesis, University of Chicago.

Dummett, A. and Nicol, A. (1990) *Subjects, Citizens, Aliens and Others: Nationality and Immigration Law* (London: Weidenfeld and Nicolson).

Dunleavy, P. (1980) *Urban Political Analysis* (London: Macmillan).

Dunleavy, P. and O'Leary, B. (1987) *Theories of the State* (Basingstoke: Macmillan).

Eade, J. (1989) *The Politics of Community* (Aldershot: Avebury).

Edelman, M. (1971) *Politics as Symbolic Action: Mass Arousal and Quiescence* (Chicago: Markham).

—— (1977) *Political Language: Words that Succeed and Policies that Fail* (New York: Academic Press).

—— (1985), 'Political Language and Political Reality', *PS*, XVIII, 1: 10–19.

Edgar, D. (1977) 'Racism, Fascism and the Politics of the National Front', *Race and Class*, 19, 2: 111–131.

Edwards, J. and Batley, R. (1978) *The Politics of Positive Discrimination* (London: Tavistock).

Elton, Lord (1965) *The Unarmed Invasion* (London: Godfrey Bles).

Essed, P. (1984) *Alledaags Racisme* (Amsterdam) (English translation: *Everyday Racism*, (Claremont: Hunter House, 1990).

—— (1987) 'Academic Racism Common Sense in the Social Sciences', Working Paper No.5, Amsterdam Centre for Race and Ethnic Studies.

—— (1991) *Understanding Everyday Racism* (Newbury Park CA: Sage).

Evans, J. M. (1983) *Immigration Law* (London: Sweet and Maxwell).

Evans, N. (1980) 'The South Wales Race Riots of 1919', *Llafur* 3, 1: 5–29.

—— (1985) 'Regulating the Reserve Army: Arabs, Blacks and the Local State in Cardiff, 1919–45', in K. Lunn (ed.) *Race and Labour in Twentieth Century Britain* (London: Frank Cass).

Evans, P. B., Rueschemeyer, D. and Skocpol, T. (1985) *Bringing the State Back In* (Cambridge University Press).

Feuchtwang, S. (1990) 'Racism: territoriality and ethnocentricity', in A. X. Cambridge and S. Feuchtwang (eds), *Antiracist Strategies* (Aldershot: Avebury).

Fielding, N. (1981) *The National Front* (London: Routledge).

Fitzgerald, M. (1984) *Political Parties and Black People* (London: Runnymede Trust).

—— (1987) *Black People and Party Politics in Britain* (London: Runnymede Trust).

Fitzgerald, M. and Layton-Henry, Z. (1986) 'Opposition Parties and Race Policies: 1979–83', in Z. Layton-Henry and P. Rich (eds), *Race, Government and Politics in Britain* (London: Macmillan).

Flett, H. (1981) 'The Politics of Dispersal in Birmingham', *Working Paper on Ethnic Relations* No. 14, (Centre for Research in Ethnic Relations, University of Warwick).

Flew, A. (1984) *Education, Race and Revolution* (London: Centre for Policy Studies).

Fogelson, R. M. (1971) *Violence as Protest* (Garden City, NY: Anchor Books).

Foot, P. (1965) *Immigration and Race in British Politics* (Harmondsworth: Penguin).

Forbes, I. and Mead, G. (1992) *Measure for Measure: A Comparative Analysis of Measures to Combat Racial Discrimination in the Member Countries of the European Community* (London: Department of Employment).

Fredrickson, G. M. (1981) *White Supremacy: A Comparative Study of American and South African History* (Oxford University Press).

Freeman, G. (1979) *Immigrant Labor and Racial Conflict in Industrial Societies* (Princeton University Press).

Freeman, M. D. A. and Spencer, S. (1979) 'Immigration control, black workers and the economy' *British Journal of Law and Society*, 6, 1: 53–81.

Fryer, P. (1984) *Staying Power: The History of Black People in Britain* (London: Pluto Press).

Gaffney, J. (1987) 'Interpretations of Violence: The Handsworth Riots of 1985', *Policy Papers in Ethnic Relations No. 10* (University of Warwick, Centre for Research in Ethnic Relations).

Gainer, B. (1972) *The Alien Invasion: the origins of the Aliens Act of 1905* (London: Heinemann).

Gallagher, T. (1985) 'A Tale of Two Cities: Communal Strife in Glasgow and Liverpool Before 1914', in R. Swift and S. Gilley (eds), *The Irish in the Victorian City* (London: Croom Helm).

Gamble, A. (1981) *Britain in Decline* (London: Macmillan).

—— (1988) *The Free Economy and the Strong State* (London: Macmillan).

Garrard, J. A. (1971) *The English and Immigration 1880–1914* (London: Oxford University Press).

Gartner, L. P. (1973) *The Jewish Immigrant in England 1870–1914* (London: Simon Publications).

Gates, H. L. (1988) *The Signifying Monkey* (New York: Oxford University Press).

—— (ed.) (1986) '*Race', Writing and Difference* (University of Chicago Press).

Gay, P. and Young, K. (1988) *Community Relations Councils* (London: CRE).

Gifford, Lord (1986) *The Broadwater Farm Inquiry* (London: Karia Press).

Gilley, S. (1978) 'English Attitudes to the Irish in England 1789–1900', in C. Holmes (ed.), *Immigrants and Minorities in British Society* (London: Allen and Unwin).

—— (1980) 'Catholics and Socialists in Glasgow, 1906–1912' in K. Lunn (ed.) *Hosts, Immigrants and Minorities* (Folkestone: Dawson).

Gilroy, P. (1987) *There Ain't No Black in the Union Jack* (London: Hutchinson).

—— (1990a) 'One Nation Under a Groove: The Cultural Politics of "Race" and Racism in Britain', in D. T. Goldberg (ed.) *Anatomy of Racism* (Minneapolis: University of Minnesota Press).

—— (1990b) 'The End of Anti-Racism' in W. Ball and J. Solomos (eds) *Race and Local Politics* (London: Macmillan).

—— (1991) 'It Ain't Where You're From, It's Where You're At . . . The Dialectics of Diasporic Identification', *Third Text*, 13: 3–16.

Glass, R. (1960) *Newcomers: West Indians in London* (London: Allen and Unwin).

Glazer, N. and Young, K. (eds) (1983) *Ethnic Pluralism and Public Policy* (London: Heinemann).

Goldberg, D. T. (1990) 'The Social Formation of Racist Discourse', in D. T. Goldberg (ed.) *Anatomy of Racism*, (Minneapolis: University of Minnesota Press).

—— (1992) 'The semantics of race', *Ethnic and Racial Studies*, 15, 4: 543–569.

Goldberg, D. T. (ed.) (1990) *Anatomy of Racism* (Minneapolis: University of Minnesota Press).

Gordon, P. (1982) 'Racial Discrimination: towards a legal strategy,' *British Journal of Law and Society*, 9, 1: 127–35.

—— (1985) *Policing Immigration: Britain's Internal Controls* (London: Pluto).

—— (1986) *Racial Violence and Harassment* (London: Runnymede Trust).

—— (1989a) *Fortress Europe? The Meaning of 1992* (London: Runnymede Trust).

—— (1989b) *Citizenship for Some? Race and government policy 1979–1989* (London: Runnymede Trust).

—— (1990) 'A Dirty War: The New Right and Local Authority Anti-Racism', in W. Ball and J. Solomos (eds) *Race and Local Politics* (London: Macmillan).

Gordon, P. and Klug, F. (1986) *New Right/New Racism* (London: Searchlight).

Goulbourne, H. (1987) 'West Indian Groups and British Politics', paper presented at Conference on Black People and British Politics (University of Warwick, November 1987).

—— (1991) *Ethnicity and nationalism in post-imperial Britain* (Cambridge University Press).

Goulbourne, H. (ed.) (1990) *Black Politics in Britain* (Aldershot: Avebury).

Greater London Council (1984) *Racial Harassment in London* (Greater London Council).

Greenberg, S. B. (1980) *Race and State in Capitalist Development* (New Haven: Yale University Press).

Gregory, D. and Urry, J. (eds) (1985) *Social Relations and Spatial Structures* (London: Macmillan).

Grewal, S., Kay, J., Landor, L., Lewis, G. and Parmar, P. (1989) *Charting The Journey* (London: Sheba).

Griffiths, P. (1966) *A Question of Colour* (London: Leslie Frewin).

Grossberg, L., Nelson, C. and Treichler, C. (eds) (1992) *Cultural Studies* (London: Routledge).

Guillaumin, C. (1980) 'The idea of race and its elevation to autonomous scientific and legal status', in UNESCO, *Sociological Theories: Race and Colonialism* (Paris: UNESCO).

Gurnah, A. (1984) 'The politics of Racism Awareness Training', *Critical Social Policy*, 11: 6–20.

Hall, S. (1977) 'Pluralism, race and class in Caribbean society', in UNESCO, *Race and class in post-colonial society* (Paris: UNESCO).

—— (1980) 'Race, Articulation and Societies Structured in Dominance', in UNESCO (ed.) *Sociology Theories: Race and Colonialism* (Paris: UNESCO).

—— (1985a) 'Gramsci's Relevance to the Analysis of Racism and Ethnicity' (unpublished paper).

—— (1985b) 'The gulf between Labour and Blacks' *The Guardian* 15 June 1985.

—— (1987) 'Urban unrest in Britain', in J. Benyon and J. Solomos (eds) *The Roots of Urban Unrest* (Oxford: Pergamon Press).

—— (1991a) 'Old and New identities, Old and New Ethnicities', in A. D. King (ed.) *Culture, Globalization and the World System* (London: Macmillan).

—— (1991b) 'The Local and the Global: Globalization and Ethnicity', in A. D. King (ed.), *Culture, Globalization and the World System* (London: Macmillan).

Hall, S., Critcher, C., Jefferson, T., Clarke, J. and Roberts, B. (1978) *Policing the Crisis: Mugging, the State, and Law and Order* (London: Macmillan).

Hall, W. (1986) 'Contracts compliance at the GLC', *Local Government Studies*, 12, 4: 17–24.

Halstead, M. (1988) *Education, Justice and Cultural Diversity: An Examination of the Honeyford Affair* (London: Falmer Press).

Hammar, T. (ed.) (1985) *European Immigration Policy: A Comparative Study* (Cambridge University Press).

Hammar, T. (1990) *Democracy and the Nation State, Aliens, denizens and citizens in a world of international migration* (Aldershot: Avebury).

Harris, C. (1988) 'Images of Blacks in Britain: 1930–60', in S. Allen and M. Macey (eds), *Race and Social Policy* (London: Economic and Social Research Council).

Hartley-Brewer, M. (1965) 'Smethwick', in N. Deakin (ed.) *Colour and the British Electorate 1964* (London: Pall Mall Press).

Harvey, D. (1989) *The Condition of Postmodernity* (Oxford: Blackwell).

Hechter, M. (1975) *Internal Colonialism* (London: Routledge).

Heineman, B. (1972) *The Politics of the Powerless: A Study of the Campaign Against Racial Discrimination* (London: Oxford University Press).

Henderson, J. and Karn, V. (1987) *Race, Class and State Housing* (Aldershot: Gower).

Hepple, R. (1968) *Race, Jobs and the Law in Britain* (Harmondsworth: Penguin).

—— (1983) 'Judging Equal Rights', *Critical Legal Problems* 36: 71–90.

Higgins, J., Deakin, N., Edwards, J. and Wicks, M. (1983) *Government and Urban Poverty* (Oxford: Basil Blackwell).

Hill, M. and Issacharoff, R. (1971) *Community Action and Race Relations* (London: Oxford University Press).

Hirschfeld, G. (1984) *Exile in Great Britain: Refugees From Hitler's Germany* (Leamington Spa: Berg).

Hirst, P. (1985) *Marxism and Historical Writing* (London: Routledge).

Hobsbawm, E. (1990) *Nations and Nationalism Since 1780: Programme, Myth, Reality* (Cambridge University Press).

Holmes, C. (1978) *Immigrants and Minorities in British Society* (London: George Allen and Unwin).

—— (1979) *Anti-Semitism in British Society 1876–1939* (London: Edward Arnold).

—— (1988) *John Bull's Island* (Basingstoke: Macmillan).

Home Affairs Committee, Sub-Committee on Race Relations and Immigration (1981a) *Racial Disadvantage* (London: HMSO).

—— (1981b) *Commission for Racial Equality* (London: HMSO).

Home Office. (1973) *Police/Immigrant Relations in England and Wales* (London: HMSO).

—— (1975) *Racial Discrimination* Cmnd 6234 (London: HMSO).

—— (1977) *A Guide to the Race Relations Act 1976* (London: Home Office).

—— (1981) *Racial Attacks* (London: Home Office).

Honeyford, R. (1983) 'Multi-ethnic intolerance', *Salisbury Review*, 4: 12–13.

—— (1984) 'Education and race: an alternative view'. *Salisbury Review* 6: 30–2.

—— (1988a) *Multi-Ethnic Education: the Burnage High School Lesson* (York: Campaign for Real Education).

—— (1988b) *Integration or Disintegration. Towards a Non-Racist Society* (London: Claridge Press).

hooks, b. (1981) *Ain't I A Woman: Black Women and Feminism* (Boston: South End Press).

—— (1990) *Yearning: Race, Gender, and Cultural Politics* (Boston: South End Press).

—— (1992) *Black Looks: Race and Representation* (London: Turnaround).

Howe, D. (1973) Fighting back: West Indian youth and the police in Notting Hill', *Race Today*, December: 333–6.

Howe, S. and Upshal, D. (1988) 'New Black Power Lines', *New Statesman & Society*, 15 July, 1988.

Hubbuck, J. and Carter, S. (1980) *Half a Chance? A Report on Job Discrimination Against Young Blacks in Nottingham* (London: Commission for Racial Equality).

Humphry, D. (1972) *Police Power and Black People* (London: Panther).

Husbands, C. (1983) *Racial Exclusionism and the City* (London: Allen and Unwin).

—— (1991) 'The mainstream right and the politics of immigration in France: major developments in the 1980s', *Ethnic and Racial Studies*, 14, 2: 170–198.

—— (1992) 'Why has there been no extreme right in Great Britain', *LSE Magazine*, Spring 1992: 4–8.

Huxley, E. (1964) *Back Street New Worlds* (London: Chatto and Windus).

Institute of Personnel Management (1987) *Contract Compliance: The UK Experience* (London: IPM).

Institute of Race Relations, *Newsletter*, 1960–69.

Jackson, J. A. (1963) *The Irish in Britain* (London: Routledge).

Jacobs, B. (1986) *Black Politics and Urban Crisis in Britain* (Cambridge University Press).

James, W. (1992) 'Migration, Racism and identity: The Caribbean Experience in Britain', *New Left Review*, 193: 15–55.

James, W. and Harris, C. (eds) (1993) *Inside Babylon: The Caribbean Diaspora in Britain* (London: Verso).

JanMohamed, A. R. and Lloyd, D. (eds) (1990) *The Nature and Context of Minority Discourse* (New York: Oxford University Press).

Jeffers, S. (1991) 'Black Sections in the Labour Party: the end of ethnicity and "godfather" politics?', in P. Werbner and M. Anwar (eds), *Black and Ethnic Leaderships in Britain* (London: Routledge).

Jenkins, R. and Solomos, J. (eds) (1989) *Racism and Equal Opportunity Policies in the 1980s*, 2nd Edition (Cambridge University Press).

Jenkins, Robin (1971) 'The Production of Knowledge in the Institute of Race Relations' (unpublished paper).

Jenkinson, J. (1985) 'The Glasgow Race Disturbances of 1919', in K. Lunn (ed.) *Hosts, Immigrants and Minorities* (Folkestone: Dawson).

Jessop, B. (1982) *The Capitalist State* (Oxford: Martin Robertson).

John, G. (1970) *Race in the Inner City: A Report from Handsworth* (London: Runnymede Trust).

Joshi, S. and Carter, B. (1984) 'The role of Labour in the creation of a racist Britain', *Race and Class*, XXV, 3: 53–70.

Joshua, H. and Wallace, T. (1983) *To Ride the Storm: the 1980 Bristol 'Riot' and the State* (London: Heinemann).

Katz, J. (1978) *White Awareness* (Norman: University of Oklahoma Press).

Katznelson, I. (1976) *Black Men, White Cities* (University of Chicago Press).

—— (1982) *City Trenches* (University of Chicago Press).

—— (1986) 'Rethinking the silences of social and economic policy', *Political Science Quarterly* 101, 2: 307–25..

Katznelson, I. and Weir, M. (1985) *Schooling for All* (New York: Basic Books).

Kay, D. and Miles, R. (1992) *Refugees or Migrant Workers? The Recruitment of Displaced Persons for British Industry 1946–1951* (London: Routledge).

Keith, M. (1987) '"Something Happened": the problems of explaining the 1980 and 1981 riots in British cities', in P. Jackson (ed.), *Race and Racism* (London: Allen and Unwin).

—— (1993) *Race, Riots and Policing: Lore and Disorder in a Multiracist Society* (London: UCL Press).

Keith, M. and Pile, S. (eds) (1993) *Place and the Politics of Identity* (London: Routledge).

Kennedy, P. and Nicholls, A. (eds) (1981) *Nationalist and Racialist Movements in Britain and Germany Before 1914* (London: Macmillan).

Kettle, M. (1982) 'Will 1982 See More Riots', *New Society*, 18 February.

Kettle, M. and Hodges, L. (1982) *Uprising!* (London: Pan).

Kirp, D. (1979) *Doing Good by Doing Little* (London: University of California Press).

Knopf, T. A. (1975) *Rumors, Race and Riots* (New Brunswick, NJ: Transaction Books).

Labour Party Black Section (1988) *The Black Agenda* (London: Labour Party Black Section).

Lambert, J. R. (1970) *Crime, Police and Race Relations: A Study in Birmingham* (London: Oxford University Press).

Lawrence, D. (1974) *Black Migrants, White Natives* (Cambridge University Press).

Layton-Henry, Z. (1980) 'Immigration' in Z. Layton-Henry (ed.) *Conservative Party Policies* (London: Macmillan).

—— (1984) *The Politics of Race in Contemporary Britain* (London: Allen and Unwin).

—— (1986) 'Race and the Thatcher Government', in Z. Layton-Henry and P. Rich (eds) *Race, Government and Politics in Britain* (London: Macmillan).

—— (1988) 'The Black Electorate and the General Election of 1987', paper presented at Conference on Black People and British Politics (University of Warwick, November 1987).

Layton-Henry, Z. (ed.) (1990) *The Political Rights of Migrant Workers in Western Europe* (London: Sage).

Layton-Henry, Z. and Rich, P. (eds) (1986) *Race, Government and Politics in Britain* (London: Macmillan).

Layton-Henry, Z. and Studlar, D. (1985) 'The Electoral Participation of Black and Asian Britons', *Parliamentary Affairs*, 38: 307–18.

Lebow, R. N. (1976) *White Britain and Black Ireland* (Philadelphia: Institute for the Study of Human Issues).

Lebzelter, G. (1978) *Political Anti-Semitism in England* (London: Macmillan).

—— (1981) 'Anti-semitism: a Focal Point for the British Radical Right' in P. Kennedy and A. Nicholls (eds) *Nationalist and Racialist Movements in Britain and Germany Before 1914* (London: Macmillan).

Lee, A. (1980) 'Working Class Response to Jews in Britain, 1880–1914', in K. Lunn (ed.), *Hosts, Immigrants and Minorities* (Folkestone: Dawson).

Lees, L. H. (1979) *Exiles in Erin: Irish Migrants in Victorian London* (Manchester University Press).

Le Lohe, M. J. (1989) 'The performance of Asian and black candidates in the British General election of 1987', *New Community* 15, 2: 159–70.

Lenton, J., Budgen, N. and Clarke, K. (1966) *Immigration, Race and Politics: A Birmingham View* (London: Bow Publications).

Lester, A. and Bindman, G. (1972) *Race and Law* (Harmondsworth: Penguin).

Levitas, R. (ed.) (1986) *The Ideology of the New Right*, (Cambridge: Polity).

Lewis, R. (1988) *Anti-Racism: A Mania Exposed* (London: Quartet).

Leys, C. (1983) *Politics in Britain* (London: Heinemann).

Lipman, V. D. (1954) *Social history of Jews in England 1850–1950* (London: Watts & Co.).

Lipsky, M. and Olson, D. (1977) *Commission Politics: The Processing of Racial Crisis in America* (New Brunswick, NJ: Transaction Books).

Little, K. (1947) *Negroes in Britain: A Study of Racial Relations in English Society* (London: Routledge and Kegan Paul).

Lloyd, C. (1991) 'Concepts, Models and Anti-racist Strategies in Britain and France', *New Community* 18, 1: 63–73.

Lunn, K. (ed.) (1980) *Hosts, Immigrants and Minorities* (Folkestone: Dawson).

—— (1985) *Race and Labour in Twentieth-Century Britain* (London: Frank Cass).

Lustgarten, L. (1980) *Legal Control of Racial Discrimination* (London: Macmillan).

Macdonald, I. (1983) *Immigration Law and Practice in the United Kingdom* (London: Butterworths).

Macdonald, I., Bhavnani, R., Khan, L. and John, G. (1989) *Murder in the Playground: the report of the Macdonald Inquiry into racism and racial violence in Manchester schools* (London: Longsight Press).

Macmillan, H. (1973) *At the End of the Day* (London: Macmillan).

Mama, A. (1989) 'Violence Against Black Women: Gender, Race, and State Responses', *Feminist Review*, 32: 30–48.

—— (1992) 'Black women and the British State: Race, Class and Gender Analysis for the 1990s', in P. Braham, A. Rattansi and R. Skellington (eds), *Racism and Antiracism. Inequalities, Opportunities and Policies* (London: Sage).

Marable, M. (1981) 'Race, Class and Conflict', *Sage Race Relations Abstracts*, 6, 4: 1–38.

—— (1983) *How Capitalism Underdeveloped Black America* (London: Pluto Press).

—— (1985) *Black American Politics* (London: Verso).

Mark, R. (1970) 'The Metropolitan Police: their role in the community', *Community* July 1970: 3–5.

Martiniello, M. (1991) 'Racism in Paradise?', *Race and Class*, 32, 3: 79–84.

Mason, D. and Jewson, N. (1992) 'Race, equal opportunities policies and employment practice: Reflections on the 1980s, prospects for the 1990s' *New Community*, 19, 1: 99–112.

May, R. and Cohen, R. (1974) 'The Interaction Between Race and Colonialism: A Case Study of the Liverpool Race Riots of 1919', *Race and Class*, 16, 2: 111–26.

McAdam, D. (1982) *Political Process and the Development of Black Insurgency: 1930–1970* (University of Chicago Press).

McCrudden, C. (1982) 'Institutional discrimination', *Oxford Journal of Legal Studies*, 2: 303–67.

—— (1983) 'Anti-discrimination goals and the legal process', in N. Glazer and K. Young (eds), *Ethnic Pluralism and Public Policy* (London: Heinemann).

—— (1987) 'The Commission for Racial Equality', in R. Baldwin and C. McCrudden (eds) *Regulation and Public Law* (London: Weidenfeld and Nicolson).

—— (1988) 'Codes in a Cold Climate: Administrative Rule-Making by the Commission for Racial Equality', *Modern Law Review* 51, 4: 409–41.

McCrudden, C., Smith, D. J. and Brown, C. (1991) *Racial Justice at Work* (London: Policy Studies Institute).

McIntosh, N. and Smith, D. J. (1974) *The Extent of Racial Discrimination* (London: Political and Economic Planning).

Mercer, K. (1990) 'Welcome to the Jungle: Identity and Diversity in Postmodern Politics' in J. Rutherford (ed.), *Identity: Community, Culture, Difference* (London: Lawrence and Wishart).

Messina, A. (1985) 'Race and Party Competition in Britain' *Parliamentary Affairs*, 38, 4: 423–36.

—— (1987) 'Mediating race relations: British Community Relations Councils revisited', *Ethnic and Racial Studies*, 10, 2: 187–202.

—— (1989) *Race and Party Competition in Britain* (Oxford: Clarendon Press).

Metropolitan Police (1986) *Public Order Review – Civil Disturbances 1981–1985* (London: Metropolitan Police).

Miles, R. (1982) *Racism and Migrant Labour* (London: Routledge and Kegan Paul).

—— (1984) 'The riots of 1958: notes on the ideological construction of "race relations" as a political issue in Britain', *Immigrants and Minorities* 3, 3: 252–75.

—— (1986) 'Labour Migration, Racism and Capital Accumulation in Western Europe Since 1945', *Capital and Class*, 28: 49–86.

—— (1987) 'Recent Marxist theories of nationalism and the issue of racism', *British Journal of Sociology*, XXXVIII, 1: 24–43.

—— (1988) 'Racism, Marxism and British Politics', *Economy and Society*, 17, 3: 428–60.

—— (1989) *Racism* (London: Routledge).

—— (1992) 'Migration, Racism and the Nation State in Contemporary Europe', in V. Satzewich (ed.), *Deconstructing the Nation: Immigration, Multiculturalism and Racism in 90s Canada* (Toronto: Garamond Press).

—— (1993) *After 'Race Relations'* (London: Routledge).

Miles, R. and Phizacklea, A. (eds.) (1979) *Racism and Political Action in Britain* (London: Routledge and Kegan Paul).

—— (1984) *White Man's Country* (London: Pluto Press).

Millward, P. (1985) 'The Stockport Riots of 1852: A Study of Anti-Catholic and Anti-Irish Sentiment', in R. Swift and S. Gilley (eds), *The Irish in the Victorian City* (London: Croom Helm).

Mishan, E. J. (1988) 'What Future for a Multi-Racial Britain?', *Salisbury Review*, 6, 4: 18–27.

Modood, T (1988) ' "Black" racial equality and Asian identity', *New Community*, XIV, 3: 397–404.

—— (1992) *'Not Easy Being British': colour, culture and citizenship* (London: Trentham Books and Runnymede Trust).

Moore, R. (1975) *Racism and Black Resistance in Britain* (London: Pluto Press).

Moore, R. and Wallace, T. (1975) *Slamming the Door: The Administration of Immigration Control* (Oxford: Martin Robertson).

Moran, M. (1985) *Politics and Society in Britain* (London: Macmillan).

Morley, D. and Robins, K. (1990) 'No Place Like Heimat: Images of Home(Land) in European Culture', *New Formations* 12: 1–23.

Mullard, C. (1985) *Race, Power and Resistance* (London: Routledge and Kegan Paul).

Murdock, G. (1984) 'Reporting the riots: images and impact', in J. Benyon (ed.), *Scarman and After* (Oxford: Pergamon Press).

Murray, N. (1986) 'Anti-racists and other demons: the press and ideology in Thatcher's Britain', *Race and Class*, XXVII, 3: 1–19.

Myrdal, G. (1969a) *Objectivity in Social Research* (London: Duckworth).

—— (1969b) *An American Dilemma: The Negro Problem and Modern Democracy* (New York: Harper and Row).

Nairn, T. (1981) *The Break-Up of Britain* (London: Verso).

—— (1988) *The Enchanted Glass* (London: Radius).

Nandy, D. (1970) 'Immigrants and the police', *Runnymede Trust Bulletin*, October.

Newman, K. (1983) 'Fighting the fear of crime', *Police*, September: 26–30; October: 30–2.

—— (1986) *Employment, Unemployment and Black People* (London: Runnymede Trust).

—— (1986a) 'Police–public relations: the pace of change', Police Federation Annual Lecture, 28 July.

—— (1986b) *Public Order Review: Civil Disturbances 1981–85* (London: Metropolitan Police).

Newton, K. (1976) *Second City Politics: Democratic processes and Decision-Making in Birmingham* (Oxford: Clarendon Press).

Nixon, J. (1982) 'The Home Office and Race Relations Policy: co-ordinator or initiator?', *Journal of Public Policy*, 2, 4: 365–78.

OECD (1986) 'United Kingdom', National Report for OECD Conference on the Future of Migration (Paris, February 1986).

Offe, C. (1984) *Contradictions of the Welfare State*, (London: Hutchinson).

—— (1985) *Disorganised Capitalism* (Cambridge: Polity).

Omi, M. and Winant, H. (1986) *Racial Formation in the United States* (London: Routledge).

O Tuathaigh, M. (1985) 'The Irish in Nineteenth Century Britain: Problems of Integration' in R. Swift and S. Gilley (eds), *The Irish in the Victorian City* (London: Croom Helm).

Ouseley, H. (1981) *The System* (London: Runnymede).

—— (1982) 'A local black alliance', in A. Ohri, B. Manning and P. Curno *Community Work and Racism* (London: Routledge).

—— (1984) 'Local Authority Race Initiatives' in M. Boddy and C. Fudge (eds) *Local Socialism* (London: Macmillan).

—— (1986) *A Different Reality: An account of Black people's experiences and their grievances before and after the Handsworth Rebellions of September 1985* (Birmingham: West Midlands County Council).

Owen, D. and Green, A. (1992) 'Labour market experience and change among ethnic groups in Great Britain', *New Community*, 19, 1: 7–29.

Palmer, F. (ed.) (1986) *Anti-Racism – An Assault on Education and Value* (London: The Sherwood Press).

Parekh, B. (1987) 'The "new right" and the politics of nationhood', in Runnymede Trust *The New Right: Image and Reality* (London: Runnymede Trust).

—— (1989) 'Between holy text and moral void', *New Statesman and Society*, 28 March, 29–32.

—— (1991) 'British Citizenship and Cultural Difference', in G. Andrews (ed.), *Citizenship* (London: Lawrence and Wishart).

Park, R. (1950) *Race and Culture* (New York: Free Press).

Parkin, F. (1979) *Marxism and Class: A Bourgeois Critique* (London: Tavistock).

Parkinson, M. and Duffy, J. (1984) 'Government's response to inner city riots: the Minister for Merseyside and the Task Force', *Parliamentary Affairs*, 37, 1: 76–96.

Parmar, P. (1990) 'Black Feminism: the Politics of Articulation', in J. Rutherford (ed.) *Identity: Community, Culture, Difference* (London: Lawrence and Wishart).

Patten, J. (1989) 'The Muslim Community in Britain', *The Times*, 5 July 1989.

Patterson, S. (1963) *Dark Strangers* (Harmondsworth: Penguin).

—— (1969) *Immigration and Race Relations in Britain 1960–1967* (London: Oxford University Press).

Pearson, D. (1981) *Race, Class and Political Activism* (Aldershot: Gower).

Phillips, A. (1991) *Engendering Democracy* (Cambridge: Polity Press).

Phizacklea, A. and Miles, R. (1980) *Labour and Racism* (London: Routledge).

—— (1987) 'The British trade union movement and racism' in G. Lee and R. Loveridge (eds) *The Manufacture of Disadvantage* (Open University: Milton Keynes).

Pieterse, J. N. (1992) *White on Black: Images of Africa and Blacks in Western Popular Culture* (New Haven and London: Yale University Press).

Pilkington, E. (1988) *Beyond the Mother Country: West Indians and the Notting Hill White Riots* (London: I. B. Tauris).

Piven, F. F. and Cloward, R. (1977) *Poor People's Movements* (New York: Vintage Books).

Pollins, H. (1982) *Economic History of the Jews in England* (London: Associated University Presses).

Powell, E. (1969) *Still to Decide* (Kingswood: Elliot Right Way Books).

—— (1972) *Still to Decide* (London: Batsford).

PREM 11/1409 (1956) 'Immigration from the Irish Republic' (London: Public Records Office).

Preston, M. B., Henderson, L. J. and Pureyar, P. (eds) (1982) *The New Black Politics* (New York: Longman).

Pryce, K. (1979) *Endless Pressure* (Harmondsworth: Penguin).

Pulle, S. (1973) *Police/Immigrant Relations in Ealing* (London: Runnymede Trust).

Race Relations Board (1973) *Race Relations Legislation in Britain* (London: Race Relations Board).

Ramazanoglu, C. (1989) *Feminism and the Contradictions of Oppression* (London: Routledge).

Ramdin, R. (1987) *The Making of the Black Working Class in Britain* (Aldershot: Gower).

Rattansi, A. (1992) 'Changing the Subject? Racism, Culture and Education', in J. Donald and A. Rattansi (eds), *'Race', Culture & Difference* (London: Sage).

Redford, A. (1976) *Labour Migration in England 1800–1850* (Manchester: Manchester University Press).

Reeves, F. (1983) *British Racial Discourse* (Cambridge University Press).

—— (1989) *Race and Borough Politics* (Avebury: Aldershot).

Reiner, R. (1985) *The Politics of the Police* (Brighton: Wheatsheaf Books).

Rex, J. (1973) *Race, Colonialism and the City* (London: Routledge and Kegan Paul).

—— (1979) 'Black militancy and class conflict' in R. Miles and A. Phizacklea (eds) *Racism and Political Action in Britain* (London: Routledge and Kegan Paul).

—— (1981) 'A working paradigm for race relations research', *Ethnic and Racial Studies* 4, 1: 1–25.

—— (1983) *Race Relations in Sociological Theory*, 2nd edn (London: Routledge and Kegan Paul).

—— (1986a) *Race and Ethnicity* (Milton Keynes: Open University Press).

—— (1986b) 'The Role of Class Analysis in the Study of Race Relations – a Weberian Perspective', in J. Rex and D. Mason (eds), *Theories of Race and Ethnic Relations* (Cambridge University Press).

—— (1988) *The Ghetto and the Underclass: Essays on Race and Social Policy* (Aldershot: Avebury).

—— (1991) *Ethnic Identity and Political Mobilisation in Britain* (Centre for Research in Ethnic Relations, University of Warwick, Monographs in Ethnic relations, No 5).

Rex, J. and Mason, D. (eds) (1986) *Theories of Race and Ethnic Relations* (Cambridge: Cambridge University Press).

Rex, J. and Moore, R. (1967) *Race, Community and Conflict* (London: Oxford University Press).

Rex, J. and Tomlinson, S. (1979) *Colonial Immigrants in a British City: A Class Analysis* (London: Routledge and Kegan Paul).

Rich, P. (1986) *Race and Empire in British Politics* (Cambridge University Press).

Richmond, A. (1954) *Colour Prejudice in Britain: A Study of West Indian Workers in Liverpool, 1942–51* (London: Routledge and Kegan Paul).

—— (1973) *Migration and Race Relations in an English City* (London: Oxford University Press).

Robinson, C. (1983) *Black Marxism* (London: Zed).

Robson, B. (1988) *Those Inner Cities* (Oxford: Clarendon Press).

Rose, E. J. B. and Associates (1969) *Colour and Citizenship: A Report on British Race Relations* (London: Oxford University Press).

Rose, R. (1985) *Politics in England* (London: Faber and Faber).

Rushdie, S. (1989) *The Satanic Verses* (London: Viking).

Rutherford, J. (ed.) (1990) *Identity: Community, Culture, Difference* (London: Lawrence and Wishart).

Ruthven, M. (1990) *A Satanic Affair* (London: Chatto and Windus).

Saggar, S. (1991) *Race and Public Policy* (Aldershot: Avebury).

—— (1992) *Race and Politics in Britain* (London: Harvester Wheatsheaf).

Sahgal, G. and Yuval-Davis, N. (eds) (1992) *Refusing Holy Orders* (London: Virago).

Samad, Y. (1992) 'Book burning and race relations: Political mobilisation of Bradford Muslims' *New Community*, 18, 4: 507–19.

Samuel, R. (ed.) (1989a) *Patriotism: Volume II: Minorities and Outsiders* (London: Routledge).

—— (1989b) *Patriotism: Volume III: National Fictions* (London: Routledge).

Saunders, P. (1981) *Social Theory and the Urban Question* (London: Hutchinson).

Scarman, Lord (1981) *The Brixton Disorders 10–12 April 1981: Report of an Inquiry by the Rt Hon. The Lord Scarman OBE* (London: HMSO).

Seidel, G. (1986) 'The concept of culture, "race" and nation in the British and French new right' in R. Levitas (ed.) *The Ideology of the New Right* (Cambridge: Polity).

Select Committee on Race Relations and Immigration (1969) *The Problems of Coloured School Leavers* (London: HMSO).

—— (1972) *Police/Immigrant Relations* (London: HMSO).

—— 1975) *The Organisation of Race Relations Administration* (London: HMSO).

—— (1977) *The West Indian Community* (London: HMSO).

—— (1978) *Immigration* (London: HMSO).

Sherman, A. (1973) *Island Refuge: Britain and Refugees from the Third Reich* (London: Paul Elek).

Sherwood, M. (1984) *Many Struggles: West Indian Workers and Service Personnel in Britain 1939–45* (London: Karia Press).

Shyllon F.O. (1974) *Black Slaves in Britain* (London: Oxford University Press).

Sim, J. (1982) 'Scarman: The Police Counter Attack', *Socialist Register 1982* (London: Merlin Press).

Silverman, J. (1986) *Independent Inquiry into the Handsworth Disturbances September 1985* (Birmingham: Birmingham City Council).

Silverman, M. (1982) *Deconstructing the Nation: immigration, racism and citizenship in modern France* (London: Routledge).

Sivanandan, A. (1982) *A Different Hunger* (London: Pluto Press).

—— (1985) 'RAT and the degradation of black struggle', *Race and Class*, *XXVI*, 4: 1–33.

—— (1990) *Communities of Resistance* (London: Verso).

Skolnick, R. (1969) *The Politics of Protest* (New York: Simon and Schuster).

Small, S. (1991a) 'Attaining Racial Parity in the United States and England: We Got to Go Where the Greener Grass Grows!', *Sage Race Relations Abstracts*, 16, 3: 3–55.

—— (1991b) 'Racialised Relations in Liverpool: A Contemporary Anomaly', *New Community* 11, 4: 511–537.

Smith, David (1987) 'Knowing your place: Class, politics and ethnicity in Chicago and Birmingham 1890–1983', in N. Thrift and P. Williams (eds), *Class and Space* (London: Macmillan).

Smith, David and Gray, J. (1987) *Police and People in London* (Aldershot: Cower).

Smith, Dennis (1977) *Racial Disadvantage in Britain* (Harmondsworth: Penguin).

Smith, G. (1987) *When Jim Crow Met John Bull* (London: I. B. Tauris).

Smith, S. J. (1989) *The Politics of 'Race' and Residence: Citizenship, Segregation and White Supremacy in Britain* (Cambridge: Polity Press).

Smithies, B. and Fiddick, P. (1969) *Enoch Powell on Immigration* (London: Sphere Books).

Soja, E. W. (1989) *Postmodern Geographies* (London: Verso).

Solomos, J. (1986) 'Trends in the political analysis of racism', *Political Studies*, XXXIV, 2: 313–24.

—— (1988) *Black Youth, Racism and the State* (Cambridge University Press).

—— (1989) 'Equal Opportunities Policies and Racial Inequality: The Role of Public Policy', *Public Administration* 67, 1: 79–93.

—— (1991) 'Political Language and Racial Discourse', *European Journal of Intercultural Studies*, 2, 1: 21–34.

Solomos, J. and Back, L. (1991) 'The Politics of Race and Social Change in Birmingham', *Research Papers No. 1* (Department of Politics and Sociology, Birkbeck College).

—— (1993) 'Race and Racism' in J. Krieger (ed.) *The Oxford Companion to Politics of the World* (New York: Oxford University Press).

Sowell, T. (1981) *Markets and Minorities* (Oxford: Basil Blackwell).

Spencer, K., Taylor, A., Smith, B., Mawson, J., Flynn, N. and Batley, R. (1986) *Crisis in the Industrial Heartland: A Study of the West Midlands* (London: Clarendon Press).

Spivak, G. C. (1987) *In Other Worlds* (London: Methuen).

Stewart, J. and Stoker, G. (eds) (1989) *The Future of Local Government* (London: Macmillan).

Stoker, G. (1988) *The Politics of Local Government*, (London: Macmillan).

Studlar, D. (1978) 'Policy Voting in Britain: The Coloured Immigration Issue in the 1964, 1966 and 1970 General Elections', *American Political Science Review*, 72, 1: 46–64.

—— (1980) 'Elite responsiveness or elite autonomy: British immigration policy reconsidered', *Ethnic and Racial Studies*, 3, 2: 207–23.

Swift R. and Gilley, S. (eds) (1985) *The Irish in the Victorian City* (London: Croom Helm).

Tannahill, J. A. (1958) *European Volunteer Workers in Britain* (Manchester University Press).

Taylor, S. (1982) *The National Front in English Politics* (London: Macmillan).

The Times (1968) *The Black Man in Search of Power* (London: Nelson).

Thatcher, M. (1988) *Britain and Europe* (London: Conservative Political Centre).

Thompson, G. (1986) *The Conservatives' Economic Policy* (London: Croom Helm).

Thrift, N. and Williams, P. (eds) (1987) *Class and Space* (London: Macmillan).

Thurlow, R. (1975) 'National Front Ideology', *Patterns of Prejudice*, 9, 1: 1–9.

Troyna, B. and Williams, J. (1986) *Racism, Education and the State* (London: Croom Helm).

van Dijk, T. A. (1988) *News Analysis: Case Studies of International and National News in the Press* (New Jersey: Lawrence Erlbaum).

—— (1991) *Racism and the Press* (London: Routledge).

Visram, R. (1986) *Ayahs, Lascars and Princes* (London: Pluto).

Walker, M. (1977) *The National Front* (London: Fontana).

Waller, P. J. (1981) *Democracy and Sectarianism: A Political and Social History of Liverpool 1868–1939* (Liverpool University Press).

Walvin, J. (1973) *Black and White: The Negro and British Society* (London: Allen and Unwin).

—— (1984) *Passage to Britain* (Harmondsworth: Penguin).

—— (1992) *Black Ivory: A History of British Slavery* (London: HarperCollins).

Ward, R. (ed.) (1984) *Race and Housing in Britain* (Centre for Research in Ethnic Relations, University of Warwick).

Ware, V. (1992) *Beyond the Pale: White Women, Racism and History* (London: Verso).

Werbner, P. and Anwar, M. (eds) (1991) *Black and Ethnic Leaderships* (London: Routledge).

Widgery, D. (1986) *Beating Time* (London: Chatto and Windus).

Wieviorka, M. (1993) 'Tendencies to Racism in Europe: Does France represent a unique case, or is it representative of a trend' in J. Wrench and J. Solomos (eds), *Racism and Migration in Western Europe* (Oxford and New York: Berg Publishers).

Wilpert, C. (1991) 'Migration and ethnicity in a non-immigration country – foreigners in a united Germany', *New Community* 18, 1: 49–62.

Wilson, H. (1971) *The Labour Government 1964–70* (London: Weidenfeld and Nicolson).

Wilson, W. J. (1980) *The Declining Significance of Race* (University of Chicago Press).

—— (1988) *The Truly Disadvantaged* (University of Chicago).

WING (1985) *Worlds Apart: Women Under Immigration and Nationality Law* (London: Pluto).

Wolf, E. (1982) *Europe and the People Without History* (Berkeley: University of California Press).

Wolpe, H. (1987) *Race, Class and the Apartheid State* (London: James Currey).

Worsthorne, P. (1978) 'Too much freedom' in M. Cowling (ed.), *Conservative Essays* (London: Cassell).

—— (1985) 'End this silence over race', *The Sunday Telegraph*, 26 September.

Wrench, J. and Solomos, J. (eds) (1993) *Racism and Migration in Western Europe* (Oxford and New York: Berg Publishers).

Young, K. (1985) 'Racial Disadvantage', in S. Ranson, G. Jones and K. Walsh (eds), *Between Centre and Locality* (London: Allen and Unwin).
—— (1989) 'The space between words: local authorities and the concept of equal opportunities' in R. Jenkins and J. Solomos (eds), *Racism and Equal Opportunity Policies in the 1980s* (Cambridge University Press).
—— (1990) 'Approaches to Policy development in the Field of Equal Opportunities', in W. Ball and J. Solomos (eds) *Race and Local Politics* (London: Macmillan).
Young, K. and Connelly, N. (1981) *Policy and Practice in the Multi-Racial City* (London: Policy Studies Institute).
—— (1984) 'After the Act: Local Authority Policy Reviews under the Race Relations Act 1976', *Local Government Studies*, 10, 1: 13–25.
Young, R. (1990) *White Mythologies: Writing History and the West* (London: Routledge).
Young, R. (ed.) (1991) *Neocolonialism*, special Issue of *Oxford Literary Review*, 13, 1–2.
Zolberg, A. R. (1989) 'The next waves: migration theory for a changing world', *International Migration Review*, 23, 3: 403–30.
Zubaida, S. (ed.) (1970) 'Introduction', *Race and Racialism* (London: Tavistock).
—— (1972) 'Sociologists and Race Relations', in *Proceedings of a Seminar: Problems and Prospects of Socio-Legal Research* (Nuffield College, Oxford).
Zubrzycki, J. (1956) *Polish Immigrants to Britain* (The Hague: Martinus Nijhoff).

Index

Abbott, D. 208–9
Abbott, S. 85, 88
Afro-Caribbean(s) 47, 57, 86, 90, 100–1, 162
Ahmed, A. S. 218
Akhtar, S. 222, 225
Alderman, G. 45
Alford, R. 199
Aliens Order (1905) 43–4, 46
Aliens Order (1920) 46–7
Aliens Restriction (Amendment) Act (1914) 46
Aliens Restriction (Amendment) Act (1919) 46
America(n) *see* United States
Amos, V. 115–16
Anglo-Saxons 40–2
Anthias, F. 219
anti-discrimination legislation 78, 236–8
Anti-Nazi League 190, 211–12
anti-racism 3, 79–80, 106–7, 114–15
'anti-anti-racism' 194–6
anti-racist alliances 198–9, 211–14
anti-semitism 44–5, 47
Anwar, M. 35, 198, 201, 205
Appignanesi, L. 218, 222
Applebey, G. 90
Asad, T. 218–19, 222–3, 228
Asian(s) 162
    East African 65–6, 135
    migrants 90, 100
Atkin, S. 210
Austria 5

Back, L. 8, 36, 118, 209, 211, 220, 223, 230
Balibar, E. 3
Ball, W. 103, 107
Banton, M. 14, 18, 26, 36, 79–80, 117, 121

Barker, M. 35, 70, 193
Batley, R. 103
Beetham, D. 100
Benedict, R. 17
Ben-Tovim, G. 100, 106, 212
Benyon, J. 92, 117, 148, 171
Berghahn, M. 47
Berkeley, H. 65
Bevan, V. 46, 56
Bhabha, H. 33
Billig, M. 181, 188
Bindman, G. 83, 85, 236
Birmingham
    race and politics in 20–1, 36, 82, 97–8, 100, 201, 222
    policing in 141–3
black(s)
    migrants 22–3, 48–50, 52–4
    MPs 209–11, 213
    politics 198–9, 214–16
    see also Afro-Caribbean(s), Asian(s)
Black Country 98
black youth 4
    alienation of 124–5
    images of 130–3
    mugging and 74, 128–9, 143–4
    see also Afro-Caribbean(s), Asian(s)
Boateng, P. 209
Bosnia 74
Bradford 97, 107, 222
Brah, A. 2, 219–20
Brent 97, 107
Bristol 47, 99–100
Bristol riots (1980) 147, 149
British Nationality Act (1948) 56–7, 58
British Nationality Act (1981) 71
British politics, race and 35, 73–4
'Britishness' *see* 'Englishness'
Brixton 74, 133, 171

Brixton riots
  April 1981   147
  September 1985   164
Broadwater Farm   148, 163, 167
Brockwell Park   134
Brockway, F.   82
Brown, C.   90–1, 109, 237
Brown, J.   142
Bovenkerk, F.   5
Burnage High School   107, 196
Butler, Lord   62

Campaign Against Racial
  Discrimination   203
Cardiff   47, 120
Carter, B.   56, 62, 121
Carter, T.   198, 203
Casey, J.   186–7, 194
Cashmore, E.   189
Castles, S.   3, 55, 69
CCCS Race and Politics Group   14,
  29, 72, 135
Cheetham, J.   206
Cheltenham   4
Chinese seamen   49–50
Clare, J.   160
Cloward, R.   199
Coates, D.   23
Cohen, P.   48, 192
Cohen, R.   5
Colley, L.   219
Collins, P. H.   2
Colls, R.   186
Colour Bar   53, 66
Commission for Racial Equality
  (CRE)   68, 80, 87–8, 90, 92–3,
  104, 108, 110, 191, 195, 218,
  236–7
  Code of Practice   92–3
Commonwealth   52, 58, 64
Commonwealth Immigrants Act
  (1962)   60–4
Commonwealth Immigrants Act
  (1968)   66, 75
Community Relations
  Commission   84, 87, 99, 138
Community Relations Councils   97,
  104

Connelly, N.   101, 104
Conservative Party   56, 70–1, 74,
  122, 195, 200
contract compliance   110–13
Cox, O.   27
Crewe, I.   205
Crick, B.   218
crime(s)
  Asian   128
  race and   143–6
  young blacks and   126–7
Cross, M.   160
Crossman, R.   65
culture, race and   15, 32–3, 219–20
Curtis, L.   40, 43

Daily Express   149, 167
Daily Mail   144, 149, 155
Daily Star   149
Daily Telegraph   144, 155, 172, 176,
  196, 224
Daniel, W. W.   80
Deakin, N.   57, 64–5, 100
Dean, D.   56
Dear, G.   163, 165
Dearlove, J.   22–3
Deedes, W.   61, 196
Deptford   150
Deva, N.   210
discrimination
  direct   87–8
  indirect   87–8
disorder(s)   *see* urban unrest
Dodd, P.   186
Dunleavy, P.   28, 95

East End, of London   4, 44–5
Edelman, M.   73, 158, 167, 176,
  178, 192, 199
Edgar, D.   189
education, racism and   106–7
Edwards, J.   103
equal opportunity   108–9
electoral politics, race and   204–5
Empire Windrush   54
employment, racism in   98
'enemy within'   74–5, 184–5, 192–3

Englishness, conceptions of 38–9, 43, 59, 183, 183–4, 220–1
ethnic minorities *see* Afro-Caribbean(s), Asian(s), black(s)
Europe 5–6
 Eastern 6, 43
 racism in 2, 31, 230–1, 233, 244–6
 Western 6
'European identity' 5–6
European Volunteer Workers 55–6
Evans, J. M. 42, 56
Evening Standard 228

Falklands War 197
feminism 2
 race and 24, 220, 223
Fielding, N. 181
Financial Times 149, 161
First World War 44
Fitzgerald, M. 35, 75, 201
Flew, A. 78, 184
Fogelson, R. M. 158
Foot, P. 62, 65
France 3–4
Fredrickson, G. M. 39
Freeman, G. 35, 52, 60, 66, 82, 181, 236
Freeman, M. D. A. 73
Friedland, R. 199
Fryer, P. 38–9, 48–9, 121

Gainer, B. 43–4, 120
Gaitskell, H. 63
Gamble, A. 241, 247
Garrard, J. A. 43, 120
Gartner, L. P. 43–4
Gates, H. L. 33
Gay, P. 99, 109, 237
gender, discrimination and 112
General Election (1987) 116, 177
General Election (1992) 4
Germany 3, 17
Gilley, S. 40–2
Gilroy, P. 14, 29–30, 35, 114, 135, 179, 183, 203, 212, 215, 216, 219, 230

Glasgow 42
Glass, R. 17
Goldberg, D. T. 2, 8, 13, 32–3, 246
Gordon, P. 47, 70, 191, 236
Goulbourne, H. 206, 221
Grant, B. 166, 209, 225
Greater London Council 97, 111, 191
Greenberg, S. B. 39
Griffiths, P. 65–6, 99
Grossberg, L. 219
Guardian, The 73, 131, 138, 144, 149, 161, 175, 183, 240
Gulf War 225–7

Hackney 97, 105, 108, 115
Hall, S. 29, 34, 73, 123, 131–2, 136, 152, 216, 219–20, 243
Halstead, M. 107
Handsworth 20, 74, 100, 126–7, 133, 141–3
Handsworth riot (September 1985) 148–9, 162
Hansard 58, 71, 72, 75, 84, 103, 121, 135, 154, 157, 164, 165, 176
Haringey 97, 105
Harris, C. 48, 56, 58, 62, 121, 219
Harvey, D. 230
Hattersley, R. 150, 153, 157
Hechter, M. 40
Heineman, B. 203
Hepple, B. 49–50,
Hirschfeld, G. 47
Holmes, C. 38–9, 43, 52, 54, 120
Holland 3, 17
Home Affairs Committee 89–90
Home Office 86, 88, 133, 191
Honeyford, R. 107, 115
Hong Kong 4
hooks, b. 2
housing, discrimination in 98, 100
Humphry, D. 123, 126, 133
Hurd, D. 165, 175
Husbands, C. 3, 189, 244–5

identity, race and 30, 31–3, 59, 219–22

immigrant(s)
 crime and 120–1
 images of 44–5
 undesirable 46
immigration 1, 6
 controls on 58–9, 62–3, 122–3
 politics of 56–77
Immigration Act (1971) 69–70
Immigration Appeals Act
  (1969) 68
Independent, The 183
India 53, 57
Indian Workers' Association 203
inner cities 116–17, 132–3
Inner London Education
  Authority 110–11
Ireland 40–1
Irish migrants 26–7, 40–3, 44, 54,
  64, 120
Italy 5

Jackson, J. A. 41, 54
Jacobs, B. 35, 72, 203
James, W. 219
Jeffers, S. 209
Jenkins, Richard 90, 109, 236
Jenkins, Roy 86
Jessop, B. 28
Jewish migrants 38, 39, 43–7,
  120–1
John, G. 123, 125, 126–7, 134
Joshi, S. 56, 62, 121
Joshua, H. 49–50, 148

Katz, J. 114
Katznelson, I. 25, 73, 96, 100,
  199–200, 213
Kaufman, G. 75
Kay, D. 54
Keith, M. 184, 230
Kennedy, P. 44
Kettle, M. 159
Khabra, P. 210
Kirp, D. 25
Kosack, G. 55, 69
Kumar, A. 210

Labour Party 7, 60–1, 69–70, 75,
  82, 195, 202, 214
 black sections and the 207–9
Ladywood 141
Lambert, J. R. 123, 125
Lambeth 97, 108
law and order, reactions to riots
  and 152–6
Lawrence, D. 99
Layton-Henry, Z. 35, 52, 60, 71,
  75, 181, 188, 202, 205
Lebzelter, G. 44
Lee, A. 44
Leeds 135
Lees, L. H. 41
Lester, A. 83, 85
Lewis, R. 195
Lewisham 141
Leys, C. 23, 174
Lipsky, M. 148, 167, 176
Little, K. 121
Liverpool 43, 47, 74, 120, 212
Lloyd, C. 5
local government, reform
  of 116–18
Local Government Act (1966) 98,
  102–3
Local Government Act (1988) 113
local politics
 race and 95–119
 political participation in 96–7
 theories of 95–6
London 42, 47, 106, 120
'loony left' 210
Lunn, K. 39, 120
Lustgarten, L. 87

Macdonald, I. 46, 52, 63, 68, 71,
  107
Macmillan, H. 62
Maitland, S. 218, 222
Major, J. 118
Manchester 97, 106
Marable, M. 25, 213
Mark, R. 123
Marxism 25
 Eurocentrism and 26
 racism and 17, 25–31

Marxism Today 209
Mason, D. 2, 13
McAdam, D. 25
McCrudden, C. 81, 87–8, 236
McGoldrick, M. 104
media, race and the 2, 143–5,
    151–2
Mercer, K. 220
Messina, A. 25, 100
Metropolitan Police 137, 140–1,
    168
migrant labour 3, 29–30
Miles, R. 8, 14, 17, 28–9, 34–5, 40,
    52, 54, 57, 60, 66, 72, 189, 202,
    245
Millward, P. 43
Mishan, E. J. 193–4
Modood, T. 223, 225
Moore, R. 20, 68, 85, 99
Moran, M. 23
Moss Side 141
Mullard, C. 201
multiculturalism 1, 221–2
Murray, N. 107
Muslims 32–3, 117–18, 222–7
Myrdal, G. 16

Nairn, T. 218
National Front 181, 188–91, 212
nationalism
    national identity and 35, 182–3,
        187–9, 196–7
    race and 184–8
Nazis 17, 212
'new' racism 3, 193–4
New Right, race and the 184–8
New Statesman 196
Newman, K. 139, 168, 175
Newnham, A. 91
Newton, K. 100, 201
Nicholls, A. 44
North Africa 5
Notting Hill 133, 135
    Carnival 139–40, 198
    1958 riots in 58, 59, 121
Nottingham 59–60, 100, 121

Observer, The 67, 97, 143, 158

Offe, C. 89
Olson, D. 148, 167, 176
Omi, M. 30, 242
Osborne, C. 60
O Tuathaigh, M. 42
Oxford. K. 172
Ouseley, H. 102, 104

Pakistan 52–3, 57
Palmer, F. 78, 114, 184
Parekh, B. 117, 219
Park, R. 14–15
Parkin, F. 26
Parmar, P. 220
Patten, J. 223–4
Patterson, S. 17, 57, 60, 63, 82
Pearson, D. 203
Phizacklea, A. 34–5, 52, 57, 66, 72,
    189, 202
Pilkington, E. 58
Piven, F. F. 199
police
    relations with black
        communities 121–2,
        127–30, 136–9
    relations with black
        youth 124–7, 130–6
    riot tactics 139–43, 165–9
policing of inner city areas 174–7
Policy Studies Institute 80, 90–1
Polish migrants 54–6
political participation 199–202
political parties, race and 7–8,
    58–68, 70–4
political science 2, 21–5
Pollins, H. 44–5
positive action 108–13
Powell, E. 74, 103, 135, 137, 145,
    150–1, 162, 182–4
Powellism 34, 67–8, 76
Preston, M. B. 25

race
    advisers 105–6
    as social category 27–9, 36–7
    class and 21, 25–6, 212–14
    immigration and 4, 49–51, 61–2,
        70–4

race (*cont.*)
  media and 32–3
  meanings of 14, 28–9
  nation and 184–8
  sociology of 6, 30–1
  theories of 1–2, 8–9
race awareness training 113–16
race relations
  in Britain 2–3, 17–21
  cycle of 14
  policies 23–4
  research on 11–12, 14
  sociology of 17–21
Race Relations Acts
  1965 81
  1968 83
  1976 72, 85–9, 104–5, 113
Race Relations Board 84–5
racial attacks 191–2
racial discourse 34
racial ideologies 1, 13, 197
racial inequality 3
racialisation 1, 5, 23, 31, 57–8,
    143–4, 230
racism
  in Britain 1–2
  definition of 1–2, 8–9, 14, 31–2
  politics of 22–3, 178–9, 234–5,
    241–4
  power and 34
Ramazanoglu, C. 2
Ramdin, B. 48, 50, 203
Rastafarianism 140, 142
Rattansi, A. 219
Redford, A. 40
Reeves, F. 35, 60
Reiner, R. 171
repatriation 50–1
Rex, J. 2, 13, 19–21, 28, 39, 99,
    127, 143, 201
Rich, P. 50, 58, 221
Richmond, A. 53, 99
Ridley, N. 112, 220–1
riots *see* urban unrest
Robinson, C. 26
Robson, B. 116–17
Rock Against Racism 190, 212
Rose, E. J. B. 57, 62, 83

Rose, R. 216
Rushdie, S. 4, 32–3, 117, 218–19,
    222–5
Rutherford, J. 219
Ruthven, M. 218, 222

Saggar, S. 198
Sahgal, G. 223
Salisbury, Lord 59–60
Salisbury Review 184, 186, 193
Samad, Y. 117, 218, 222
Samuel, R. 38, 219
Saunders, P. 22–3, 95
Scarman, Lord 89, 148
  description of riots 154
  on positive action 116–17
Scarman Report 72, 148, 155–6,
    159, 169–71
Scotland 42
Second World War 2, 43, 51
  black American soldiers in 53–4
Seidel, G. 180, 183
Select Committee on Race Relations
    and Immigration 73, 85,
    128–30, 138–9
Sheffield 106
Sherman, A. 47
Sherwood, M. 53
Shyllon, F. 48
Sim, J. 172
Sivanandan, A. 52, 62, 69, 85, 114,
    198, 203
Skolnick, J. 158
Slavery 27
Smethwick 65, 99
Smith, D. 80, 85
Smith, G. 53
Smith, S. 100, 109, 230
social movements 214–16
Soja, E. W. 230
Solomos, J. 8, 29, 36, 73, 74, 84,
    90, 92, 103, 107, 109, 117–18,
    148, 171, 184, 186, 209, 211,
    223, 228, 236
South Africa 13, 16, 39
Southall 141, 148
Sowell, T. 94
Sparkbrook 20, 100

Special Patrol Group 139–40
Spencer, S. 73, 236
Spivak, G. 33
Stoker, G. 96, 105, 118
Studlar, D. 25, 205
Sun, The 144–5, 149, 210, 238
Sunday Telegraph 162, 198

Tannahill, J. A. 55
Taylor, S. 181, 190
Tebbit, N. 228–9
Thatcher, M. 70, 96, 118, 157,
    187–8, 193, 221
Thatcherism 196
Thrift, N. 96
Times, The 66, 121, 122, 125, 166,
    173, 208, 224
Tomlinson, S. 20, 99, 127, 143, 201
Tottenham 148
Toxteth 148
Troyna, B. 179

underclass 20–1
United Nations, racism and the 79
United States of America
    Civil Rights Movement in
        the 24, 88
    immigration to the 15
    racism in 2, 39
    riots in 148
    sociology of race in 13–17, 25
urban politics
    race and 101–5
    urban left and 105, 109–10
urban programme 103
urban unrest 139–43, 147–79
    explanations of 149–52
    impact of 102, 169–71
    policing and 165–9
    politics of 158–64
    racial disadvantage and 156–8
    social causes of 157, 171, 239–41

Urry, J. 95

van Dijk, T. A. 180, 184, 195
Vaz, K. 209, 225
Victorian England 42
Visram, R. 49

Walker, M. 188
Walker, Patrick Gordon 65
Wallace, T. 49–50, 68, 148
Waller, M. 42
Walvin, J. 40, 48
Ware, V. 2, 220
Weir, M. 199–200, 213
West Indian(s) *see* Afro-
    Caribbean(s)
West Indies 53
West Midlands 98–9, 161
Whitelaw, W. 149, 157
Widgery, D. 212
Wieviorka, M. 230–1
Williams, J. 179
Williams, P. 96
Wilson, H. 64
Winant, H. 30, 242
Wolf, E. 39
Wolpe, H.,
Wolverhampton 82, 212
Women Against
    Fundamentalism 223
Worsthorne, P. 152–3
Wrench, J. 228

Young, K. 99, 101, 104, 108
Young, R. 33
Yugoslavia 73–4
Yuval-Davis, N. 219, 223

Zubaida, S. 19, 21–2, 234
Zubrzycki, J. 54

Race and Racism in Britain

Race and Racism in Britain

Second Edition

John Solomos
Reader in Public Policy
Birkbeck College
University of London

St. Martin's Press   New York

First published in Great Britain in 1989 as
Race and Racism in Contemporary Britain
First published in the United States of America in 1993

Printed in Hong Kong

ISBN 0–312–09980–0 (pbk.)

Library of Congress Cataloging-in-Publication Data
Solomos, John.
Race and racism in Britain / John Solomos. — 2nd ed.
p.   cm.
Rev. ed. of: Race and racism in contemporary Britain.   1989.
Includes bibliographical references and index.
ISBN 0–312–09980–0 (pbk.)
1. Great Britain—Race relations.   2. Racism—Great Britain–
–History—20th century.   3. Blacks—Great Britain—Politics and
government.   4. Blacks—Great Britain—Social conditions.
I. Solomos, John.   Race and racism in contemporary Britain.
II. Title.
DA125.A1S62   1993
305.8'00941—dc20   93–15200
                                                           CIP

To the memory of Cleopatra, Solomos, Styliani and Yiannis, who missed out on the opportunities I have enjoyed, but whose experiences remain with me

Contents

Preface to the First Edition   xi

Preface to the Second Edition   xiii

Introduction   1
    Recent trends and developments   2
    Key questions   3
    Racism in contemporary Europe   5
    Focus of study   6
    Plan of the book   9

1 Theories of Race and Racism   13
    Introduction   13
    Approaches to the study of race relations   14
    The sociology of race in Britain   17
    Politics, power and racism   21
    Critiques of the race relations problematic   25
    Culture, community and identity   31
    What kind of alternative?   33
    Summary and conclusion   35

2 Historical Background and Context   38
    Introduction   38
    The historical context of racism in Britain   39
    Anglo-Saxons and Celts   40
    Political and ideological responses to Jewish immigration 43
    Race and labour in the early twentieth century   47
    Summary and conclusion   51

3 The Politics of Race and Immigration since 1945   52
    Introduction   52
    The post-1945 conjuncture and European migration   53
    Migration, colonial labour and the state: 1945-62   56
    Immigration and racialised politics   59
    Immigration controls and state racism   61

The 1962 Commonwealth Immigrants Act 63
The changing terms of political debate 64
Institutionalising immigration controls 68
Immigration and race since 1979 70
Prospects for reform 74
Summary and conclusion 77

4 Race Relations Policies and the Political Process **78**
Introduction 78
Racism and racial discrimination 79
Race relations legislation in context 80
The origins of anti-discrimination legislation 82
The genesis of race relations policies 83
The 1976 Race Relations Act 85
From policy to practice 89
Proposals for reform 91
Summary and conclusion 93

5 Urban Politics and Racial Inequality **95**
Introduction 95
Concepts and models of local politics 95
Race and local politics in historical perspective 96
Processes of racialisation 98
Models of policy change 101
Policy change and conflict 102
Pressures for change and their impact 105
Resistance to change 106
Positive action and new initiatives 108
Training and racial equality 113
Changing forms of local governance 116
Summary and conclusion 118

6 Race, Policing and Disorder **120**
Introduction 120
Race, crime and disorder 120
Alienated youth and ghetto life 124
Policing minority communities 127
Mugging and street violence 130
Racialisation and popular images 136
Policing and violent disorder 139

Race, crime and statistics 143
Summary and conclusion 146

7 Protest, Racism and Urban Unrest in the 1980s **147**
Introduction 147
Disorder and urban unrest 147
Explanations of urban unrest 149
Law and disorder 152
Racial disadvantage and urban unrest 156
Alienation and powerlessness 158
Power, legitimacy and political disorder 160
Policing after the riots 165
Scarman and beyond 169
The changing politics of policing 174
Summary and conclusion 178

8 Racism, Nationalism and Political Action **180**
Introduction 180
Changing forms of racial ideology 181
Conceptions of race and nation 184
New-right ideologies and national identity 186
Neo-fascist politics 188
The politics of racial attacks 191
Racialised politics and the enemy within 192
Naturalisation of racism 193
Anti anti-racism 194
Nationalism and the interests of the majority 196
Summary and conclusion 197

9 Race, Politics and Mobilisation **198**
Introduction 198
Political participation and exclusion 199
The context of black political participation 200
Origins of black political mobilisation 202
Forms of black political organisation 203
Anti-racist politics and political alliances 211
The politics of race and class 212
Politics, social movements and reform 214
Summary and conclusion 216

10   Race, Culture and Social Change   **218**
     Introduction   218
     Imagined communities   219
     Multiculturalism, identity and the nation   221
     Rushdie and Islam   222
     Nationality and immigration   227
     Social and economic change   229
     Summary and conclusion   231

11   Changing Dynamics of Race and Racism   **233**
     Introduction   233
     Racism, politics and ideology   234
     Equality or symbolic reforms?   235
     Protest and social change   239
     Rethinking the politics of racism   241
     Racism and nationalism in Europe   244
     What kind of future?   246

Guide to Further Reading   249

Bibliography   252

Index   273

Preface to the First Edition

I would like to thank all the colleagues, students and friends who have helped me to articulate the arguments which are developed in this book. Since 1982 I have taught a number of courses on the politics of racism and related issues, and this has allowed me to test out some of the early versions of chapters included in this volume. I also owe a special debt to my former colleagues at the Centre for Research in Ethnic Relations, University of Warwick, who provided support and a challenging intellectual environment in the initial stages of writing. My present colleagues in the Department of Politics and Sociology at Birkbeck College have given me the space and encouragement to complete this study, and without their support it would have been much delayed. A number of other academic colleagues have given me help and support, in particular Bob Benewick, John Benyon, Mike Cowen, Andrew Gamble, Clive Harris, Bob Jessop, Michael Keith, Bob Miles and Solomos Solomou. Equally I have benefited from the superb collection of materials on race relations brought together by Heather Lynn at Warwick, which has no doubt saved me many hours of searching. At Warwick I received valuable administrative and secretarial support from Rose Goodwin, Gurbakhsh Hundal and Charlotte Wellington. At Birkbeck I have benefited from the invaluable secretarial support of Audrey Coppard and Harriet Lodge. My students at Birkbeck during 1987–88 were the unknowing recipients of some parts of this book in the form of lectures, and their comments helped me to sharpen my ideas and to organise this volume somewhat differently.

I owe a deep debt to my publisher, Steven Kennedy, for his support of the project despite unforeseen delays. At a personal level my family has provided me with necessary emotional support. Friends in Birmingham and London have seen the project develop and helped me to relax when I needed to. George and Ian were good company on our various trips to watch West Bromwich Albion, and they and the 'Baggies' deserve a special thanks. Christine Dunn helped to keep me going even when the labour got too much. This book is dedicated with much love to my grandparents.

Birkbeck College, London   JOHN SOLOMOS

Preface to the Second Edition

For the second edition of this book I have chosen to rewrite all the chapters and to add additional material. This is partly the result of the pace of change even in the relatively short period since the first book was produced. Already in the past few years political debates about racial and ethnic issues have taken on new forms in both Britain and other European societies. Racist and nationalist movements have helped to further politicise debates about the role of immigration and the position of ethnic minorities. We have also seen the emergence of new forms of political and social mobilisation by minorities themselves. The changes I have introduced also reflect my own continuing attempts to come to terms with some of the key issues which this book covers. This can be seen in the new material included in Chapters 1, 5, 6 and 10, as well as in the changes I have introduced in other chapters. In including this material I have listened to the suggestions both of my students and my colleagues, and I hope this makes this edition more useful to both the specialist and the general reader.

In producing the second edition of this book I am grateful for the help and advice I have received from a number of colleagues and friends, who have helped me to revise and elaborate my argument. My greatest debt is to Les Back with whom I have worked closely over the past three years and who has influenced the content of a number of chapters in ways too numerable to mention. My students at Birkbeck College have proved a critical and supportive audience and they have helped me to clarify my ideas. The participants in the Workshop on the Politics of Racism, which has met at Birkbeck since 1988, have helped me to develop my ideas in a number of productive directions. In particular I am grateful to Clive Harris, Michael Keith and Syd Jeffers who have all helped to keep the Workshop a friendly place to try out tentative ideas. Terry Mayer and Joanne Winning have provided a supportive environment at Birkbeck while I was producing this second edition and made sure I was not overwhelmed by administration and that I kept to my deadline. Steven Kennedy once again encouraged and supported the production of this edition. Since the production of the first edition the 'Baggies' have introduced me to the delights of third division football, an experience that has proved too much at times but which has at least allowed me to visit many new grounds and produced many enjoyable Saturday afternoons looking on the bright side of life.

Birkbeck College, London   JOHN SOLOMOS